Running a successful self-catering holiday home

The complete guide to setting up and managing a holiday let in the UK

Samantha Bennett

Copyright ©2023 Samantha Bennett

All rights reserved.

Published by WhisperWing Press 2023

Disclaimer: This guide is provided for general informational purposes only. The author and publisher are not engaged in rendering legal, financial, or professional advice. Readers are advised to consult relevant professionals for specific advice pertaining to their individual circumstances. The author and publisher cannot be held responsible for any discrepancies, changes, or inaccuracies that may occur beyond the book's publication date. It is always advisable to consult official sources and directly contact relevant establishments for the most up-to-date and reliable information.

Contents

1	Introduction
7	Chapter One: An overview of the holiday let business
24	Chapter Two: Which property to buy and where?
60	Chapter Three: Listing sites and holiday let agencies
75	Chapter Four: Setting up an Airbnb listing
141	Chapter Five: A brief guide to setting up listings on other sites
165	Chapter Six: Selling direct – setting up your own website and calendar
189	Chapter Seven: Legals and finance
205	Chapter Eight: Housekeeping
220	Chapter Nine: Renovating and furnishing a holiday home
300	Chapter Ten: Top tips for running your let
340	To conclude

Introduction

If you have purchased this book, then you are most likely either thinking about setting up a holiday let or are in the early stages of your holiday let journey. Maybe you are looking for further guidance and advice to help improve an existing let. This book will be helpful for all of these scenarios. I have decided to write the kind of guide to holiday letting which I wish had existed when I had started out in the business over 18 years ago. I have a great deal of experience in the field and have run several holiday lets of my own very successfully in this time as well as helping to establish and manage lets for clients, along with carrying out consultation work on interiors and renovations. I am a 'Superhost' on Airbnb and have lots of experience with the other major holiday let listing platforms as well. I have experience of running multiple holiday lets successfully, from city centre homes and flats in popular tourist areas, to town houses, country manors and little cottages in remote villages. I feel that this has taught me some very valuable lessons regarding different holiday let models and the best way to market, run and maintain them, all of which I can pass on to you.

My holiday let journey has not always been a smooth or easy one, but it has been a fascinating experience which has equipped me with a wide range of skills along the way and a greater understanding of people and all their quirks and preferences. The holiday let market can be incredibly lucrative for those willing to work hard and take a proactive approach towards the realities and practicalities of the business. Through this guide I will help you avoid many of the pitfalls that typically befall new hosts and help you to quickly establish a successful holiday let business of your own. Since being established in 2007, Airbnb has been largely responsible for the massive expansion and development of the global holiday home market. The landscape of holiday letting has changed at an astonishing rate over the last ten years in particular - whether for good or bad, is up for debate. There has certainly been something of a backlash against Airbnb in recent years with talk of small communities and city areas becoming dominated by the company, with talk of 'greedy' landlords spoiling some communities and areas for other people. I have always tried to be a reasonable and considerate holiday let landlord and not impact neighbours or communities in a negative way. I have refurbished and improved many homes and sold some on for a healthy profit when I have decided to move on, but always leave a home in a much better state than I found it. I feel that I have given many people wonderful holiday memories and provided emergency homely accommodation at short notice at a reasonable price for a variety of travellers. I have been responsible for employing a number of local tradespeople to help in the renovation stages of my businesses and have employed many local people to help run them, from handymen, to plumbers, cleaners, gardeners and laundry companies. One of the most common complaints about holiday lets is that they, and the guests, hurt the local economy – that housing stock is removed for local people and little money is put back into the community. I do have a lot of sympathy for people in this situation and for residents living in areas saturated by holiday lets or those living next door to holiday properties with lax rules and disinterested landlords. I always encourage and advise my guests on visiting local sights, shops, cafes, restaurants and other small local businesses - I feel that tourists can support and enhance local communities when gently coaxed in the right direction. I always create a home which is smarter and better maintained than it previously was. I ask guests to be respectful and mindful of any neighbours. I do believe that all these measures help to counteract some of the negative aspects that holiday homes can bring to an area. Being a holiday let landlord is rarely an easy or lazy route to making money. People will always want self-catering holidays. Long gone are the days when we booked guest houses, bed and breakfasts, cottages and hotels with little information about them and simply hoped for the best, often to be sorely disappointed upon arrival. Guests' expectations have never been higher and the review systems and easy access to information and photography on holiday listing sites means that consumers can generally be very choosy these days when looking for their perfect holiday accommodation. Anyone looking to move into this business will soon find out that it is not a job where you sit back and let the money roll in – there is *a lot* of work involved, from setting up your holiday let, to running and maintaining it successfully. The initial setup is certainly one of the busiest and most difficult phases of the business and is the most important part of the process in terms of getting things right in order to help secure future success.

Running and maintaining a holiday let usually requires a lot of hard work too. There are many other skills and tips which can be useful to know once your let is up and running, especially in terms of maximising your occupancy and revenue, keeping costs down, maintaining high standards and marketing your let to as wide an audience as possible. Many holiday let landlords will be extremely reluctant to share their top tips with you, but this is where the value of this book lies – I will tell you everything I wish I had known at the start of my journey. The potential returns on holiday lets are excellent, and with the increased regulation on buy-to-let rentals and landlords by the UK government, with increasingly stringent rules and difficulties in removing bad tenants, it is easy to see why people have turned to this market instead. It allows you to be your own boss, with flexible working hours and you will never be stuck with the "tenants from hell". You have the potential to earn a great deal more from shorter holiday breaks compared to a regular rental, but there will be a lot more work involved with high expectations from your guests.

It has never been easier to run your own holiday let, in terms of free online holiday listing websites such as Airbnb, online holiday agencies and a large range of social media and marketing platforms, but this has also meant that the market has become saturated in some places – it is an increasingly competitive market, where holiday let landlords need to up their game in order to survive and thrive. Nine percent more holiday lets are forecast to join the business over the coming year, so it is becoming increasingly necessary to outshine your competitors. The reviews systems can be brutal – the consumer has a lot of power to make or break businesses. It is not a business for the faint-hearted. You need to have steely nerves, dedication to detail and a thick skin. Administration and computer skills, customer service experience, an eye for design and basic DIY skills are all helpful to have, although all can be learnt or improved quickly along the way.

Partly due to Airbnb, along with an increasing number of regular rental landlords moving into the holiday let sector, the UK Government has started to tighten up holiday let legislation. Wales has recently further increased its stay requirements on holiday homes and local Welsh councils have the power to greatly increase tax on second homes, so it is something to bear in mind, as other parts of the UK may follow suit. Scotland has also recently announced new legislation and licence requirements for holiday homes and Edinburgh has become the first place in the UK to be registered as a designated short-term rental control area due to a severe affordable housing shortage. Tourist hot spots, popular cities or locations with a shortage of local housing including rental homes need to be researched carefully by those considering setting up a holiday let in such places. The government is currently looking at introducing planning permission requirements for new owners of holiday lets in England as well. There are minimum occupancy requirements which need to be met in order to qualify as an official furnished holiday let within the UK (more on this in chapter seven), so you need to be realistic about how occupied your let will be. If you fail to meet these requirements, then your property may be taxed as a second home. It seems that second homes are going to increasingly be subjected to higher taxes, judging by recent changes that have taken place in Wales and due to a general shortage of affordable housing in the UK. As I will discuss later, you do not need to always buy in a typically popular tourist area in order to run a very successful holiday let, so avoiding potentially difficult UK 'hot spots' isn't always a bad thing.

I will be covering every aspect of the holiday let business, from deciding what kind of property to buy and where to buy within the UK along with advice on legal requirements, taxes, business rates, costs, how to optimise revenue, how to set up online listings and practical advice on running a holiday let – be it a single room in your home, an annex, or multiple properties. I also offer in depth advice on renovations, furnishings, housekeeping, administration, finances, customer service, difficult guests, reviews, online calendars, how to market your let and how to manage your own website and calendar.

A holiday let can be a very fulfilling and profitable business. I hope to save you a great deal of time and money by imparting some of the hard-earned knowledge I have amassed over the years.

Wishing you the best of luck on your holiday let journey!

Samantha Bennett

Chapter One

An overview of the holiday let business

There is no such person as a 'typical' holiday let landlord. I have met so many different types of people with different types of let, and a wide range of people looking to move into the business over the years, and each person is unique. In my experience, the busy 'investor' holiday let landlord will dedicate time and effort in the setup phase of the business, often to then have the let fully managed by an online holiday agency, or by a business manager who will list their property for them on various listing websites and/or manage their own website and calendar for them, along with arranging housekeeping and even accounting. If you have a full-time job already, this business model may work well for you. Never underestimate how much work is involved in the day-to-day running of a holiday let. There will be guests who need to talk to you urgently, or times that you need to drop everything to deal with an emergency. There is also a surprising amount of administration involved in the business – it is easy to double-book, forget to log new bookings, send a welcome email with access instructions to a guest or update your housekeeping team with a new clean, not to mention accounting and managing your calendars in general, along with maintenance and so on. If you have a busy full-time career already, then I advise that you either employ a manager or have the let fully managed by one of the many online holiday let agencies. If you want more involvement in the running of the business, then I would recommend that you do not have more than a part-time job, or at the very least have a job which is flexible, in terms of expectations and office time. I have known people with creative, yet flexible jobs (think artist, freelance designers and writers) who have managed to successfully run several holiday lets, but this is because they are generally not in full office hour jobs. Some of them have even taken over the housekeeping duties of cleaning and laundering, to maximise profits, when their other work has been quiet. The flexibility of freelance work can lend itself well to managing a holiday let on the side.

The holiday let business is also very suited to stay-at-home parents, or those on a career break with young children. You can be around for school pick-ups and most of the work can be done during the day or evening. Always be aware that if you are planning to be fully responsible for the running of your let, that it is an open-ended business – there are no completely 'closed' hours. You will find yourself dealing with calls, emails and issues during evenings and weekends. There will be more issues when the let is busy, so weekends and school holidays can be your most hectic times; be sure that you are happy to take on this responsibility. I would strongly recommend that your holiday let is not located more than an hour away from your own place of residence and is preferably as close as possible, if you are going to be solely responsible for its operation, especially if you have young children.

I have noticed a large increase in older, often retired, people setting themselves up as holiday let landlords. It can be a very good extra source of income in retirement and these people have more time generally to dedicate to the business. Bear in mind that if you want to maximise your profits by doing a lot of the work and maintenance yourself, that it can be a very physical job. I have found renovations and maintenance extremely physically challenging at times. A lot of the work involves lifting, scrubbing, cleaning and moving furniture. Even with the best housekeeping team in the world, and an excellent handyman on call, you will find yourself having to carry out tasks which involve strength and stamina, especially in emergencies, or at short notice.

Whilst anyone can set up and run a holiday let, some people are suited to it better than others. You don't have to be an IT whizz these days – setting up a free online listing has never been simpler, and these sites are becoming more and more user-friendly over time, in my experience. The listing sites are very intuitive and most of them have the technology to explain to you, step-by-step, what needs to be done via an automated 'bot'. I will cover setting up online listings in greater detail later on in the book as there are some quirks and pitfalls to be aware of. You need to be well organised and good at administration in general. Keeping accounts and spreadsheets is strongly advisable, or a record of costs and receipts at the very least, if you plan to have an accountant help you. Whilst holiday listing sites are good at sending reminders and confirmations of bookings, you will still need a foolproof system to ensure that no guest is ever forgotten or that a property is not accidentally double-booked. You will spend a few hours most weeks just on 'admin'. The more marketing, calendar management and listing improvement you do, the more time you will spend on admin, but this is a way to improve your business and increase bookings and revenue. It can be an open-ended task and it is up to you how much work you put into the business, beyond the essential messaging and calendar management once you have set up your listings and/or website. I find that it becomes intuitive over time – you will often notice a surge in bookings or interest after making changes or improvements to your listings or websites, or after some canny marketing or price adjustments. If you set up a listing and never add or update information or photos and choose a base rate and simply stick to it, you will probably not maximise your potential revenue. As with the hands-on physical management of your let, the more time and effort you put into the admin and marketing side of things, the more financially rewarding your business will be. Hosts who are constantly looking to improve their online administrative activity and marketing as well as keeping a close eye on their property in terms of maintenance and improvements, will always be more successful than an unengaged host.

Customer service is a key part of the job as a holiday let manager. You need to know how to talk to guests and to communicate with them in a friendly and helpful way, however challenging some of them can be at times. The role is very much about serving the public – if you are not prepared to be friendly and patient then this might not be the right job for you. There will be many occasions when you are dealing with rude or entitled guests and you will need to stay calm and polite. People will frequently ask silly or repetitive questions and you will have to reply to all of them in a reasonable manner. Of course, if someone is being abusive or doing something illegal, then you will have to act assertively and decisively, as certain behaviours should not be tolerated, but hopefully you won't find yourself in this position. Most guests are friendly and reasonable, and you may find that interacting with a variety of people from different backgrounds is actually very rewarding, especially if you plan to meet them in person. Giving people a wonderful holiday experience can be very gratifying. If customer service, which includes biting your tongue and smiling through gritted teeth on occasion, is something you feel you don't want to do, then you will need to re-consider entering this business, unless you plan to have your let fully managed. You need to be prepared to listen to guests' feedback and take any suggestions or comments seriously. Some of the most successful holiday let hosts are those who continuously look to improve their business through feedback and innovation and choose not to be offended by any negative comments and instead utilise them to improve the holiday experience for future guests. Being easily offended and sensitive will not be helpful to this business.

I have noticed a growing trend in guests treating me like a hotel concierge at times – some guests have very high expectations of service from the holiday let owner with frequent questions and additional requests for things that would not usually fall to the owner. I provide as much information as possible in advance about the house, local area, amenities, grocery shopping, restaurants and pubs, but it is noticeable that a lot of guests do not read the guides or check the local information book or leaflets and will still message me with questions that are easily answered by the house manual, holiday listing or in the welcome email that I always send a couple of days before arrival. Your time is valuable, so anything which helps to free it up is worthwhile. I will share tips later in the book on what to have in your let and what information to include to decrease burdens upon your time. I also tell guests to email me in the first instance and to phone only in an emergency, having had guests ring me repeatedly about every little detail or query in the past. This is not practical if you have any other sort of responsibilities or job in your life. I have shared typical messaging templates later in the book to help with pitching your communication in a friendly, but professional tone.

You need to be prepared to roll up your sleeves and get your hands dirty in the holiday let business. There have been many times when I have wondered what I was doing, when I have found myself trying to clear drains, pick up dog mess by the front entrance of a house, sorting through dirty mixed recycling which has not been collected, removing part of a dental brace from a blocked sink or a used sanitary pad wrapped up in tissue inside a drawer (yes, really!). It is not a glamorous job, however much you outsource tasks. I usually use housekeeping services for cleaning and laundry, and a range of builders and handymen for renovations and repairs, but there are always jobs that no one will do for you, that are missed by housekeeping, or that need to be done immediately, rather than next day, and it will invariably be you doing the worst kind of emergency tasks – blocked toilets, drains and sinks along with loose or broken toilet seats are the most common emergency situations. Disposable gloves are your friend. Previously a bit of a germaphobe, the job has been surprisingly good for making me a little more robust and tolerant towards things I previously would not have wanted to touch with a barge pole. You will learn to get things done quickly and efficiently and turn off your disgust when time is against you. A healthy revenue and bank balance will hopefully compensate for these unpleasant tasks!

If you have some basic DIY skills, this can be immensely helpful. There is a woeful shortage of handymen and instantly available builders at the moment in the UK. I would say that 90% of issues can be fixed without a handyman, but having a toolbox and some basic knowledge of DIY will save you a great deal of stress and money. I only had a very basic knowledge and ability when I started out, but I have come on leaps and bounds since then and now have a well-stocked toolbox for most things that tend to need fixing. Holiday homes take a pounding, in terms of wear and tear, and it is not unusual to get a call or email from a guest every week during busy times regarding something which requires fixing. It is very stressful trying to get something fixed, often with little notice, especially on same-day changeovers. Guests often like to tell you about the broken shower, loose tap, toilet seat or blocked drain on departure day as they did not want to disrupt their holiday by having a handyman visit. I will attach a useful 'essentials' list for your toolbox and spare parts store later in the book, when I talk about top tips for running and maintaining your let. So far, we have established that you will be an administrator, accountant, customer service agent, occasional cleaner and handyman if you choose to enter the world of the holiday let. The next big question is whether the economics will stack up for you, in terms of revenue, costs and your time. You need to decide what your time is 'worth' if you plan to run the let mostly by yourself and if the potential stress of dealing with the public in a customer-service role pays you well enough for this. You need a sound financial plan. You must decide your set-up budget – the cost of the property and any renovation and furnishing costs and be realistic about your potential revenue and running costs. Setting your base nightly rate is key to the business, although you will learn to alter it accordingly for busy and quiet periods. Check out comparable businesses and hotels in your area – never assume that you can make more than a competitor because your home will be better furnished or more stylish, although this certainly increases your chances. There is usually a ceiling on the price that a landlord can charge – there will be listings for properties at preposterous prices online, but this does not mean that they will be renting out at this price. It is noticeable that some lets have astronomically high prices but with little occupancy – I cannot help but think that some of these homes might be using the holiday let label illegitimately. The government is currently cracking down on second homes 'posing' as holiday lets with little actual occupation, so this is likely to change. The more research you do, the more comparable existing lets you look at on listing sites, with an eye on occupancy, and time of year, the more you will get a true sense of your potential earnings.

Free online listing sites such as Airbnb, Booking.com, VRBO/Holidaylettings.co.uk and Trip Advisor are very useful for research and checking out typical nightly rates in your area of for your type of listing, as you can easily search by types of property, number of bedrooms and area. Their commission will generally range from 3% up to 15%, so bear this mind when considering nightly rates. It is also worth looking at the holiday let agencies which have more control over your listing and tend to offer fuller management services, in return for higher commission. They also usually demand a certain amount of exclusivity for your property availability on their calendar and commission can typically range from 15% up to 60% depending on the agency and their level of management. I will discuss holiday let listing sites and holiday let agencies in more detail later. Be aware that some properties will advertise ludicrously high nightly rates but will not necessarily be booked at these rates. I can only assume that some holiday let owners are deliberately limiting their bookings on purpose at certain times of the year - their homes are officially 'available' but few will book at those prices. It may be to fulfil availability criteria to trade as an official holiday let. The government is increasingly cracking down on 'false' holiday let landlords, so it is not a route that I would advise you take. Required occupancy rates are generally being raised over time by the government to prevent this. Always research several properties to get a sense of the true, average nightly rates and check their occupancy. Bear in mind that some calendar blocks may be just that - blocks - rather than actual bookings.

Once you have a sense of your potential average nightly rate and occupancy for the type of let you wish to run, then you need to consider running costs as well – the largest being cleaning, utilities and tax (more on this later). If you plan to have your let fully run by an agency, then these costs will also be significant, potentially taking up to half your revenue or even more. Once you have a rough idea of potential revenue, this needs to be offset against your time and commitment to the business. You may decide that there are better and easier ways in which to invest your money. Never underestimate the value of your time and remember that the holiday let business can be all-encompassing. Although it will be flexible and there will be quiet times, there will also be very busy and stressful moments as well and a certain amount of required admin per week, along with site visits from time to time. Maximising your income will involve running the let to the best of your abilities – being on-call for your guests, making frequent visits to check everything over, maintaining your let to a high standard, and being highly involved in general. You will need to be dynamic with your calendars, keeping an eye on demand and pricing and adjusting as necessary to optimise your revenue. You will learn when to drop prices in order to fill last-minute availability, and how to raise prices in advance for early bookers - it is part learned intuition in the end, and part keeping an eye on the market and your competitors.

There will be a baseline where it becomes unprofitable to rent out your home and it is a good idea to decide this at the outset, once you have a clear idea of running and changeover costs. You may notice other businesses undercutting you, but this may be because their running costs are lower or because they are carrying out the housekeeping themselves, for example. I have a one-bedroom rural cottage but can never match the £50 per night that some properties offer nearby when my cleaning fee is £60 and laundry is £20 (plus expensive LPG heating and sundries such as toiletries, milk and biscuits, logs and kindling etc.) I can only assume that cheaply priced competitors are mortgage-free houses or annexes run by owners who live on site or close by and manage their own cleaning and possibly laundry too. It can be a very good side earner for a farmer with a converted barn on site. My strengths here are that I offer a very pretty and characterful home, beautifully renovated with lots of extras and mod cons, which I market carefully on several listing platforms including on my own website, whereas some of my competitors look a lot more basic and have limited online exposure. Some guests are looking for cheap and cheerful, others want an Instagram-worthy cottage and are happy to pay extra for it. Each type of let has its own place and customer in the market and you need to find yours. Recent studies show that budget accommodation and high-end luxury accommodation are the two most resilient types of holiday let business during an economic downturn and that the middle range of let tends to feel the pinch first. However, even within the larger, middling range of holiday lets, you can still ensure that your let stands out among the competition through careful management and presentation.

You will have periods on your calendar that remain empty. The holiday let market is very dynamic in general and will respond to the economic climate almost immediately – every other holiday let owner, holiday agency and housekeeping agency will agree with this. Any economic downturn is often *immediately* reflected in reduced bookings and quiet weeks for a holiday let. A regular rental will tick along nicely and predictably. If you want guaranteed income and not too much stress, then this line of business may suit you better, even though the potential earnings may not be as high. It may be worth you simply testing the waters of the holiday market initially with a view to swapping to a regular rental if things aren't working out after a year or so. I know a lot of regular landlords have looked to sell or convert their homes to holiday lets due to increasing rules and regulations, but it does seem that the UK government is beginning to tighten up holiday let legislation as well, so it may not be such a big shift to move back to the regular rental market if your holiday home already meets a number of health and safety markers. There is a shortage of regular rentals at the moment and rental prices have been increasing recently. It may be that regular rentals become a lot more attractive to investors again, despite the increased regulation from government, especially if the holiday let market begins to struggle due to saturation or an economic downturn. Try to bear this in mind during the renovation or furnishing phase of your project, as you may find that the kind of tenants you want to attract later on may not match up with your renovation style. Holiday homes do get a battering, but long-term tenants will typically cause more damage and wear and tear, so you might not want to give your holiday home a very expensive makeover if you have half an eye of converting to a regular rental later.

You also need to keep in mind that it can be a slow burn at the start of the holiday let journey – you won't initially have any reviews and it is reviews which generate confidence in potential bookers or repeat-bookers at the start. It is a business that is cumulative - the better you run it, the busier it becomes over time. Repeat bookers and direct bookers will usually become your preferred type of guest and best source of income. You will hopefully end up with guests you know and trust, which is always preferable to hosting strangers. Direct bookings mean you will not have to pay listing site commission and be at the mercy of public reviews. You will need to hold your nerve a little at the start of your journey as you are building something new and guests can be extremely wary of new listings, thanks to some of the Airbnb horror stories they've read online. To get the ball rolling I always recommend starting off with lower prices and good deals. Not everyone automatically leaves a review so you will need to chase guests a little for these, without pestering too much - I wouldn't ask more than once. Extra attention to detail and friendliness in your messages, along with a few extra goodies such as a good bottle of wine or chocolates can encourage a good review, although you do need to be wary about these being mentioned in a review, or becoming something that is expected from guests. However, if it's not mentioned as something included with the rental in your listings you should generally be okay to slightly spoil your first few sets of guests. I have friends who have a policy of only ever booking newly listed holiday homes, as they have found that they tend to be immaculate, before any general wear and tear sets in, and offered at a good price.

Allow a minimum of one year to see how your business fares, preferably two, before you decide whether to continue or change tack. My properties always seem to start turning a good profit by the second year in general. It takes time to establish the business, solve any teething problems and to build up reviews and return guests. Fake reviews are, quite rightly, greatly frowned upon. Listing sites have tightened up security and loopholes in recent years, so it has become much harder to do this. Some landlords have allegedly been known to get fake bookings from family members and to reimburse them for the payment, thereby just losing the listing site commission, in exchange for a good first review. It shouldn't be necessary to go to these extremes though if you can tempt your first guests with relatively low prices or special deals. I have always found myself increasing my nightly rate significantly after about six to twelve months, once I have several good reviews under my belt.

As I have explained, there is a lot more volatility and uncertainty in the holiday let market compared to regular rentals, so it can be an unnerving experience at times, especially in the early days. Pressure is greatly reduced if your finances mean that you are not dependent on a certain level of revenue at any point – this is probably why many people view the holiday let business as a game for wealthy people, although this hasn't been my experience.

Mortgage rules are a very important element of planning your let; a holiday let is not subject to the same tax rates and rules as a regular rental property. You will require a holiday let-specific mortgage if you plan to buy a holiday home with one. If you plan to rent your own home, or part of it as a holiday let, you will need to inform your mortgage company who may not allow it, meaning that you must remortgage elsewhere. You will also need to obtain holiday let home insurance - as with holiday let mortgages, these can also work out more expensive than regular home insurance. I am aware of many holiday landlords who have never admitted the true status of their holiday let to their mortgage company, and have a property which is officially classed as a general buy-to-let property, when it is actually a holiday let, but I strongly recommend that you do not go down this route, as there are serious legal and financial implications if you are found out. Your insurance can also be invalidated if it turns out that your property is not registered correctly. If your house is destroyed by flood or fire, or if a guest is seriously injured at your let, you could stand to lose everything if the mortgage and insurance company discover that you haven't registered your let correctly. Holiday let home insurance should cover you, your property and your guests and is essential. Outrightly owned lets, an existing on-site annex, or inherited properties are obviously much less of a risk and a lot less stressful to run, from a financial point of view, but you will still need to ensure that they are correctly insured.

There are investors who like holiday lets due to the various tax breaks and exemptions that they can benefit from, along with the possibility of the property increasing in value over time. However, do not forget to factor in Capital Gains Tax for any increase in your property's value if you decide to sell. Some investors run multiple holiday lets for all of the above reasons. You will find that they will tend to optimise their income by renting out different types of properties. I know one landlord who has several city centre lets, plus a couple of cottages in very rural locations. Generally, the city lets have always performed the best, in terms of there never being a particularly 'quiet' season, but, post-pandemic, he has seen a massive surge of interest in his rural lets, with people looking to escape the towns and cities. He finds that when one type of let is less busy then the other often helps to plug the financial gap and diminished occupancy. Current rules on 'averaging' if you own more than one holiday let means that you can 'spread' your declared occupancy across a number of lets, which is very useful if one or two are underperforming. City lets are now picking up again, due to businesses reopening and international travellers returning. The holiday let market is always in flux and you need to be able to move and adapt with it. I would say that running more than two holiday lets becomes a full-time job, if you want to be fully involved, especially during peak holiday seasons. Taking time off for yourself can become problematic if you end up with a portfolio that you fully manage. I like to have control of my listings and properties, so I only outsource this when I am on holiday by paying the manager of my housekeeping company extra to manage my lets whilst I am away. I give guests her phone number and contact details if I'm not going to be around, in case of any problems, plus a list of my tradespeople in case of any maintenance issues. I still have to deal with bookings and enquiries, however, even when on holiday. Apart from that, I seem to manage running several without too much of a headache, but none of them are more than an hour and a half's drive away which helps.

The more things you can automate, the easier your life will be. Key safes with codes automatically emailed to guests a day or two before check-in, message templates (most listing sites now have these features), plenty of information provided beforehand and on arrival, smart thermostats and clear instructions on how to use appliances will all help to reduce the amount of time you spend on your computer, speaking to guests or visiting to fix problems. Being super prepared in advance and fixing any problems as soon as possible and ensuring that the details of your let are up to date means that hopefully over time it will become a smoothly oiled machine requiring less and less communication between you and guests and fewer site visits to replace or fix things. Choosing the right furnishings, appliances and finishes in the first place can save you a lot of time and problems in the long term, as I will discuss later in the book.

Chapter seven is a very important chapter in terms of legal requirements, health and safety and tax implications for a holiday let. Occupancy rates are an important part of deciding whether you will be able to trade as an official furnished holiday let. As well as ensuring that you're fulfilling various legal and financial rules, being aware of how the system works can also provide a number of tax breaks and exemptions. Many holiday lets are run as small businesses and, depending on where your holiday home is located and what its rateable value is, you may be able to claim small business relief and avoid having to pay business rates. Expenses and set-up costs can be deducted from your pre-tax profits. The cost of setting up your holiday rental can also be set against income tax, which is not the case for normal buy-to-lets. If you make a loss in your first year, perhaps due to the cost of setting up a holiday let, this loss can be carried into the second year, and beyond, if necessary, for tax purposes. There can also be financial benefits when it comes to Capital Gains Tax and pension payments.

Be prepared for the first year of trading to be a steep learning curve and a time when most problems and faults become apparent. It can sometimes feel like an onslaught of issues and problems in the early days, but each time you discover or fix a problem or improve a feature in your property, you improve your business and make your future life a little easier. The value of this book chiefly lies in the fact that I can help you avoid a lot of common mistakes in the initial set up of your let, hopefully saving you a lot of time and money, along with offering tips for maximising your profit and maintaining a successful let.

Key points

- It is very difficult to run a holiday let alongside a full-time job. Consider employing a manager or using a holiday let agency in this case.
- Holiday lets can be suited to part time workers or those employed with flexible working hours, stay at home parents or retirees.
- Holiday lets can be a good place for investors to put their money – especially through buying multiple lets and using averaging to fulfil occupation requirements.

- Owning a property outright, either as an existing annexe, inherited property or investment will mean that you can ride out economic storms and downturns with less risk and stress.
- Rules on Capital Gains Tax, VAT exemption on renovation costs and reduced or exempt business rates can help make the holiday market attractive to investors. Always check the latest legislation before proceeding.
- Whilst the holiday let market can be very lucrative, it is also a very volatile place and responds almost immediately to economic events or downturns.
- Allow at least one year before judging your own success as it takes a year or two to get established.
- Consider setting up your home in such a way that swapping to the regular lettings market, if necessary, wouldn't be too difficult.
- Check out a number of existing holiday lets online to get a sense of prices – do not forget to factor in running costs and listing site commission though. Be wary of lets with ludicrously high nightly rates - they may well not be booking out at these rates.
- If you plan to run your own lets, be prepared for a lot of physical and often unpleasant tasks. Tradespeople and handymen aren't always immediately available, and cleaners do not always notice everything that requires attention.
- DIY, administration and IT skills, along with customer service experience are all helpful but not essential.
- Before you take any further steps, research mortgages if you plan to have one as you will require a holiday let specific mortgage. Do not risk invalidating your insurance by having the wrong kind of mortgage. You will require holiday let specific insurance as well.

- The first year of running your holiday let will be the most difficult and busiest, especially if you plan to renovate first. Lots of elements of the business can be automated, so once your systems are in place, things will get easier.
- Your time is valuable – do not undersell it or forget to factor it into your costs.

Chapter Two
Which property to buy and where?

Choices, choices. Stay close to home if possible

If you have purchased this book, then you may just be starting out on your holiday let business journey and looking for a property to buy. Perhaps you are still considering several areas within the UK. You may be looking at areas that you can see yourself retiring to one day, or somewhere you enjoy holidaying in with a view to using your holiday let for your own holidays as well as renting it out. You may be looking for a second home which you only plan to rent out occasionally, or you may wish to purchase a purely profit-focussed business where maximum revenue and minimum costs are your chief concerns. I always advise that a chief deciding factor in your location search for a holiday should be distance from your own home. If you want to have any hands-on level of involvement with your holiday let, and if you will be heavily involved in the renovation and running of your let, I strongly advise buying as close to your own home as possible. I still advise this even if you plan to have it fully managed by a holiday let agency and/or housekeeping staff, as you will still find yourself in emergency situations where you have to be there in person, usually at short notice. I have a rule of not buying a property more than two hours' drive away, but it is always better to be as close as possible in my experience. If you happen to already live in a tourist destination or vibrant town or city, then that simplifies things, as you have an easy ready-made market on your doorstep and an area, you're already familiar with, which is always a distinct advantage, although the higher house and flat prices will reflect this. This, however, will most likely be offset by the fact that your market will hopefully be lucrative. Do not buy a distantly located let because you have friends or family living there who say they are happy to help run the business, do your cleaning or keep an eye on it for you. I know of several people who have gone down this route and it never ends happily and can easily sour a previously good friendship or relationship. You need to view your holiday let as a serious business, not a little side earner which relies on favours from friends and family. Housekeeping is likewise a serious business and cannot be something that you rely on non-professionals for, long-term. People will be happy to help in an emergency, but not all the time. It is noticeable that the more successful holiday homes are those with the most involved and present owners. The attention to detail and high level of upkeep that owners tend to provide will ensure good reviews and increased bookings. No one will look after your let or maintain it as well as you will.

A fully managed letting service via an agency will be expensive and maintenance and cleaning issues will probably be overlooked. You may struggle to find a fully managed service in some areas, especially if they are particularly rural. You may find that employing a private individual housekeeper may be preferable to paying for a fully managed service from a lettings agent, in terms of cost, efficiency and communication. If you can find a good cleaner or housekeeper who is happy to keep an eye on maintenance jobs as well as supplies and everything else connected with your property, then you may be able to consider a let located more than two hours' drive away. However, I would still recommend occasionally visiting your holiday home to check things over.

Country retreats are increasingly in demand, especially following on from the pandemic of 2020, where people were desperate for fresh air and space - even remote homes in unlikely places can be surprisingly successful if marketed correctly. Country homes, gardens and the great outdoors continue to trend on social media, and it is something that a lot of country cottage lets are continuing to tap into via canny marketing.

Coastal areas are always very popular and command some of the highest prices during peak holiday season but can struggle out of season. Cornwall should be approached very cautiously due to its severe local housing shortage. I can imagine that it is an area that will have to address the housing shortage problem sooner or later, possibly with increased occupancy requirements, licences or increased tax for second home and holiday let owners, as is happening in Wales. According to a recent Guardian article, coastal Airbnb homes have increased in number by 56% between 2019 and 2022, compared with an increase of 15% in non-coastal areas.

City and town destinations are likewise also very popular, with people looking for experiences including dining, culture and history. Hospitality in cities has been incredibly busy over the last few years, again probably partly in reaction to the lockdowns of 2020 and 2021 – restaurants and activities often need to be booked well in advance to guarantee a place. It is a surprising phenomenon given the cost-of-living crisis that the UK has recently suffered from. The demand for weekend breaks and family self-catering UK holidays means that holiday lets in cities, towns and villages in popular areas have been very busy over the last few years. In the years that I have been a holiday let landlord, there have been periods, from time to time that are very quiet where it feels that the market will never bounce back, but it always has done, so far.

If you are looking to buy a property you will need to carefully choose a budget and stick to it if possible. I strongly recommend that you carefully research the set-up and running costs involved and remain realistic about the potential achievable occupancy and revenue before putting in an offer on any home. The UK has suffered from uncertain economic times recently. Luxuries such as holidays can often be the first thing people cut back on during times of economic strife. However, there are recent studies that suggest that holidaymaker numbers are set to increase over the next few years. It has been suggested by one study that people are increasingly cutting back on physical items such as larger houses and new cars rather than on 'experiences', like holidays and travel at the moment.

There are boom years and lean years in this business, and revenue and occupancy can never be fully predicted or guaranteed. Do not over-stretch yourselves in the buying phase for this reason. There will be quiet months. A regular rental won't usually generate nearly as much rental income as a holiday let, but it will tick by with predictable revenue and costs. Holiday lets are a lot more unpredictable and probably not suited to those with uncertain finances or large mortgages which are reliant upon the revenue from the let. I would not rely on a holiday let as a sole source of income either for these reasons. Some areas of the UK have been somewhat oversaturated by holiday lets; you will need to check out the competition and other lets' occupancy and rates to get a sense of how much demand there is prior to buying a home in a popular area. I always advise first time holiday letters to buy smaller rather than bigger to test the waters first – there is a lot to learn in the first year or two of trading, and you don't want to be stressed about finances and struggling to clear your mortgage on top of this. You can always up-size to a larger property in the future once you have gained confidence and experience, but I would always start with something quite modest.

The house buying market can be very volatile - attempting to buy at a 'low' and avoiding the 'highs' is almost impossible. Many people suffered 'buyers' remorse' after overstretching themselves during the boom years of 2020-22, especially as the market cooled quickly in 2023, but as we have seen many times in the past, things can pick up very quickly again. Hopefully you will be in a strong position as a possible chain-free buyer which again will be very attractive to sellers regardless of the state of the housing market - if it is a difficult market for sellers then you will be in a very strong position. Some holiday let owners are very pragmatic in their house hunts and stick firmly to a set of criteria and will happily put several cheeky offers forward to several suitable properties and then simply pick the best bargain overall. It's a good approach if you are looking to maximise profit and minimise costs and plan to run your let for a reasonable length of time; however, if you buy a house that is struggling to sell for a reason, it is likely that it might not perform as well as a holiday home and may be difficult to sell in the future. Road noise, problematic neighbours, awkward rights of way and so on will upset holiday guests just as much as a homeowner, but any resultant bad reviews could seriously hurt your business. On one hand it is best not to fall in love with your rental property and to remain professional and dispassionate about it. This will allow you to focus purely on profit and to be less upset by the ravages that it will almost certainly be put through by guests over the years. On the other hand, a property that has something extra attractive or special about it may rent out more easily and will probably sell more easily one day. A compromise somewhere in the middle is probably a good bet – a home that is good enough, at a reasonable price and that can be easily renovated or redecorated to look more attractive.

If you plan to use the holiday let yourself, then there will be a stronger emotional connection, which can be a good and/or bad thing. It means you will be looking for a home that you love – hopefully others will love it too, but you will need to avoid the easy mistake of overly personalising things too much towards your own taste. You will also need to be mentally prepared for guests not always appreciating or treating your beloved home as you would like them to. However, you may be an excellent holiday let landlord, as you are more likely to keep things in good repair and have a home that is clearly loved and cared for – this is always noticed and appreciated by guests. If you have high expectations of guests and want your holiday home to be always kept immaculate, then it might not be the right business for you. However, if you're happy to share your lovely second home with others whilst balancing this with a slightly detached view of the house as a business, then the holiday let model may suit perfectly. There are lots of ways to minimise any problems, additional costs and disappointments, including guest damage – tips on this later.

If you want to rent out a room, an annex, or even your own home, if you are planning to be living elsewhere for a short period, then it could certainly be worth testing the local short term rental market, even if you don't live in a typically popular tourist area or beauty spot. Always contact your local planning office to check the current legislation and rules before renting out all or part of your own home. You will require holiday let insurance and will need to inform your mortgage provider who may not agree to short lets in your property meaning that you may need to re-mortgage. Whether you're prepared to make the necessary changes and additions to your home for this kind of business and whether the set up and running costs still leave room for a decent profit is something else you will need to research carefully. Renting out your own home, a room or annex is also quite a different ball game, psychologically, as you will be more emotionally invested in your business. One host I knew had an attached wing to her property which she rented out to holiday guests. However, she found it very difficult to give her guests the space and privacy they required and was a little too involved, day-to-day, mainly from a fear of people doing things 'wrong', causing damage or making a mess. She began to struggle to fill her dates due to negative feedback from some guests which noted that she could be rather intrusive and fussy at times. The house was well presented and comfortable, but her business soon folded as she could not ultimately cope with other people staying in part of her home. On the other hand, some hosts thrive with guests on-site or in an annex and enjoy meeting them in person and sharing local information, but they tend to have much more relaxed personalities. If you like your privacy, and/or are very protective of your belongings and grounds, then renting your own home, or part of it, may not be suited to you. I know one host in a coastal tourist area who has a modest annex which he lives in during the summer when renting the larger half of his home and then moves back into the larger half for the autumn, winter and spring. He makes an excellent living from the business although views the additional income as a fantastic 'bonus'. He is also very easy-going, which probably helps if living in close proximity to guests.

There are a number of new listing sites springing up which are tapping into the more informal market of private rooms within people's homes – which is similar to how Airbnb started. If you're interested in renting out an individual room or annex within your home, then these may be worth looking at. Homestay.com is one of the largest and would be worth checking out, although prices typically range from £15 to £40 per night for a private room. If you are happy to share your space, and possibly a bathroom and kitchen, then it could be worth considering, but it is quite a different world to the formal holiday let market. In response to the cost-of-living crisis and new competition, Airbnb is currently re-launching its private room side of the business, 'Airbnb Rooms', which is focussed on helping guests find individual rooms within hosts' homes, so it seems that there is a renewed demand for this type of accommodation for guests.

There have never been so many different types of holiday homes available to visitors – from lodges, caravans, shepherd's huts, garden buildings, old railway carriages, teepees, glamping pods, one-bedroom flats to ten-bedroom manor houses and so on. Setting up a successful holiday let is a two-prong process in the first instance – choosing the right area and the right type of home is key. Searching on popular free holiday let listing platforms such as Airbnb, Booking.com, VRBO and Trip Advisor will give you a chance to see what else is already out there and have a sneaky peek at their calendars, prices and occupancy. You can also search by month, number of bedrooms, type of property and there is usually a map search function as well if you want to look beyond your starting search point. Bear in mind that most free listing sites charge varying amounts of commission for bookings, typically ranging from 3% up to 15%. Also check out the various holiday let online agencies such as Sykes Cottages, English Cottages, Country Cottages, Perfect Stays, Rural Retreats, Unique Homestays and so on for ideas and inspiration. Again, be aware that the owner will be paying these agencies a large chunk of commission – typically anything from 15% up to 60%, depending on the service.

Where possible try to find a gap in the holiday let market – if there isn't a gap, then look for the least saturated area of provision. You may find a glut of one-bedroom flats in your preferred area available at a disappointingly low nightly rate, but a shortage of family homes, for example. Or you might notice that the single glamping pods up the road command twice the price of the two-bedroom terrace cottage and cost a fraction to buy – but then you may notice that they are empty for half the year. You need to get a sense of the different types of properties' performance all year round. You may notice that most of the local family holiday homes look rather tired and dated and feel confident that you can corner that market in your area with a funky modern home with excellent facilities which appeals to younger families, groups of friends as well as older people. A modest two-bedroom cottage in a village five miles away might be booked up for the next year or not at all. The basically furnished pet-friendly terrace home with small yard might be booked up months in advance at an excellent rate because it offers something different to all the luxury one bedroom holiday flats. Research is key as no area and home are exactly alike. The one trend which will be unmistakable is that the well-presented homes are always more booked up than the tired-looking ones. Even if you go down the pet-friendly route, I cannot stress to you enough the importance of how you present and furnish your home. Even the most ordinary or tiny holiday let can be very successful if beautifully laid out and styled. More of this in chapter eight.

City and town lets

Most cities and towns will be visited for their vibrant shopping scene, nightlife, culture and tourist attractions. Generally speaking, city lets will rent out more than town lets, unless it is a very picturesque town or one with a major tourist attraction or similar on the doorstep. The more picturesque and historic a city, the higher the house prices, rental prices and the busier the holiday let. Airbnb has shown us that every part of the UK can be monetised, in terms of short-term visitors, and even the most unlikely and un-picturesque cities and towns usually have their points of interest. Not all guests are on holiday – there will be people travelling for business, for weddings, for hospital appointments, to visit children at university, to visit family and for a myriad of other reasons. You need to identify your potential market early on and target this in your house hunting and final set-up. There may not even be a 'typical' market to cater for in some cases – you may be able to appeal to all of the above in equal measure with a genuine mix of types of guest throughout the year. You may find that your let is better suited to longer term stays and find yourself booked up for a few weeks by each guest. There are often renters desperate for accommodation for a few weeks if they have left their rental home and have a gap before the next one is available, or if they are waiting on a house sale - if you reserve your calendar for longer stays only, then you may find yourself surprisingly busy with these types of guest - just bear in mind that you may lose your official holiday let status as a result and some of the financial advantages which come with this - see more in chapter seven. It may still be worth the swap though. Some hosts claim that too many short stays break up their calendar, preventing longer stay guests from booking. It will be a case of trial and error in the early days if your home is not based in a typically touristy area. Urban areas will generally mean that you will receive more bookings from a wider range of renters, including those looking for longer stays.

Always check your local authority's planning department in case there is any additional holiday let legislation for your city or town – London has slightly different stay and tax thresholds to other parts of the UK and Edinburgh is a designated control zone meaning that planning permission must be sought to set up a holiday let or convert a residential home into a holiday let there. Some cities are talking about introducing visitor taxes for holiday accommodation providers, as already happens in some European cities, so always check for the latest rules with your local council.

If your city or town is primarily focused on its nightlife, then you may need to focus on younger people and larger groups. If your town or city does not have much in the way of tourist attractions, then you need to find out who is visiting and why and find out how busy the hotels are and what they are charging per night. Generally, the more areas of interest a city or town offers, the more successful your let will be, as you will be appealing to a wide variety of people for year-round interest. However, less touristy cities and towns can usually offer homes and flats for sale at a much more competitive price, and this can be offset against the fact that your holiday home may not be as busy or lucrative as those in typically touristy areas. You may find that your let may not even end up functioning as a holiday let, but rather as short stop-gap accommodation for those visiting your town or city for a variety of reasons. Even within the typical tourist hot spots you will find yourself hosting guests who are there for non-holiday reasons, especially out of season, and these guests plug a very important gap during quieter months in my experience.

It is a good idea to check out the rates and occupancy of other holiday lets, guest houses and local hotels before deciding to rent out a holiday home in a less typically touristy town or city. Check out properties within your vicinity on the large free listings sites, including Airbnb and Booking.com, along with any more localised agencies which often list by county. Airbnb and Booking.com can be very useful sites for research and for when you come to list a property in a less touristy area, as business travellers and other non-tourist travellers will often turn to these sites, in particular, when looking for short stays. Both sites are keen to encourage business travellers with various incentives and specific schemes available on their sites to appeal to this kind of guest. They will also encourage hosts to offer longer stays and discounts for people on work placements, or in need of stop-gap accommodation for any reason.

It is also definitely worth adding your holiday let to Google maps as people will often search on Google Maps for accommodation close to a work site or event if they have an early start or a long way to travel. You can also search Google maps for accommodation, which is another good way to find and check out your potential competitors. A large town or city with attractions will usually be a better bet, in terms of maximising profit and occupancy, but it is becoming an increasingly saturated market in many places, and you will pay a lot more for a home in these areas. Cities with large populations, a shortage of affordable housing and rentals, or high numbers of existing holiday lets are more likely to be targeted by local councils in the near future for additional taxes and possible restrictions though, and this is already starting to happen in Scotland and Wales, so looking beyond these types of area may pay off in the long term. Research is key here if you do decide to find a 'bargain' in a lesser-known area. If you have a mortgage to pay, buying in the wrong area can be financially disastrous. Likewise, buying a super expensive flat in the middle of your thriving city may not bring the income you had hoped for if every holiday homeowner around you is having to slash nightly prices due to an economic downturn and/or oversupply of similar holiday lets. There is an increasing shortage of regular rental homes and flats across the UK, so there is always a safety net in terms of swapping to this market, if it works for you. If you have half an eye on making this swap later and are simply 'testing the waters' for the holiday market first, then this will obviously influence the type of home you buy and how you furnish it.

I have run an extremely profitable home on the edge of a popular tourist city – I noticed a gap in the market for a modest family sized home with parking, slightly set back from the centre of things, as the city was so busy with stag and hen groups at night and the one-bedroom flats were very expensive and did not feel like particularly good value. Many flats couldn't be rented out as holiday lets in any case due to clauses in the building contracts. There were enough tourist attractions for families in the city centre and beyond and I realised there would be plenty of interest from these types of groups. It was around a fifteen-minute walk into the city centre and I aimed my market towards tourists and families with lots of local information and a clean, modern but family-friendly interior and set-up. My guests were glad of the relative peace and quiet, neutral styling, enclosed garden, additional space, and probably most of all, the parking, compared to the city centre. People would typically visit the city centre on foot, or by bus, and also take day trips to the countryside and coast. They would also typically stay longer than the weekend city visitors. I was happy as I was able to buy a larger property, compared to the expensive flats that I had looked at first, and this house increased in value at a much greater rate than the flats I'd previously looked at, when I came to sell some years later. It was incredibly successful, despite being a very ordinary small three-bedroom semi-detached home on a small estate. A modest home can still make a very successful let, especially if it is bought at a good price – my biggest discovery in this business is that it is quite often the smaller, cheaper homes that are the highest yielding, percentage-wise.

The city centre can be a noisy place. Some people, (usually younger guests), will put up with noise and difficult or no parking, especially if the flat/home is close to a railway station, in order to be in the centre of a vibrant city. However, do not forget that you, your cleaning team (if you plan to use them), and any maintenance or tradespeople, will normally require somewhere to park. Parking permits can further complicate things – this is worth looking into in detail if you're looking to buy in an area with limited or restricted parking. Some councils provide one permanent permit, others have a tear-out booklet type system. Either can easily be accidentally taken by the guest on the day of departure, and you can bet that the next guest will complain or mark you down for it. It will not matter that it was not your fault that the permit was missing, although reimbursing guests for any car park costs will certainly help reduce the potential for any negative feedback. It is another headache that I've always tried to avoid. Each council is different, but you definitely need to clarify the parking situation before proceeding with a purchase in an area with restricted or permit parking. Even if you buy a flat with underground or gated parking, this can present other problems to solve in terms of providing guests access upon arrival, along with security issues – private apartment car parks can be difficult for guests to access if they use a key fob or require a registered vehicle. You may not be allowed to fit a key safe on an apartment building. The concierge may not want to hold keys for you - for the car park or flat - and paying someone to meet and greet guests on your behalf will be costly and complicated. Likewise, will you want to be available at all times for meet and greet, including for guests whose flight was delayed and need to be met at 1am? Never underestimate the practicalities when house and flat hunting. The holiday let business can take up a lot of your time and energy as it is, without having additional worries such as lost parking permits or late arrivals needing you to let them into a car park. City lets close to a city centre, railway station and/or car park can be a little more immune to the parking issue, but provision of a private parking space is always infinitely preferable in my experience if you want to avoid additional stress. London is probably one of the few places where people will not expect parking.

City centres can be a very competitive place to run a holiday let – there are likely to be a range of budget and high-end hotels available to guests, along with many holiday flats and homes. Hotels are having to price themselves increasingly competitively, especially during the current economic downturn, so you will need to monitor and compare their prices, as well as checking out the holiday let competition in advance. Always check out the going rates before you even start to house hunt and make your calculations and predictions using prices at the lower end of the scale. I notice that the very central holiday homes generally receive more mixed reviews, however luxurious they are. This is usually due to city centre noise, disruption, noisy neighbours, traffic and parking issues, which usually cannot be controlled by the owner in any case. High demand and lots of visitor attractions, bars and restaurants on the doorstep, usually means that these businesses still thrive despite the downsides and an occasional poor review, but it is definitely getting more challenging for holiday let hosts due to more people moving into this market, especially for small flats. Look for homes in quieter side streets, wherever possible, or at least those with secondary or triple glazing. Air conditioning is becoming increasingly necessary during hot summers, but not many flats currently have it, and many guests will not want to open windows due to noise and pollution. For this reason, you tend to get a glut of poorer reviews for city centre flats during the summer months – heat and noise are the two biggest complaints. You will need to invest in several good fans, preferably with a very quiet setting for nighttime, if you have a city centre home. The novelty of running a city centre flat or home soon wears thin if you are faced with a barrage of complaints about noise every week and those bad reviews can soon mount up. Check out the street of your choice at all times of day. It might be relatively quiet in the evening, but full of delivery vans or a noisy recycling collection in the morning for example. You need to get a sense of the levels of noise throughout the day. Being close to a bar may be very problematic on Friday and Saturday nights for most guests, but if your target audience is made up of partygoers and hen groups, then it might be perfect. Good local city hotels will often have excellent insulation and soundproofing, usually with triple glazing, and air conditioning, so you have tough competition, unless you can significantly undercut them in price or have other appealing features which they lack. Hotels are increasingly offering 'apart-hotel' (apartment hotel) set-ups, whereby guests have access to a basic kitchenette – this seems to be in direct response to the success of holiday lets, as they have realised that people want the luxury of a hotel with the option to self-cater at the same time. Along with other flats, Apart-hotels will likely be your biggest competitor, if you have a luxury one- or two-bedroom flat.

    Holidaymakers tend to fall into two camps – those who want the experience of a hotel; to have breakfast provided, and sometimes dinner, with minimal effort required, and sometimes a spa and pool. Those looking to book holiday homes are usually looking primarily for the flexibility that self-catering offers and usually consist of larger groups or families. They want to save money by avoiding restaurants and want a well-equipped kitchen. Booking several rooms in a hotel will nearly always work out a great deal more expensive than renting a home with two or three bedrooms. Although some hotels allow pets, it's still not overly common, especially in a city or town centre. If you're prepared to offer something different – for example, a luxury city home that allows pets, preferably with a yard or small garden, you may find yourself inundated with bookings.

In the town or city, you will find that a large portion of your income will come from short breaks, and weekend stays will be your most popular nights. Two-night stays will be very popular, all year round, but you will need to decide if this is economically viable, in terms of the changeover costs which can be very high, for cleaning and laundry agencies. Sometimes changeover costs mean that a minimum stay of three nights is required, but obviously with most people working Monday-Friday, longer stays will not book as easily. There is a large swathe of retired travellers who are always on the lookout for a quieter out-of-season visit, but whether this is enough to fill your calendar adequately is another matter. The working from home phenomenon has certainly helped in recent years; if you have a good WIFI signal, you are more likely to get people booking three nights or more, and managing to work from your let, if necessary, for a day or so. The Friday-Sunday two-night stay will always be the most popular option, but you will need to mark up your prices to allow for the changeover costs, which can be quite high, or alternatively add a cleaning/laundry fee to your holiday listing. If you're in a popular city, you will probably find that you only have to offer two-night stays during the quieter months of November-February or if you have two-night gaps to fill between other bookings on your calendar. Most hosts select a minimum of three-night stays due to changeover costs, or charge more for two-night stays and offer discounts if guests book three or more nights. Properties with two or more bedrooms tend to get more week-long stays through school holidays and the summer months, although it does depend on the area.

City centres are very popular with stag and hen groups, and groups of young people in general. You need to decide whether you will accept these groups - there is always a tick box for this option on the holiday let listing sites. I have always avoided them, as I think the potential for the resultant noise is not fair on neighbours, although I know people who specialise in this field, offering basic accommodation for larger groups, who claim that it can be very lucrative and that the all-female and all-male groups can be surprisingly well-behaved and tidy. These types of let typically have several bunk beds in each bedroom, basic yet modern décor with very few breakables and stain-resistant furniture and flooring. You will certainly experience at least a few instances each year where a horrible mess is left behind – but if everything is easy to wipe down and nothing is too expensive to replace then it might not bother you too much if the returns are good. Budget hotels generally cater quite well to these groups, so you might find that you cannot compete within that price bracket in any case. Always research your competition first. We should avoid pigeon-holing guests – my biggest surprise, as a holiday let manager, is that some of my worst behaved guests have been the mild-mannered well-to-do family who have left the home in a terrible state. Likewise, I have had small groups of young friends down for the weekend who have gone clubbing and drinking until the small hours and have left the house immaculate; it can be hard to predict who the 'difficult' guests will be – other hosts and cleaning companies will concur with this.

Important note: if you are looking at city or town centre flats, carefully check the terms of the lease as many blocks of flats, especially those in popular city centres, have a clause that does not allow them to be rented out as holiday lets or sublet by the owner. Some unscrupulous landlords ignore this, but you will almost certainly be reported by disgruntled neighbours if you choose to ignore the rules.

Guests looking to stay just outside a city or town centre are usually searching for a quieter area. If you're considering the outskirts of a city or town then make sure you're able to offer this and/or other advantages – e.g. parking, more space and bedrooms, a garden, cheaper rates, easy access to motorways and A roads and so on. If you are happy to welcome pets, you will find that you can be very successful with this business model – many city centre flats will not accept them. A pet-friendly holiday home situated on the edge of a city or town with a garden within reasonable walking or driving distance can be very popular indeed. You can look even further afield, for example a quaint village 10-20 minutes' drive from the city centre, for the same reasons – this attracts guests looking for a country retreat with the option of visiting the city a few times. I know several people with cottages in this situation, which are very popular with a range of visitors and get booked up well in advance. You will generally be able to buy a larger, more impressive property this way, although bear in mind that some villages do not take kindly to holiday lets in their midst. You need to be prepared for some disgruntled neighbours; however considerate you try to be. It is usually preferable to buy a detached home, or to at the very least avoid any shared parking/rights of way in this instance, as some neighbours can be quite territorial and wary of outsiders. Do your best to be a good landlord, whichever circumstance you find yourself in – be mindful of neighbours and the kind of guests you will attract. No one wants to live next door to a noisy party property, bins of overflowing rubbish or recycling boxes piled high with empty beer cans and wine bottles. Many holiday home landlords now stipulate a curfew on noise to try to minimise disruption to neighbours.

The most typical city centre let will usually be a flat for two people. This market may look saturated, and you will be in more direct competition with hotels who can often offer additional facilities such as a spa, restaurant and room service. If you do decide to go for this market, you generally need to have a very stylish and high-end finish, with a focus on quality which needs to be maintained at all times. The boutique holiday let experience is becoming the norm for many travellers. Think quality beds and bedding, high-end furniture, original art on the walls, good quality toiletries and sundries, a coffee machine, sophisticated sound system and TV etc. You may want to consider leaving breakfast sundries or a voucher for a nearby cafe as well as this is the other way that hotels typically outperform holiday lets. The main advantage that the one-bedroom apartment has over the hotel is the kitchen, so always make this a focal point, in terms of appearance, functionality and advertising - paying for dinner each night makes the hotel a much more expensive option overall for travellers. The other option for a city centre let is something more modest and no-frills, which can work if your running costs are minimal (i.e. you do the cleaning and possibly the laundry as well), although guests will obviously pay less for this. Holiday lets are becoming more sophisticated and luxurious over time, as competition increases, so there is always a gap in the market for something simpler and cheaper. But even basic accommodation needs to be decent – you cannot get away with shabby furniture, uncomfortable beds and dirty carpets. In my experience, it is worth paying that bit more on furnishings and fixtures at the beginning as the smarter-looking lets will always book first and be busier, regardless of rates. It always surprises me how some holiday homeowners don't realise that just changing a tired old sofa or some dated curtains could probably push up their rates or occupancy significantly. People are swayed to book a holiday let usually within the first few seconds of viewing the photos, so do not ever underestimate the importance of the first photographic impressions and appearance of your holiday home.

One of the big draws of city lets for investors is that there is no completely 'quiet' season – you will have guests visiting all year round. In city centre lets with more than one bedroom you will have more families book during school holidays and will be able to increase your stay requirements over these periods typically to four to seven days minimum, depending on the market at the time. Avoid having more than one bedroom furnished with a double bed, however, as twin bedrooms will open your home up to more types of guest groups. Fewer changeovers significantly reduce running costs, although guests are more likely to book longer stays if they are discounted in some way – Airbnb typically encourages you to offer weekly discounts. My city lets attract a wide variety of guests from couples, groups of friends to wedding guests, people working in the city for a few days, parents of students and so on. A one bedroom let is going to be couples mainly unless you decide to have a sofa bed in the living room for occasional use to increase occupancy. A sofa bed will encourage bookings from couples with a single child, or possibly two small children, or groups of two or three as well. I have always decided against the sofa bed, as judging by colleagues' experiences, it creates a bit of a 'student dig' atmosphere and more complaints – the sofa bed is usually not as comfortable as a regular bed and guests can end up short of living space. There will be more wear and tear, with four people effectively crammed into a space meant for two. In my experience, if people are planning to cram more friends into your one-bedroom home, they will bring their own air bed and bedding, in any case (often regardless of whether you have stipulated no more additional guests in your terms). Never leave spare linen or duvets in cupboards as it will certainly be used for unplanned guests to kip on the sofa and you will find yourself with double the laundry and clearing up for the next changeover. If you do decide to maximise your occupancy via a sofa bed, then consider adding a surcharge to allow for the extra time and laundry and try to buy a good quality one. It's also worth adding a mattress topper, as sofa bed mattresses tend to be very slim.

I have a colleague who always advises anyone looking to move into holiday letting to limit themselves to three bedrooms, especially if it is their first property and/or based in a city. It is good advice, especially if you want to avoid large, noisy groups of friends. There are more short stays and more changeovers for a city home, and the running costs are therefore higher, so a smaller property is better suited to this. It will generally get more wear and tear, having year-round interest, so a smaller property will be easier to maintain. The lower buying and set-up costs of a smaller property can often mean that these sorts of properties are surprisingly successful in terms of net yield – additional bedrooms can have diminishing marginal returns. I would usually recommend first time holiday let landlords to start small in any case whilst they learn the business and not over-invest at the start. Never underestimate how much work is involved in keeping a holiday let looking smart! The one-bedroom flat needs to be immaculate to compete with the local boutique hotel. Hotels can be an extremely expensive way for a family to visit a town or city, so a city centre home of two or three bedrooms can be very attractive, and all the more so during school holidays. Be prepared to drop your prices out of season and to accept smaller groups though. I never charge by group size/number of guests in any case – it's simpler and easier to charge per holiday as most likely you'll be paying the cleaning agency the same for each changeover and the difference in laundry prices is minimal.

Village, countryside and coastal lets, including holiday parks

If you happen to live in a beautiful part of the country, it certainly makes sense to scope out your local area for a holiday home. Even if your area is not typically a 'touristy' area, you would be surprised at how many people are looking to 'get away from it all' – for peace and seclusion. But you do need to be financially prepared for quiet months on the calendar – this is usually off-set against the lucrative busy summer months. November to February (except Christmas and New year which are usually very popular) will be the quietest months and you will find yourself offering shorter breaks, and two-night breaks, if viable (versus cleaning/changeover costs) during these months. If you are happy to clean and launder, then your costs will be significantly lower. If you require housekeeping services, then your first port of call is to check whether there is a cleaning and laundry agency who service the area – this has been my biggest struggle with the business at times. Holiday letting is a very fast growth area, so even quite remote areas are finally responding with cleaning and laundering companies springing up in previously un-serviced areas. But always check this before falling in love with your dream property in the middle of nowhere. More typically touristy areas will always book more easily and quickly, but platforms like Airbnb are useful in that they encourage people to look beyond a search area, via the listings page, or on the map. Your property may not always book up first, but once all the cottages have gone in the famous village five or more miles away, you'll be next on the search list. If your prices are competitive enough, or your home enticing enough, then some people will prioritise you above the homes in the middle of the tourist village or town in any case. If you are looking at a remote area you may find that you need to be a bit more competitive with pricing and services and your home made to be as desirable as possible to compete with the homes in neighbouring, better-known villages. You need to focus on what your property can offer, compared to the competition – be it a beautiful garden, privacy, wildlife, a nearby lake, an amazing view, a beautifully decorated or original-looking home, a hot tub, attention to detail and so on. A beautiful finish and good photography will stand you in good stead amongst the competition, as will canny marketing – think getting a feature in an interiors magazine, or a beautiful blog-type Instagram account showcasing the best of your home or area. Even tiny homes, if well decorated, with quirky and interesting features can be surprisingly successful. It always amazes me how a tiny shepherd's hut often costs more to rent than a two-bedroom cottage, because it looks sweet and interesting, with fairy lights, fire pit and hot tub.

If you do not live in the countryside, but are looking to buy a rural let, maybe with a plan to use it as a holiday home for yourself as well, it is best to live no more than two hours away in my experience – that is if you wish to have any involvement in the running of the business. Even if you plan to have your holiday home fully managed (including listings, bookings and changeovers) by an agency, there will be occasions when you need to physically visit and anything more than a four-hour round trip will not be enjoyable or practical. One to one-and-a-half hours away is generally my limit. A burst pipe or major incident may well require you to visit. There are holiday home agencies who will fully manage your let, but they will generally take a large commission, and you will find maintenance call outs, sundries and supplies will be provided at a premium rate. My experience with agencies is that they will never care for your property or guests as well as you could. They remove a lot of day-to-day stress, but you pay a high price for this, and you will probably be disappointed the next time you visit and notice all the things that have not been taken care of. Reviews will generally start off well and deteriorate throughout the year as things are missed or spoiled through use. Some of the high-end holiday let agencies are not too affected by this however, if they are the only listing provider, as they generally have control over the reviews and may not share the very bad ones, even if they claim to. There is little incentive for them to do so. Airbnb is a more open and fair listing site in this sense at least, for guests. A holiday let agency will choose your cleaning team and laundry provider – things can quickly deteriorate, in terms of upkeep, decoration, supplies and general attention to detail when your property is fully managed for you. I have stayed at holiday cottages run by agencies and a slight air of neglect is often noticeable. It depends whether this will bother you greatly, or if it does start to impact your business – i.e. if disgruntled guests find another platform to review you on, or you have no repeat-bookers etc. I do feel we have a serious duty of care, as a holiday provider, to ensure guests arrive at a clean, well-equipped home. Not all holiday let landlords have this sense of obligation, and maybe they save themselves a lot of stress, upset and money as a result – but generally I find that people notice the extra effort and attention to detail that is put in and do appreciate it, which leads to good reviews, and therefore more bookings and repeat bookers. Even if you plan to be very hands-off, you will still need to visit at an absolute minimum of once a year to check things over or to do maintenance/replacement of furnishings even if you are fully managed. You might be lucky and find a holiday let agency that takes care of everything, including redecoration, maintenance and replacing broken items, deep cleans and so on. Whilst this is more likely at a very high-end level, with a very high commission to match, I have yet to find one.

Seaside holiday lets are another market in themselves – extremely popular during the summer months, but can struggle out of season, unless there is something very special about them. People will travel to a large, beautiful house for a short stay or special occasion, out of season, in my experience, but most of your income will be made between May and September, with June to August being the most profitable months. Houses will cost a great deal more if there is a sea view or close proximity to a beach. Be aware that being very seasonal, coastal lets could potentially struggle to fulfil minimum occupancy clauses set by the government for you to qualify as a holiday let and you could find your let taxed as a second home. If the revenue is good enough from the summer months, however, this may not deter you in any case. But tread very carefully if you're considering Wales as local councils have been given powers to tax second homes at a much higher rate if they do not meet the occupancy requirements set by the Welsh government.

There are few bargains to be found when searching for coastal properties – even amongst those homes which require complete modernisation. The boom spots of Cornwall, Dorset and Devon are always the most popular for holidaymakers, followed by upmarket coastal resorts on the south-east and east coast – think Whitstable, Rye, Camber Sands, Southwold and so on. Northern coastal areas can also be very popular but are not as busy as the south or as expensive. Northumberland is beautiful and relatively unspoilt compared to the south, but you will still pay premium prices in the desirable coastal areas here as well – Bamburgh, Craster and Alnmouth are lovely and Seahouses is very popular during the summer months.

Whitby, Filey, Scarborough, Robin Hood's Bay and Tynemouth are all desirable seaside towns in the northeast. Blackpool in the northwest is always busy – especially for the summer and the autumn Illuminations. The Welsh coast is very popular with holidaymakers and has a lot of beautiful, unspoilt coastline, along with popular seaside towns such as Mumbles, Aberystwyth, Rhossili and Tenby, to name just a few. The capital, Cardiff, and Swansea are also popular and thriving city coastal destinations. The Pembrokeshire Coast is the UK's only coastal National Park and is a very popular holiday destination, along with Anglesey and the Gower Peninsula. However, as I discuss in more detail in chapter seven, the Welsh government is beginning to crack down on the holiday let market, in terms of taxation and occupancy, so tread very carefully here and do your research. As always, some cheaper spots can be found the further inland you move, or in the slightly less picturesque areas between the better-known towns, but rental income potential will reflect this. Overall, my feeling is that Wales is best avoided as somewhere to purchase a holiday home due to current legislation.

Scotland has miles of beautiful, unspoilt coastline and lots of islands, but it is a long journey for many, especially in the northern regions and not many people will be prepared to brave the weather out of season. There is a thriving market for holidays in Scottish rural areas and the national parks in particular, along with cities (especially Edinburgh) and coastal and island homes, but unless you live within a couple of hours' drive, I would not consider buying into this market. If you do, then you will probably find some more reasonably priced bolt holes in more remote areas and there are a lot more miles of undiscovered and unspoiled rural areas in Scotland than anywhere else in the UK. However, whether you can get properties in these areas serviced by cleaners and a laundry service will be another matter. Again, be very careful if considering Scotland, due to recent new legislation which has tightened up holiday let rules (see chapter seven).

Overall, there are few 'undiscovered' areas on the British coastline though and it's a market I've generally avoided due to the initial set up cost, house prices and seasonal dips. You will attract more families and those with dogs in this market and will need to be prepared for sand everywhere – sand and dogs (or even just sand), means that you need a very robust, practical home. There is understandably a lot of resentment in Cornwall at the moment towards the holiday let market, due to a chronic shortage of housing, and it would not be unfeasible to imagine the council beginning to crack down further on holiday and second homeowners in the near future. Large, detached coastal properties can command incredible prices during peak season in Cornwall, but they will have a purchase price tag to reflect this.

There are many holiday parks around the UK, especially on the coast, made up of older bungalows, lodges and caravans, which stipulate purely holiday use, so these may still be worth looking at, and will cost a lot less than a 'real' home due to the restrictions usually imposed on them. The older bungalows are probably a better idea than more recent lodges and static caravans, as they often date from the 1960s or 1970s, and are more permanent that the lodges or caravans which will need to be replaced after a certain number of years as per the park policy – this is why caravans and lodges do not hold much value and can be difficult to re-sell. Annual park fees can be another major running cost as well. However, the quality and building materials of these old bungalows can often be questionable. I have seen some older ones recently which have clearly been renovated and can look very smart with new windows, redecoration and landscaping. The utilities/heating system can often be outdated and the build quality not very high – they may be prone to mould and damp in winter. Some of the parks have definitely seen better days and may not appeal to a younger crowd looking for Instagram-worthy glamour. You may find that a renovated holiday bungalow in a park does very well for families and groups of friends through the summer months, if you are able to maximise your occupancy and profits, and if the park fees are not too high. I would not buy one of the modern, and usually more expensive, lodges in the newer parks now springing up, however lovely the finish and setting, as the park fees will be high and its long term value very questionable – a new lodge or caravan will lose value faster than any other type of home and although lodges will seem like a good bargain compared to a permanent home, its value will always be capped by its status as a holiday home. Sometimes the parks will insist on managing the bookings if you sublet your lodge, and may charge commission, or there may be a rule against subletting. Always read the fine print if you're looking at the holiday park route. It's worth considering for places like Cornwall, as at least it does not always impact on the difficult local housing situation if the park is purely for holiday use. Many of these parks will close for a month or two in the winter.

Basic holiday let legal information to consider in your search:

I cover legal requirements for holiday lets in the UK in chapter seven in detail, but it is worth noting here that legislation is being tightened up throughout the UK at the moment. Wales has increased its occupancy thresholds for properties to qualify as holiday lets and councils' power to increase tax by up to 300% on second homes. Scotland now requires holiday let owners to apply for a licence. It has also introduced the first short-term rental control scheme, which currently applies to Edinburgh, due to a severe lack of affordable housing and rentals there. Planning permission is now also required to set up holiday let in Edinburgh and each case is treated by its own merits, with no guarantee that you will be able to proceed. I would tread very carefully if you are considering Scotland and Wales. It seems that there is a move by the UK government to tackle the issue of the shortage of available housing and affordable rentals in certain property hotspots, so do bear this in mind in your search, as taxes and restrictions seem likely to increase in these areas in the future. Always check current legislation and rules with your local council, as well as the government website, when researching a specific area. Some cities, such as London, can also have their own set of additional requirements or slightly different thresholds and rules.

Remember to bear in mind the UK 31 day limit rule which applies to short term holiday let occupancy rules (more about this in chapter seven). Stays *can* be extended beyond 31 days, but it can impact whether you fulfil occupancy criteria which then determines whether you will be able to continue trading as a holiday let. As there are various financial benefits to being classed as an official furnished holiday let, the government are working to ensure that all holiday let owners are genuinely and fully striving to run a holiday let business rather than simply trying to avoid certain taxes or costs for a second home or buy-to-let property or looking to profit from capital gains.

Also, be mindful of clauses on blocks of flats which can prohibit you from renting them out as holiday lets and check any service charges for leasehold properties and apartments.

Popular destinations by recent polls:

The ten most popular UK regions for the summer holidays in 2021 (source: BBC):

1. North Wales
2. Cumbria
3. Cornwall
4. Devon
5. North Yorkshire
6. Yorkshire Dales
7. Peak District
8. South Wales
9. East Anglia
10. Dorset

The ten fastest-growing UK regions for summer 2021 (BBC):

1. Peak District
2. Somerset
3. East Anglia
4. Yorkshire Dales
5. Southern Scotland
6. Heart of England
7. Central Scotland
8. Devon

9. Northumberland

10. Cornwall

Top ten areas to buy a holiday home in the UK in order of best financial returns (data from Sykes Holidays April 2023):

1. Dorset

2. Peak District

3. Northumberland

4. Yorkshire Dales

5. Somerset

6. Devon

7. North Wales

8. Highlands and Islands

9. North York Moors and Coast

10. South Coast

Top 15 most popular UK holiday and short break destination cities (source; AV Travel):

London, Edinburgh, Bath, York, Belfast, Bristol, Brighton, Newcastle, Manchester, Cardiff, Liverpool, Durham, Norwich, Glasgow, Birmingham

Top 20 UK Staycation (UK visitors) spots according to a Daily Mail article, April 2023:

1. Yorkshire
2. Cornwall
3. Scottish Highlands and Islands
4. Cumbria
5. Northumberland
6. Devon
7. Norfolk
8. Berkshire
9. North Wales
10. Isle of Wight
11. Dorset
12. Derbyshire
13. London
14. Scottish Borders
15. Buckinghamshire
16. Suffolk
17. South Wales
18. Cambridgeshire
19. Central Scotland
20. Somerset

Key points

- Buy as close to your own home as possible - preferably never more than two hours' drive away. The most successful lets usually have hands-on owners.
- If going ahead with a more distantly located let, then consider using a fully managed service via a lettings agency or employing a housekeeper/cleaner who is happy to deal with maintenance and other potential issues. You should still aim to visit occasionally.
- Do not underestimate travelling time and the frequency that you will need to visit.
- Do not rely on local friends or family to help run your holiday let if you do not live nearby.
- Holiday lets can do very well in popular tourist areas, but markets can sometimes get saturated and property prices will reflect the desirability of an area.
- Choose a budget and stick to it when property searching – I would advise starting with something modest.
- Research running and set-up costs of your let along with realistic potential earning before committing to buy. Always underestimate revenue in your calculations.
- Check out the provision of cleaning and laundry companies before committing.
- The holiday let market can be very volatile, be wary of over-stretching yourself financially.
- Research holiday let mortgages carefully if you plan to take one out – not all mortgage companies will cover holiday lets. Your insurance could be invalidated if you do not have the correct type of mortgage.

- Check with your local planning department and the current government guidelines for any holiday let legislation or restrictions.
- Be very wary of buying in Wales due to recent changes in legislation.
- Proceed with caution if considering Scotland due to increased restrictions and laws. Edinburgh is particularly problematic, and you cannot assume that you will be able to set up a new holiday let there.
- Check with your local planning office if you are thinking of letting out a room or annexe at your own home. You will still require holiday let insurance and you will need to notify your mortgage company who may not consent to you renting part, or all, of your home to paying guests.
- Look at properties on free online listing sites to get a sense of the prices that people are charging for different properties in various areas. Bear in mind that these sites will typically be taking a commission of between 3 and 15%. Also look at properties on holiday agency websites for inspiration and pricing guides – agencies will generally be charging owners a higher commission than the free listing sites, anything from 15% to 60%. Also use Google Maps to check out other holiday lets in your chosen area.
- Look for a gap in the market – sometimes it's a good idea to look beyond the obviously popular areas. Not all guests are holiday makers.
- Unless you are considering London, I would always advise that your let provides some kind of parking provision. One or more allocated parking spaces are always preferable.

- If considering flats and apartments, always check the lease carefully as some have clauses which prevent them from being sublet or used for short term lets.
- If considering an apartment, plan how guests will access your flat and where keys will be collected from – concierges may not be happy to hold keys for your guests and there may not be anywhere suitable to put a key safe on the outside of the building.
- A property with a maximum of three bedrooms is usually advisable for a first let.
- Cities are likelier to have year-round interest and occupancy than rural or coastal areas.
- Consider parking provision - even if you don't believe your guests will need it, your cleaners, builders and tradespeople may require it. Most guests will expect some kind of parking unless your let is in London.

Chapter Three
Listing sites and holiday let agencies

Having found and bought a suitable holiday home, you will probably want to start running your business as soon as possible. Along with undertaking any renovation and furnishing works, one of the first things to decide is whether you wish to market and sell through one of the many online holiday let agencies, independently through free online holiday let listing sites, and/or direct through your own website, or a combination of several of these options.

Holiday let agencies

Broadly speaking, online holiday let agencies are typically geared towards non-city destinations and tend to focus on rural, village and coastal homes. Some examples of popular holiday let agencies include Sykes Cottages, Holidaycottages.co.uk (who also own Gorgeous Cottages and Ingrid Flute Cottages amongst others), English Cottages, Perfect Stays, Boutique Retreats, Olivers Travels, Sawday's and Rural Retreats. Most areas in the UK will also have a number of smaller more localised holiday agencies operating there too. Town and city lets tend to be managed by more specialised local agencies dealing with a specific area, usually with an office situated in the town. These tend to have less marketing power and exposure than the large nationwide agencies, although most will have an online presence. Most agencies take payment in the form of commission from bookings, although some also have joining and/or annual fees as well. Generally, commission is quite a bit higher for holiday homeowners when using a holiday let agency, compared to the free online listing holiday let sites.

The main difference between the free online listing sites, such as Airbnb, holidaylettings.co.uk/Trip Advisor, Vrbo/Expedia, Booking.com and a holiday let agency site is that agencies will tend to manage your holiday home bookings, calendar and payments on your behalf. You will probably have little or no communication with guests or potential guests. The holiday let agency claims to offer a closer relationship with the holiday let owner than the free independent listing sites, with the agency vetting and checking the property and owner prior to listing the let – not everyone with a holiday home will be accepted, especially by the high end and luxury holiday let agencies. Some agencies will only accept certain properties onto their books and may have a checklist of amenities and standards that properties must meet in order to be considered.

Each agency will have a slightly different business model and you may find that you are able to have more involvement in the booking and guest communication process in some cases, depending on the agency. Generally, most agencies are geared towards managing your let for you, particularly the calendar and booking process. Many of them will offer different tiers of service and a sliding commission scale to suit different needs and budgets, typically ranging from 15% up to 60%. Some may have a joining or annual fee as well. Some will just charge one large joining or annual fee and will not take any commission. Many agencies will be able to fully manage your let – from setting up the listing, providing photos and marketing, arranging housekeeping, bookings, updating your calendar, communicating with guests and arranging maintenance and so on. Some will let you pick and choose in terms of what you want them to do. It is quite common for an agency to be keen to manage your calendar, bookings and communications with guests, but let you arrange the housekeeping and maintenance. Indeed, I often find that agencies can be reluctant to take on housekeeping and maintenance roles, as they can be the most challenging part of the business. Personally, I haven't ever been prepared to pay a large chunk of commission purely for them to manage my calendar and guest communications. I think the main value in using a holiday agency is if you really don't have time to manage your let yourself and are looking for a fully managed service, or if you have a very high-end property which will rent at a high rate, and you want the professionalism and kudos that a top end agency can offer to represent your business. Another reason to consider using an agency is if you live some distance away and cannot be on hand to deal with issues and maintenance - you will most likely require a fully managed service in this case.

 I notice that smaller locally based agencies often get booked up quickly by holiday let owners and are often reluctant to take on new clients, especially if they're successfully managing the housekeeping and maintenance element of their clients' businesses as well. Fully inclusive local agencies (those who are prepared to run every aspect of your holiday let for you) are hard to find. This is probably because their commission doesn't tend to be as high as the national agencies', plus they're experts in their local fields, with a good working knowledge of local services. Their smaller size means that they can only stretch their services so far, hence the difficulty in finding one. If you can find a local agency which is prepared to manage your bookings, housekeeping, and general maintenance, you should seriously consider letting them manage your holiday home (depending on their commission and reputation of course). I would not be inclined to go with a localised holiday let agency which only offered to manage your bookings and calendar though, as you will still be paying substantial commission, but for relatively low exposure to potential guests compared to the larger national agencies. If the smaller agency also has calendar exclusivity requirements (e.g. you need to reserve a set number of weeks for the agency each year) then you may want to avoid it. Some housekeeping companies offer to help with calendars and bookings as well, although this is rarer and I think it is better to find an agency which specialises in the booking and listing process, rather than a housekeeping business offering it as a sideline.

Most agencies will usually demand a certain level of exclusivity from your holiday let in return for their services and pricing model. Some will expect full exclusivity, which means that you cannot advertise anywhere else, and others will request that you keep a certain percentage of the calendar free for them each year and that you notify the agency of any bookings you make outside of their calendar so that they can update it accordingly. There will be more room for error once you're dealing with multiple calendars, so make sure that they have a good reputation and calendar system if you decide to go down this route. Agencies will often dictate fairly restrictive terms when it comes to calendar availability and often limit the number of dates you can use the home yourself, especially during peak season. You will have to give up a degree of control over your property.

Some customers, especially older people, are very wary of the free holiday listing sites such as Airbnb and feel more comfortable booking through an official holiday let agency, and this is another way in which the holiday let agency works well for some owners. However, you will often find the same homes on the 'exclusive' holiday agency sites also listing independently on Airbnb, usually at a much lower price. Many of the free independent holiday listing sites have insurance built into their contracts these days, so it isn't usually any riskier for guests to use them instead of an 'official' holiday let agency in any case. It is easier for agencies to hide bad reviews, as they manage their own listings and control what can be seen on their websites. I have found a lot of holiday let agencies do not really live up to the high expectations they promise. The national agencies can have a lot of homes on their books and can sometimes struggle to give the same attention to detail that an owner might provide. If they are managing everything, including housekeeping, they will be setting up contracts with local cleaning and laundry companies, but will rarely check the standard of work or keep a close eye on the details of the day-to-day running of the let. They are most likely to become aware of a problem or something which requires attention when they receive their first angry email or low rating for a cottage from a guest. The upside is that they will have to deal with the guest, instead of you. Of course, you do have the option to have the agency fully manage the let whilst still making regular site visits yourself to do any necessary repairs and deep cleaning or any or the other myriad of little jobs which are often overlooked. However, in this case you are not really benefiting from one of the main perks of using an agency, which is to remove the pressures and time demands involved in running a holiday home. All agencies are different, so I recommend researching them thoroughly and finding genuine customer testimonials before choosing one. Also check their terms and conditions very carefully before committing to a contract with them.

 The biggest advantages of using a holiday let agency for most holiday homeowners is being able to hand over most or all the tasks, stress and management of running the let, along with giving confidence to wary holiday makers by being a well-known name in the business with exposure to a wide audience. They will often offer a lot of advice and guidelines for your let and will usually provide professional photography as well.

I do find that agencies tend to underprice accommodation, sometimes quite significantly – I was once quoted 60% less than I was currently charging for a week's stay at a holiday let I manage when I enquired about typical revenue via one of the large national agencies. With a basic starting rate commission of 22% + VAT, plus a joining fee and additional cleaning and laundry costs, I would have struggled to make much profit at all. Be very wary of looking at agencies first when trying to get a sense of potential revenue for this reason. They will fill your calendar quickly and easily at a lower price, and have excellent exposure and marketing power, but you may have little profit to show for your let at the end of the year. If a good profit is not essential to you and you are looking to let a home with minimal stress and involvement, then it is worth considering. Given that councils are beginning to increase council tax for empty second homes in particular, I can imagine that there will be homeowners looking to avoid this by turning their second homes into holiday lets. Bear in mind that a full calendar will also translate into higher maintenance and running costs; if your profit is already fairly minimal or flat due to high commission, you could potentially end up losing money overall once these additional costs are factored in. Holiday let agencies will sometimes insist on setting your pricing. Also, it is not always possible or easy to make immediate changes to your occupancy and pricing throughout the year as you can on the independent listing sites where you have complete control over your calendar. Some agencies will decide on 'base' prices at the start of the year and stick to them regardless of performance.

Some large holiday let agencies:

Sykes Cottages, Rural Retreats, Perfect Stays, Classic Cottages, Cottages.com, Premier Cottages, Pass the Keys, Coast and Country, Sawdays, holidaycottages.co.uk, Original Cottages, Boutique Retreats, Olivers Travels.

There are many more holiday let agencies based around the country, along with localised ones which focus on certain areas or counties which may be worth looking at, especially in scenic, popular places, coastal areas and national parks. Some of these will also have a local office in a tourist area with an office for walk-in trade. City holiday let breaks are more typically booked through Airbnb, Expedia/VRBO, Trip Advisor/Holidaylettings.co.uk, Booking.com, along with smaller local city-based holiday let agencies. Some regular rental agencies also now encompass holiday lets as it is a growing market and they often have city centre offices. Some of the large holiday let agencies own several businesses and will advertise your property on various sister sites, with the same pricing and descriptions, for maximum exposure.

Independent holiday let listing sites

I prefer to use free, independent listing sites for my holiday lets due to a lack of any calendar exclusivity clauses, lower commission and their large, international customer base. They are usually free to join and make money by charging you and/or guests commission per stay. The best known and biggest independent online holiday home listing site is currently Airbnb, but it is worth bearing in mind that it is certainly not the only one. I also use Booking.com, Vrbo (also links to, and replicates listings on, Expedia) and Trip Advisor (links to, and replicates listings on, holidaylettings.co.uk in the

UK plus acts as a referral site for other unconnected listing sites). Booking.com is probably the second most used website for guests searching and booking self-catering accommodation, in my experience, followed by Vrbo (previously called Owners Direct and Home Away), which seems to be expanding, and it is connected to the large travel agency Expedia. I find that I get more international travellers from this site. I do not get many bookings directly from Trip Advisor these days, and the company seems to be moving towards more of a referral service model of business, which links to the best bookable prices on other listing platforms including Booking.com. It should still be possible to book directly through Trip Advisor and its listings are replicated on holidaylettings.co.uk for UK hosts and guests. It also connects with other sites including FlipKey, Niumba, House Trip and Vacation Home Rentals which are more international. There are lots of other free online listing sites, but I would only focus on a few of the larger ones listed above, possibly just Airbnb to start with, whilst you're finding your feet. Most of the major listing sites tend to be completely free to list on and will take commission from each booking you receive. The larger listing sites are also geared up to export and import changes to your calendar with their rivals – if you get a booking on one site, it is possible to automatically block the dates on other listing sites if you link up the calendars. Most of them use the same i-Cal application.

   Unlike holiday let agencies, the independent listing sites are open to all hosts. They will still need to vet your business and verify you before allowing your listing to go live, but it is usually a very straightforward process. All of the sites have easy to use technology which will guide you through the process of setting up your listing. You will initially have to provide your own photography, but some companies, particularly Airbnb, will offer free professional photography once your listing has been up and running for a while. All of the listing sites allow guests to review properties and most of them allow hosts to review or score guests, except for Booking.com. You will be responsible for setting your calendar prices, discounts, weekly prices and so on. You will communicate directly with guests, although payment will be handled by the listing site and forwarded to you once the guest has checked in, minus any commission.

When setting my prices on the various listing sites, I factor in their commission and any other costs - this means that my prices vary from site to site. I will sometimes add a cleaning and laundry fee on sites which charge higher commission, or simply raise the nightly rate. Generally, customers will shop around and choose the best price for them - they may find your listing on one site, but book through another. Some owners will block peak periods on the sites which charge more commission, if they feel confident that the dates will book easily elsewhere. If you want dates available on one listing site, but not another, then avoid synching your calendars as calendar blocks are exported automatically otherwise.

To summarise; Booking.com charges owners the most commission at between 10 and 20% of the overall price paid by the guest (this varies depending on the property and location, but typically I have always been charged around 15%), followed by VRBO/Expedia at around 8%, whilst Airbnb and Trip Advisor/Holidaylettings.co.uk both typically charge owners around 3% commission. Most sites will also charge a small payment fee for processing the payout. Booking.com is the only site which currently only charges the host, with no additional fees payable by the guest. The other sites make money by adding 'guest fees' which are usually a variable percentage of the overall booking price and by charging owners a small commission. Please note; Airbnb has started to change its payment/commission model in some countries and for some new hosts and this could be a change that is rolled out further afield. Check the payment and commission terms carefully when signing up to Airbnb so that you can price your accommodation accordingly. I currently pay 3% as do most UK hosts but be mindful of any potential changes that could be introduced.

Consider looking at alternative listing websites if you are looking to rent out a room within your own home or an annex. Listing sites such as Homestays.com specialise in this field and are expanding quickly. Prices will typically range from £16 to £40 per night for an individual room and guests will often expect to have access to your kitchen and living spaces. A large room with an ensuite and basic kitchenette or an annex with its own facilities would be ideal for this set up, and would command a higher price, but lots of people list a single room on the site and are happy to share bathrooms and living spaces with their guests. A lot of younger people are turning their back on sites such as Airbnb due to the damage it is doing in some communities and are happy for a simpler, cheaper experience when travelling. Airbnb is one of the few large international listing sites which does still list individual rooms to rent within hosts' own homes so is still worth considering as well, if you are looking to do this. I think they are aware of the new competition springing up and are currently trying to make the individual room rental model more appealing on their site by encouraging hosts to make the experience more personal and friendly through a variety of means including more host information and quirky extras. This side of their business has recently been re-launched and is called 'Airbnb Rooms' - it's partly due to the cost-of-living crisis and is also trying to appeal to younger travellers who want to stay at simpler and cheaper accommodation. The average price for an Airbnb room in the UK is £59 according to the co-founder of the site.

You may also like to consider listing on alternative and ethical listing sites such as Fairbnb which is a free listing site which diverts some of the host commission towards local schemes and charities in the area that the home is listed – it is a business model which tries to actively support local communities.

I find that the listing companies are somewhat opaque about their 'guest fees' and do not always state them clearly for hosts, and they can vary depending on the type of property and its location and can change over time. They will be a percentage of the overall accommodation cost and will be listed separately in the payment summary of each booking. Having gone through my payment pages and various terms and conditions pages I can summarise some average/typical guest fees; Vrbo is typically around 12%, Trip Advisor/Holidaylettings.co.uk is typically anywhere between 8-16% depending on the property and area, and Airbnb typically around 10-15%. Booking.com does not charge the guest additional fees. Bear in mind that these charges can be altered by the company at any time. I will discuss managing your own website and calendar later, but being aware of guest fees and commission on the free listing sites is very useful when it comes to pricing your own calendar competitively on your own website in order to encourage direct bookings. As I will explain later, the direct booker is the best type of booking and guest in my opinion.

Key points

- Holiday let agencies will usually take higher commission from hosts, compared to independent listing sites, in return for a more tailored, personal service. They will usually arrange payments and communication with guests. Some will also help arrange cleaning and laundry, although it will be at an additional cost. Expect to pay commission anywhere from 15 to 60%, depending on the area, property and level of service you require. Some will have joining fees.
- Holiday let agencies can be suited to hosts who do not plan to be involved in the day-to-day running of their lets and some are geared towards luxury properties. Some agencies will only accept certain properties onto their books and may have a checklist of amenities and standards that properties have to meet in order to be considered.
- National holiday agencies worth checking out; Sykes Cottages, Holidaycottages.co.uk, Perfect Stays, Boutique Retreats, Olivers Travels, Sawdays, Classic Cottages and Rural Retreats. Also check out smaller local agencies.
- Downsides of using a holiday let agency; they will often demand a certain amount of exclusivity from your calendar, and you may be limited in terms of how often you can stay at the property. The fees can be very high. The larger national agencies are unlikely to keep your property in top notch condition – they will be using the local available cleaning and laundry services, but details and maintenance issues can sometimes be overlooked. Many agencies are keen to deal with bookings,

payment and guest communication but some will not cover cleaning, laundry and maintenance. It may be difficult or impossible to tweak your prices and occupancy requirements throughout the year.
- Upsides of using a holiday let agency; some people trust official holiday let agencies more than free listing sites. The high-end national agencies can be suited to luxury properties and will market them accordingly. The large national agencies have a large audience and will have a proper marketing department working for you. They will typically take professional photographs and guide you through the listing process or set up the listing on your behalf. You will rarely need to communicate with your guests directly and most issues or feedback will be dealt with by the agency. Local agencies will have access to local information and are more likely to be able to help with housekeeping, laundry and maintenance.
- Independent holiday listing sites: these are open to all hosts, usually free to join and will generally charge lower commission than holiday let agencies. There are usually no calendar restrictions. Independent holiday let listing sites to consider include Airbnb, Booking.com, Vrbo (linked to Expedia) and Trip Advisor (linked to holidaylettings.co.uk). Hosts set up their own listing, usually using automated software which guides them through the process. You will communicate directly with guests, set your nightly and weekly prices and any discounts by yourself on the independent sites. The site will handle payments and forward your payment, minus commission, once the guest has checked in. You can

tweak prices and occupancy requirements as and when you want to. You have complete control over your calendar.
- Start with Airbnb initially – it is the largest free listing site, very international and is one of the easiest to use and typically charges hosts a low commission of around 3%. Guests are charged additional booking fees.
- Booking.com generally charges one of the higher commissions for hosts, typically around 10 to 20% depending on the property and location. It has a large international following and does not charge guests additional fees.
- Vrbo/Expedia typically charges hosts around 8% commission. Vrbo is a growing website with a strong US database, but it does have an international reach. Vrbo charges guests additional booking fees.
- Trip Advisor / Holidaylettings.co.uk typically charges hosts around 3% commission and also charges guests a booking fee. Trip Advisor increasingly seems to be acting as a referral site which links to other companies such as Booking.com, but guests can book directly through them and their sister site, Holidaylettings.
- Roomstays is a listing site which advertises private rooms or annexes in people's own homes – its prices are generally lower than regular holiday let sites. Airbnb has recently relaunched its private room business, Airbnb Rooms, due to increased competition and more people looking for budget-friendly, personal accommodation.
- Most of the main free listing sites use the same i-Cal calendar software, meaning that calendars can be

linked and updated automatically by bookings on other sites.
- Factor in the commission charged by the different listing sites when setting your nightly prices and any additional fees.

Chapter Four
Setting up an Airbnb listing

An introduction to Airbnb

A large part of the success of Airbnb is in its straightforward format, for owners and guests, along with its international reach – it is the best-known holiday let listing platform in the world and is used in most countries. It is relatively easy to set up a new Airbnb listing and you are guided through it by an online bot from start to finish. Whilst the calendar is easy to use, I will discuss some of the features which can be a little less obvious to find for the first-time user. Airbnb has tightened up its regulations in response to criticism in recent years, meaning that they will now require full ID and proof of who you are before your listing can go live. The main advantages of Airbnb for me are low commission per booking, (typically around 3%), a large international customer base and the ability to vet and review guests and respond to reviews. Airbnb adds an extra 'guest fee' which is usually around 14% of the accommodation price added for the guest to pay. However, they have recently started changing their fee structure in some countries and for some new hosts, so check this carefully when you set up your listing in case they apply the new fee system to you. The new system increases host fees to around 14% and completely removes the guest fee. There is a chance that these changes will be further rolled out across the board, so keep an eye on this. However, it seems that most UK hosts are still mostly being charged around 3% for the time being. The bulk of my bookings now come from Airbnb and private bookings, so it is the obvious place for a new holiday homeowner to start. Airbnb, whilst best known for regular holiday rentals, still advertises individual rooms within private homes and guests can easily search the database of listings by the type of accommodation they want, be it a holiday cottage, private room within the host's own home, caravan, teepee, tree house or glamping pod and so on. It is suited to many different types of guest and budget.

Guests like Airbnb for its payment handling and promise of refunds in certain cases if things go wrong. Hosts are automatically insured, for free, by their program, 'AirCover', against liability (up to $1 million USD) and damage (up to $3 million USD), and Airbnb says it will offer hosts help and support if there are any problems with guests or bookings. However, I always recommend that hosts (and guests) have their own insurance in place in any case. There have been horror stories in the press of hosts having their properties trashed by fake bookers holding parties and so on and not being suitably compensated, although Airbnb had increased its guest-screening process including more careful ID checks, along with hosts having the option to ask guests to agree to rules and terms in advance of their stay.

Airbnb is often chosen by guests looking for a unique home-from-home experience and by those who wish to self-cater. It is now a firm favourite with families, but young and older couples also favour it for the freedom it gives when travelling, ease of booking and the sense of staying in a proper home as opposed to a hotel – it usually works out cheaper than hotels too. I found that guests tended to be friendlier a few years ago, and I think many assumed they were staying in my personal home, as this was very much the original model of the business – people renting out a spare room and airbed (hence 'Airbnb') or their own home when they were away.

There are still guests who hark back to these 'golden' days of more personal experiences, where they often would make friends with the host and family or stay in someone's home with all its belongings and personal effects, but over recent years the whole business has become a lot more professional, although there are still plenty of personal homes and private rooms available to book on the site. However, these days, most guests now expect a more professional holiday let experience and have quite high standards. I have incidentally recently stayed in someone's second home via Airbnb and found the cleanliness lacking, and the profusion of personal objects left out, including toothbrushes, half-used food in the fridge etc., rather unnerving, so this model is not for everyone (me included). I think most guests would object to this in any case, especially if they are paying the equivalent of a professionally run holiday let for the honour of staying in someone's slightly messy home – some people might prefer this 'authentic' experience, however, especially if it is at a reduced price. If you are thinking of renting a spare room or your own home or second home, do bear in mind that it generally has to be done to a proper standard, but more on this later.

Airbnb has had a lot of bashing from guests recently due to the extra 'unseen' fees added by hosts (typically for cleaning and linen, for example) which have historically only become clear once the guest comes to pay, along with Airbnb's guest fees. Airbnb have recently made this more transparent so that guests can see the full price of the accommodation at the point of booking. Some hosts have removed additional cleaning fees and simply increased their nightly rate in response to this – some have claimed that they have increased bookings and revenues by doing so.

Much of the information and advice below will be applicable to other listing sites. Just to note; sometimes the website set up can be a little confusing for newbies initially. You can choose 'calendar view' and alter the nightly prices here, but to edit the actual listing, you need to click on the top right button 'menu' then select 'listing' and then proceed from there to change or add any details to your existing listing. If you have more than one property, you will select from between them on these buttons and they will be displayed here. You can add multiple properties to one account and use the same email and bank details, or you can add different bank accounts for different properties. Airbnb will manage payments and will release your payout 24 hours after guests check in to your home and it usually takes a few extra days for the money to reach your account.

I strongly advise setting up your listing on a PC or laptop as it is much easier to do this on a larger screen than on a mobile screen – the editing and calendars are a little different on the mobile app and desktop sites. I would recommend downloading the mobile Airbnb app once your listing is up and running, so that you can keep an eye on your business and reply to messages and bookings easily, even when you are out and about. It's generally easier to sort out calendar changes and trip length requirements on a PC rather than the app, especially when you are new to it.

Setting up an Airbnb listing

Listing details, descriptions and photography

The following sections appear under 'listing basics' when you set up a listing. First go to Airbnb.co.uk and click the top right-hand button 'Airbnb your home'. It will immediately show you the rates of properties close to you and average prices (assuming your computer doesn't have your location blocked). Airbnb is very much geared towards nervous newbies and offers new hosts the option to be guided by a more experienced 'Superhost' ('Superhosts' are holiday let owners who score consistently well in review scores and have a generally good track record, including few or no cancellations from the host). There is help via the Airbnb Community, which is made up of other hosts who can offer help and answer questions - this is useful for general queries, although I find that specific account or guest issues usually require help from an Airbnb agent instead.

They also offer a gentle introduction to your first hosting, which is always the most nerve-wracking experience of all, by letting you book a guest with lots of other stays under their belt, with good feedback. I imagine that this avoids new hosts running for the hills if they're unlucky enough to get a difficult guest for their first booking. There are lots of useful facts and FAQs in the introductory pages.

Once you have gone through this you can then press 'set up' and follow the next steps which establish your identity and contact details. I would avoid signing up with a social media account or with Apple or Google, all of which are offered as alternative means of signing up, and instead keep it simple with a regular email and phone number by pressing the red 'continue' button. This will also avoid having your business tied to another type of account which you might wish to close for any reason one day. Airbnb will not share your personal email with guests, but you will receive notifications of bookings and communications from guests and Airbnb to your email.

Listing title

You want something short, snappy and memorable which mentions your property's best features. Characters are limited, so think carefully about this. I always advise holiday let owners to 'name' their property, preferably with something upmarket/enticing sounding, preferably with a unique name, using 'Cottage' or 'House' in the title, depending on whether it is a country or town/city location. A name is always more memorable, guests will find you more easily if they search for you again. If you plan to have your own website and to allow direct bookings, it will allow guests to find you outside of the listing sites. You do not need to officially add this to an address – you keep your house number and road name and include this in the directions, it's just a case of adding a house name plaque to your property and adding it to the top of your address. If your let is in a desirable area, put this in the title, and, if there's room, add how many people the home sleeps – i.e. 'Seashell Cottage, near Padstow, sleeps 5', 'Harebell Cottage, 30m from Bamburgh beach, sea views, sleeps 4', or 'Fenwick House, central Bath townhouse, sleeps 3', for example. If you are somewhere quite isolated or rural then use a superlative about the countryside or mention a peaceful or private location. If you are very centrally located in a town or city, then try to indicate this if you have space. If your property is very high-end with luxurious furnishings and appliances, then try to use the word 'luxury' or similar in the title as well. Guests will usually be using filters such as area, size of home, including bedroom numbers etc., so it's not essential to mention this in your title, but I think it helps to make things as clear as possible.

Listing description

The next section is a more comprehensive listing description where you have 500 characters to play with, which is not as many as you might think once you start writing it, so focus on the best aspects of your let, in order of importance, and keep things clear and simple. People are sold by the idea of your property usually within the first couple of sentences and they may not even bother reading beyond this section of your listing. Do not be shy of using superlatives. Use at least one 'stunning', 'characterful', 'beautiful' or 'luxurious' (assuming this is true!) Try to be as positive as possible whilst also honestly describing your property. Tell guests if your house is detached, if it has good views (you must mention a sea view if you have one), how many people it sleeps, how many bathrooms and bedrooms it has, if it's a central city location, if it's peaceful and how close it is to any major tourist attractions, famous villages, cities or towns. If you have parking in a city or town location also mention this – if you have room on the listing title also mention it there as well. Favourite guest facilities which may be worth mentioning include hot tubs (always number one on the most requested additional facility by guests), followed by barbecues, bike storage, gardens and wood burners. If you live close to a great pub, restaurant or cafe definitely try to mention this here, as it is another top guest favourite – guests love to be within walking distance of a pub in particular. For example, 'Milthorpe Cottage is a beautiful, detached period cottage situated five minutes' drive or a 15 minute picturesque walk from stunning Sandy Bay beach. This characterful, comfortable home offers 3 bedrooms and sleeps up to 6. Hot tub, secure bike storage, barbecue and log burner. Quiet location with large garden.' If your flat is a little small or in a noisy area, stress its upsides – 'very central', 'wonderfully convenient' and emphasise its décor or style, especially if it has a high-end or 'luxury' finish – mention any particularly good pubs, bars or restaurants within easy walking distance, along with any visitor attractions nearby. It is usually worth using some abbreviations and avoiding written numbers to save characters. The more positive information you can squeeze into this section, the better.

Photographs

This is probably one of the most important elements of your entire business and online presence. You will need good photos of all the main rooms, including bedrooms, kitchen, main bathroom (plus ensuites if you have them), living room and any other reception rooms, along with some high-quality external photos, including the facade of your home and any outdoor space you might have. Smart phones have really come on in recent years, and now a decent phone will generally take good enough pictures for your listing, or at least to tide you over with, if you plan to pay for professional photography later on. If you have a good camera, or a friend with a good camera, then certainly utilise this as well. Airbnb sometimes offers free professional photography once your listing is up and running. It is in their interest to showcase your property to its best advantage, so I have always been offered it at some point or other, but do not rely on this offer, as you could be waiting for a while. Airbnb's photographer will automatically upload the photos of your let to the listing once they've been edited, and you can then decide if you wish to keep them all, or you can change the order of them. I have had good and bad Airbnb photographers over the years. Some of the photos are excellent and I haven't changed them yet, despite some of my furnishings having been altered since they were taken. Some were poor on one occasion, and I deleted most of them and then hired my own photographer instead.

If you do need to take your own photos, then make sure that the property is immaculate. I remove bins and hide wires or anything ugly before photographing my let. I advise switching on any table lamps to give rooms a welcoming glow. I generally avoid switching on the main ceiling light, unless the room is particularly dark as they can give off a somewhat yellow, depressing light. Slightly dark, gloomy photos will not encourage anyone to book. Many hosts like to stage rooms with vases of flowers, or trays with cake and tea, although this can be frowned upon as mildly false advertising if you don't plan to have fresh flowers or complimentary food in the let. A lot of holiday hosts do stage photographs, and it can perhaps encourage potential guests to picture themselves on holiday there and give a sense of luxury and potential. Some will have a breakfast tray complete with croissants and coffee on the bed, or a tray of afternoon tea laid out in the living room by a lit fire with candles and a throw draped casually over the sofa. It's a matter of personal choice, as other hosts will show their homes in an empty, tidy state, similar to those used by estate agents.

If you can afford it, then I strongly recommend that you hire a professional photographer, as they will make your home look as good as possible with the best lighting and will occasionally use a wide-angle lens to fit as much of each room as possible into each photo. I often find that my own photos can make the rooms look squished and fail to capture enough of the space in each shot. However, I would be wary of an overly exaggerated wide-angle lens which can make the property look much bigger than it actually is as this could lead to disappointment and negative feedback from guests.

If you are setting your listing up during the winter, then still take external photos of the home and outdoor spaces, but make sure you update them in the spring and then the summer and ensure that the best summer shots are used before any other pictures in the photo order. I like to include photos from different seasons in my rural holiday lets, but I always prioritise the sunny photos, in terms of order, as they showcase the home to its best advantage.

Order your photos carefully. It's usually best to have an external facade photo as your main and first photo, if you are letting a house, followed by the living room and then either the next best reception room or bedroom. If your home doesn't have a particularly attractive or interesting facade, then consider using room photos first. People often decide whether to book after viewing the first few photos, so these are the most important ones. If you are letting a flat, then generally I'd advise putting the living room photo first, followed by the bedroom, then kitchen and bathroom, leaving external shots until last. If you have an impressive garden, hot tub, balcony with a view or pool, then include this photo early in the order of pictures. I try to update photos from time to time, especially if I feel that I have upgraded the space in some way. I also add seasonal photos of the surroundings and of any tourist attractions, although I put these at the end of the photo list, as the main home is more important. If you live very close to a remarkable attraction, however, then it may be worth inserting a photo of this fairly high up in the photo ranking and try to give a sense of your home's proximity to the place, if possible. Some hosts take a distant photo of their home and highlight it in some way to show its placement within its surroundings, especially if they are impressive. You could also consider using a screenshot of Google Maps with your home labelled on it (useful for illustrating proximity to famous sites and popular attractions), or even an aerial photo if you have access to a drone with a camera.

The space

In this section you can go into greater detail about your property's set-up and any special features and facilities. Comfortable and pocket sprung mattresses and bed sizes are worth mentioning, along with quality bed linen and professional cleaning and/or laundering. A lot of families with small children will greatly appreciate things like blackout blinds and curtains, so also mention this here, along with any cots, highchairs and toys that you provide. Stress how well your kitchen is equipped here as it's one of the biggest strengths of self-catering accommodation versus hotel rooms and mention any useful appliances such as a washing machine, tumble dryer, dishwasher, microwave etc. Coffee machines are also very much requested from guests – I do not provide them as they break down and no one ever cleans them, but a cafetière with some complementary coffee is appreciated at the very least. Tell guests about your entertainment systems on offer – sound systems, radios, speakers, what kind of TV you have (including size if it's large) and any satellite or streaming services included such as Netflix and Amazon Video etc. It is surprising how many guests go away to spend a great deal of time indoors watching TV and playing music even if they're surrounded by beautiful hiking terrain or famous landmarks - each to their own! Any gaming systems, board games or outdoor play equipment is therefore also worth mentioning. Let guests know what supplies and sundries are supplied in this section as well – coffee/tea/sugar, biscuits and milk on arrival, for example, a basket of logs for the log burner, shampoo and soap, kitchen basics such as foil, salt, pepper and oil. I find that guests ask about these things most frequently – it would be even more so if I didn't list them here. Hopefully it will save you some time answering emails, along with encouraging guests to book a house where lots of little extras are provided as people often like to travel as light as possible. Again, use superlatives wherever justified. Describe your home in a way that entices guests to book – emphasise your home's good points, character, aesthetic appeal or styling. Mention if your home is in a quiet area, if there are nice views, or list some more places of interest nearby with travelling distances and/or walking times. If you are renting out an apartment, mention any shared facilities which will be accessible to guests, such as a roof terrace, gym or pool. If you have a garden describe it in greater detail along with mention of garden furniture, barbecue, hot tub or fire pit. Include information about clothes drying equipment, such as an indoor airer or rotary outdoor dryer, as guests usually expect to be able to wash and dry clothes, and this is another thing that gives self-catering the edge over hotel rooms. A lot of items will be mentioned in the 'amenities' tick box section of your listing as well, but it is worth describing them here as well, in fuller detail.

Guest access

In this section, clarify what type of accommodation you are offering – especially if you are letting an annex or room in your home, for example. Will the guest have access to the whole house, including the kitchen or living room, or are they offered one room with an ensuite, or part of a larger house, for example. Is the property a completely detached, private let or will they just have access to part of a house or an attached annex? Is there a shared path, garden or car park? Is the let an apartment in a block of eight other apartments with use of a roof terrace or other facilities? Will they be able to use the gardens by your house, if you're letting out an annex on site, or is there a separate garden just for guests' use? In short, do not allow any confusion in precisely what you are offering, accommodation-wise. I also use this section to briefly describe what system I have in place for guests on arrival – for example, a key safe with code emailed to them a day before, or a meet-and-greet arrangement. It's worth mentioning any steps or staircases to be expected on arrival – from the car park or to the front door, for example, and inside the property as some older guests struggle with them.

Other details to note

This is a useful section which informs guests of any other things not covered by other parts of the listing, or somewhere to stress anything important. I tend to include health and safety information – e.g. guests use the trampoline at their own risk, children be aware of the fire escape window etc., or to stress important rules such as a strict ban on animals or smoking or restrictions with parking or vehicle size and type. I once had guests arrive with an unexpected caravan who pulled into the tiny car park which was shared with the neighbours, and after this I added a note here about no large vehicles, caravans or camper vans due to restricted access and parking space. Not all guests will think about checking if their vehicle will be suitable for the type of parking you provide. Lack of mobile reception, low doorways or beams or anything that might be fundamental to the guests' health and safety or use of the property or which could sway their decision to book your home, not covered by other parts of the listing, can be mentioned here. Add any features of the property which could be difficult for guests with mobility restrictions. There is another section for rules and policies which covers basic house rules so you may not wish to double up on those here.

Other things in the listing basics section include number of guests and a listing status button (allows you to edit the setting before making it 'live' and bookable or if you wish to snooze bookings temporarily).

After the basic list, there is a tick list of amenities – make sure you fill this out as thoroughly as possible as the more amenities and facilities, the better, as far as guests are concerned.

You then put the address in the location section following this and mark the approximate position of your home on a map – you can choose not to divulge the exact address until after someone has booked. Generally, it is best to put the full address here as sometimes guests only seem able to access it 24 hours before arrival, which is no good if they wish to pre-book a grocery delivery, for example. I also give them the full address of the property in my first booking confirmation email.

Airbnb will prompt you from time to time, once your listing is up and running, to add information on additional amenities. This is usually a tick-box exercise which involves adding further detail about your facilities. It is worth filling these out as they appear as guests clearly respond well to lots of information and it could help your position in the rankings as you will be flagged up as an active and responsive host.

This is followed by a 'neighbourhood description'. It is a good chance to showcase the positive things about your let – be it amazing views, friendly neighbours, privacy, seclusion, lovely walks from the doorstep, proximity to famous landmarks, a great bakery or pub. Try to give potential guests a sense of what to expect in their immediate surroundings. If the house has close neighbours or is semi-detached, or terraced, it's worth gently asking guests to be mindful of neighbours and to treat them respectfully. You can set 'quiet' hours in rules and policies as well. You should mention any areas shared with neighbours and any expected etiquette or behaviour related to these and any expectations regarding shared parking spaces.

Next, in 'Getting around', it is worth mentioning if you recommend that guests have a car – this is very important for rural lets. I run a cottage in quite a remote area and always mention that a car is *essential* as there are no shops or pubs within easy walking distance. I have guests defy this advice, taking long, slow train journeys and infrequent taxis to get there and usually there is some trouble for them in terms of getting there very late or complaining about the lack of shops or where to get supplies from once they have settled in. I once had a guest who arrived by taxi continually ring me about problems and requests for additional logs and so on, even though I make it quite clear on the listing that we only supply one complimentary basket of logs. I relented and gave him the key safe code to the log store, on the promise that he would reimburse me, but he never did. I haven't offered this to other guests since. You live and learn in this business. I also find that guests who arrive by taxi or train to rural lets are often late checking out which can be very disruptive if you have cleaners waiting to access the home and/or a same-day changeover – they rarely pre-book taxis (which will usually involve a long waiting time in remote locations) or will try to stay in the home longer so that they can avoid hanging around at the station. Be very firm with your check out times – many hosts now threaten additional fees for late check-outs due to the cleaning schedule and changeover day being frequently disrupted by guests not respecting the given check out time. City and town centre lets are not such a problem in this instance as there are usually plenty of cafes and places that guests are happy to visit if they have a later train.

I also give approximate distances to the nearest shops, pubs and restaurants and some of the bigger attractions in this section. If you have a city centre home or flat, then it is worth mentioning the distance from the nearest train station and travelling time by taxi or foot, and any underground or metro stations nearby and travelling distances to some famous landmarks or places. It is also worth listing the nearest airport, its distance and the travelling time. Any tricky terrain or roads that can be impacted by poor weather are also worth a mention here.

'Property and rooms' is a very self-explanatory tick-box section which clearly marks out what bedrooms, beds and bathroom arrangement you have. Accessibility and guest safety are, likewise, self-explanatory, tick-box sections.

Pricing and availability

Pricing and availability is the next part of the listing to fill out after listing details. It has a useful tool at the top of the page which automatically works out a typical three-night stay, which is calculated using your base prices, plus any guest fees.

In 'nightly price' you can set a basic everyday price for your accommodation. This is a 'base' price which will be shown to guests when scrolling through listings and will be the price that your calendar is initially and automatically filled up with, although you will almost certainly decide to tweak it according to time of year, especially for weekends, school holidays, public holidays and for last minute availability. Some guests get quite irate about 'misleading' base prices- i.e. a property advertises itself as typically charging £100 per night, but is actually priced around £150-180 for most of the year bar a few days in January, for example. I think it's better to try to show a typical average price, taking into account peak and low seasons, as some guests will choose not to book on principle if they feel misled. Also, you will find that some guests are choosing to search for more expensive, luxurious accommodation – they want to treat themselves and will pay accordingly. As long as you are not overpricing your home or exaggerating its attractions, then this shouldn't be a problem. Bear in mind that your calendar will be automatically filled with this price for however far ahead you choose to allow booking – typically 12 or 18 months. You will then probably want to alter some of the pricing for holidays and busy or quiet periods. Remember to update the calendar pricing each month, as a new month is released each month for the 12- or 18-month period in advance. I have been caught out by early bookers snapping up public holidays or special dates at a regular base rate or for a shorter occupancy than I would have liked by not updating my calendar quickly enough. You need to be aware of Bank holidays, public holidays and school holidays well in advance and make a note of them. Research your competition in order to help price your let – look at other Airbnb properties and check out other holiday sites, considering commission or guests fees that may be incorporated into the nightly price. Be mindful that Airbnb will often encourage you to price down, rather than up – they are keen to get your calendar filled, but you need to weigh this against your running costs. I only really listen to Airbnb's pricing advice when I have last minute availability to fill and need to price it competitively or during quieter spells. After setting your base prices you can easily change the price of any specific dates on your actual calendar.

Airbnb has a function called 'smart pricing' which automatically selects pricing on your behalf, considering local trends and booking information on the site. I have never used this as I find that Airbnb nearly always underprices. The calendar will often suggest typical or comparable pricing for your let, but it is often on the low side, in my experience. It can be a useful tool for late bookings, in terms of showing how competitive you need to be in order to fill any empty dates or those which are proving difficult to book, but I certainly would not rely on it for busy periods or for dates quite far removed in the future. It is a switch that you can turn on or off, and I find that the website really does push for you to use it, so be careful not to accidentally click on it or agree to it when prompted, unless you wish to use it.

After smart pricing, you can select year-round weekly and monthly discounts by applying a percentage discount. It is particularly useful for smaller properties, especially city or town flats, to make them appealing for longer stays as they tend to book out much more easily for short stays. It can become uneconomical for guests to book flats for more than a few nights if the changeover costs are incorporated into the nightly price, so a weekly discount makes a longer stay a lot more affordable. Alternatively, if you have a more modest nightly price plus a separate cleaning/laundry fee to cover the changeover costs, then you may not want to add a weekly discount. I generally avoid using weekly discounts for larger homes which have higher running and maintenance costs and tend to get booked more easily for longer stays in any case by families during school holidays. I do not recommend applying a weekly base discount to larger properties all year round. You will need to rely on week-long stays for the bulk of your revenue for larger family homes to cover costs and make a decent profit. You can always drop the nightly price or add a custom discount for specific dates during quieter periods if you wish. Again, I find that Airbnb pushes for a big discount and will often suggest a discount of 20% or more, but generally a 10 to 15% discount would be adequate.

I do not offer a monthly discount for any of my properties, as stays of more than 31 days do not count towards 'holiday let' occupancy and can affect whether your property will still be classed as a furnished holiday let at the end of the financial year (see more in chapter seven). If you find you are attracting lots of longer stays then you may have to accept that you may not potentially be classed as an official holiday let after a year or two and will be taxed accordingly. I find that longer-stay guests create more damage, use a lot of heating and electricity and also often expect weekly free laundry and cleaning. I would make it clear on your listing that stays of more than a week will not automatically include additional cleaning and laundry, unless requested and that it will be supplied at an additional cost - it is possible to request additional payments from your guests via Airbnb. You may wish to make it part of your terms that longer stays must pay for weekly cleaning and laundry and allow cleaners in, as guests rarely clean properly and you may have a lot of deep cleaning to do when they check-out otherwise. I rarely have guests book longer than a week and those that enquire after longer stays are often looking for large discounts during dates which are easy to fill in any case. I have found that holiday guests, particularly families, who stay for as long as a fortnight are more likely to leave properties in very poor shape, so I generally set my calendars to a limit of ten days. You might find that your target audience for your home is looking for longer stays, in which case set your occupancy rules, calendar pricing and long-stay discounts accordingly. It is probably worth considering longer stays outside of touristy areas, where you may be attracting people on short-term work contracts, those visiting families or looking for accommodation between house moves etc. Many hosts report that professionals staying long-term at their properties are generally well behaved and do not make too much of a mess, as they are generally out for most of the day.

    I tend to offer good discounts for weeks between November and February, which are the quietest months. 'Custom length of stay discounts' allows you to set other discounts for different stay lengths, but again, these are geared at much longer stays of several weeks, and you are unlikely to be able to continue to register as an official holiday let if you have too many long stays. There are a number of economic advantages to being classed as a holiday let which I will outline in chapter seven. However, some hosts find that longer stays can be very profitable - it depends on your area and type of guest.

There are then options to apply discounts for 'early bird' bookers and 'last minute' bookers, but I don't tend to bother with these, preferring to drop my price manually on the calendar, where necessary. I rarely offer early bird offers, especially for peak periods, as there is no need usually. However, you may want to try this if you are initially struggling to drum up bookings in the early days of your business. Be wary of having too many different types of special discount applied to your calendar, as it can be hard to keep track of them all and you may forget when you have applied them and drop your calendar price on top of the discounts by accident and find yourself rather out of pocket.

Additional fees

This section allows the owner to apply any extra fees to the booking cost such as for cleaning and laundry, or for additional guests. I have been advised never to charge more than 10% of the total stay cost for additional fees, which I think is a good rule of thumb. I have currently removed additional fees on my listings completely as I have seen evidence that suggests that guests' goodwill tends to be eroded by the idea of hidden 'extras' and that they are less likely to book because of them. Instead, I have slightly raised my nightly rate, and have indeed seen a surge in bookings. However, cleaning and laundry will be two of your biggest costs and you may find it helpful to charge guests something towards them, especially if you find you are attracting a lot of shorter stays. I have never charged my guests the full cost of cleaning and laundry in the past but even with a nominal fee towards these things I have sometimes received some negative feedback in response. I think many guests would be very surprised by how expensive these things actually are, and the online vitriol aimed at holiday let owners currently seems most bothered by these extra, 'greedy' fees. However, consider them carefully, as you may find that short stays, especially of two nights, are unviable, once cleaning and laundry are factored in. Adding fees, even just a percentage of the actual cleaning and laundry costs, might help you offer shorter stays. For now, I am generally replacing cleaning and laundry fees with a slightly higher nightly booking rate instead and offering bigger discounts on weekly bookings. I have had to raise the nightly rate most for short stays of two or three nights to make them economically viable. Even if you do your own cleaning and laundry, this represents time and money, so should not be seen as something that costs 'nothing'. People will often compare the Airbnb model unfavourably towards hotels who offer 'free' cleaning and laundry and employ a team of staff. However, most hotels will cost significantly more per night, especially for larger groups of people, usually without the provision for self-catering or a living room space or garden. For smaller properties and flats which are in direct competition with hotels I generally would avoid adding any extra fees, even if it still works out less than a hotel room, as, psychologically, guests will still often feel hard done by due to extra fees. I would increase the nightly price and offer a weekly discount instead. I find that guests tend to leave holiday properties in better condition when they have not been charged a cleaning fee as they can otherwise feel that it is a service they have paid for and want their money's worth by leaving a lot of mess for the cleaner. They will more likely resent any checkout requests and will be less likely to honour them - e.g. putting rubbish outside, sweeping fireplaces and washing up before leaving.

There are various types of other fees on the list which can be filled out accordingly, but I would avoid any more fees than absolutely necessary, as it is a big deterrent to guests. You have the option to charge more for additional guests – this could be useful if you have a sofa bed or pull out bed option which requires additional bedding, for example, but generally I find that cleaning companies charge me a flat rate to clean a home, regardless of whether all beds have been slept in, and so I therefore give a flat nightly rate. I often have guests hint strongly to me that they expect a discount if their party size is smaller than the maximum number of guests the property can accommodate, but I do not offer this as my costs will not be very different, bar the cost of a couple of sets of bedding and towels to be laundered, which is fairly minimal. The cleaning is always the biggest changeover cost. If you are doing your own laundry, you could offer a small discount if all bedrooms are not going to be used, to entice guests to book, as a goodwill gesture. However, I often find that guests (probably children) are likely to jump or sit on beds even if they have not been slept in, and all rooms will usually require a dust and vacuum, regardless.

You also have the option to set a weekend price here for Fridays and Saturdays, throughout the year – again, your calendar will automatically fill with this price once you select it. It can save time changing all your base prices at the weekends but remember to tweak them for quieter or busier periods, so generally choosing an average price between peak and quiet periods is a good bet at this stage. Fridays and Saturdays are always the more popular days for guests, regardless of area, especially if you offer two-night breaks. Due to changeover costs, I only tend to offer two-night breaks as last-minute options, or if I have a two-night period created on my calendar between two other bookings. I sometimes charge a little more for Sundays during summer months, but Friday and Saturday are usually the most expensive dates on my calendar. A lot of hosts offer a minimum of three-night stays and finding a two-night stay can sometimes be tricky for guests, so you may find that you can raise the price of these nights to a point where it is profitable. I often have guests asking to book two- or three-nights during school holidays for larger properties, but I rarely offer this, as generally I find I have enough longer-stay bookings that it is unnecessary, and changeover costs should be considered. Weekend pricing is most important for city and town lets in my experience, especially outside of the summer months, when most of your guests will be looking to book weekend breaks.

Trip length

The next section allows you to specify minimum and maximum trip lengths. Like pricing, there is a choice for the 'base' number of days for both, but then you can customise it for other specific dates (see 'custom trip length' below). I usually set my minimum base stay to three days and my maximum base stay to ten days, having personally had bad experiences from fortnightly guests and not wanting guests to stay more than 31 days so that I can ensure that I fulfil my occupancy criteria as an official furnished holiday let. Ten day stay guests do not often have the expectation of an additional cleaning and linen changeover mid-stay either, whereas guests staying for a fortnight often expect it to be provided free of charge during the second week, which will eat into your profit. It is harder for cleaners to clean when guests' belongings are in place and if you don't arrange a mid-stay clean, then you will find that the end of stay clean will take a lot longer after two weeks. Two-night stays can be unviable or provide minimal profit, due to changeover costs – if you have a two-night stay gap on your calendar or want to try and entice a weekend booking if you have last minute availability then by all means offer two nights for those specific dates. You will need to increase your nightly rate though in this case. My minimum stay for larger properties during school holidays is always a week, usually specifying a Saturday-to-Saturday booking, so people generally can only book one week, which I prefer, before moving on to the next guests. If you have a different model in mind, then certainly try it – you can always change your mind later if things don't go to plan. If you are looking for business traveller guests, away from tourist hot spots, you may be happy to offer 31 days maximum, as they will not be around much during the day, and the property will not take such a hammering, maintenance-wise, as a family home during school holidays. Longer stays do not tend to be so troublesome for smaller properties and one-bedroom apartments, in my experience – I would not automatically offer weekly cleaning, but if a guest requests it, then I think it's fair to charge for this, especially if you have already applied a weekly discount to the price. I would usually offer a change of linen per week, requesting that guests strip the beds and put towels and linen in a bag by the door to be collected, and that new linen be dropped off for the guest to make up the bed with themselves. I would not offer more than this, unless you do your own cleaning and linen and don't mind changing everything yourself. A cleaning company will usually charge you for their travel and time to do this and can sometimes be reluctant to do this at all if they are busy with full cleans at other properties. Some hosts find that longer stays can be very profitable, even if it impacts their holiday let status (more on occupancy rules and the perks of being classed as an official let in chapter seven). Lots of short stays can deter potential longer-term guests from booking, but it is a question of your preferences too. Sometimes it is a case of trial and error until you find your ideal booking and length of stay preferences.

Custom trip length

This is a very useful function on Airbnb that I use a lot. It allows you to maximise your profits and control your calendar during busy periods. You can select any range of dates and apply rules for the minimum stay. It works via drop-down boxes and will suggest monthly date ranges, but generally it is best to click on the last option 'specific dates' which will allow you to select a specific date range from the calendar – always double check you are in the correct month and year as it sometimes jumps around unexpectedly after you've selected a start date. For larger family homes I usually select school holiday dates and request a Saturday check-in and changeover with a minimum stay of seven nights. I find that guests favour a Saturday for school holidays, due to issues of traffic on a Friday evening if they work Monday to Friday – they can travel first thing on a Saturday instead. Obviously, check if your cleaner or cleaning company has a preference or any restrictions before setting this, as some private cleaners tend to prefer a weekday clean to a Saturday. It's useful to also bear in mind public holidays – for Bank holidays I usually select the Friday to Sunday dates, with a rule that guests can only check-in on the Friday, with a minimum of three nights' stay. Bank holidays are always very popular so always try to get the three full days booked from Friday to Monday at a higher rate if possible. For smaller properties such a one-bedroom flat, I will still set similar rules for public and Bank holidays, but generally request stays of four or five nights maximum during peak periods, as couples often tend to do shorter breaks in my experience, although you can try to tempt them to stay longer by applying a weekly discount or a custom weekly price. You can end up with the odd two- or three-night gap this way, but they often fill very quickly during peak season, and you can usually increase the nightly rate on a shorter stay as they are harder to come by for guests during peak season. Remember to update this section each month, due to early bookers looking for short stays during peak times a year or more in advance. If you do not restrict check-in days or holiday lengths for popular dates and school holidays in time, someone will come and ruin your calendar with a Wednesday to Sunday stay in your large family home in August if you are not careful – and they will expect you to honour it (guests have little sympathy for owners crying that they had not had a chance to update their calendar yet). Airbnb are quite reasonable, however, and I find if you have made a mistake, or someone has booked something that should not have been bookable, you can usually undo it, although there can be penalties, in terms of your place in the listing rankings, and even financial penalties, if you let guests down without good reason. You should always try to message Airbnb first if this happens - if you simply cancel a booking without reason, you are more likely to be penalised in some way.

Airbnb has recently updated some of its calendar settings, and it appears to have removed the option to select check-in days on the 'custom trip length' lists. A lot of people have struggled with this, so there is a chance that it will be reintroduced to this section of the listings. However, don't panic if this is not the case - you should still be able to select check-in day preferences via the new 'professional hosting tools' which have recently been introduced - I will discuss these in greater detail later in this chapter. These new tools also allow you to set more customised discounts. Contact Airbnb if you cannot find them.

Whilst you could manage everything electronically, I personally find it is helpful to have a file binder with paper printouts of all the months, up to 18 months in advance, with days and dates written on them. I mark school and public holidays on this calendar, along with any bookings. For bookings I write the name of the guest, mark the dates they've booked with a line, mark the day that the cleaners will be coming and put the price, to check against my bank statement. I also put which listing site they booked with here, or if they booked directly. It is so helpful to have a physical print-out and would advise all owners to have this back up to refer to. It has saved me from making costly mistakes or forgetting bookings in the past and encourages me to make a note of holidays and popular dates well in advance. A useful website, in terms of checking school holidays and public holidays is www.termdates.com. It's worth checking a few counties, as well as different dates for England, Northern Ireland, Scotland and Wales, as school holidays can be spread over several weeks, and are often staggered.

Calendar availability

This section allows you to specify a minimum notice period in terms of accepting bookings. On 'advance notice' you can choose from 1, 2, 3, or 7 nights' notice. I usually put one day's notice as it allows me to entice last-minute instant bookers and I usually have the houses ready and clean on the day of departure in any case and use cleaning agencies who can usually clean at fairly short notice. If you have a single, private cleaner, then you may wish to increase the notice period. If same-day changeovers are potentially problematic for you, then you can also select a 'preparation' period which automatically blocks a day or so from before or after a booking to give you a day or more to clean. Again, as I use cleaning agencies, I mark this box as 'none' for preparation time. I find quite a large proportion of my bookings will be last minute ones and are very useful during quieter periods. Notice periods are most useful when you have selected to allow instant booking. If you do not select instant booking, then you will be able to decide whether you wish to accept a last-minute booking request or not. Even if you have your notice period set to a few days or more in advance, last minute guests can still request to book and you can decide if you are available to host at the last minute - to allow this make sure you tick the box below 'advance notice' which allows guests to send last minute booking requests regardless of your notice settings. If there is any question about your cleaner or agency being able to step in at short notice, then ensure you do not allow instant last-minute bookings as Airbnb will penalise you for cancelling.

'Availability window' allows you to select how far in advance guests can book – I usually set this to twelve months, as it can be a headache keeping an eye on school and public holidays up to 18 months or more in advance and you are more likely to get cancellations, which are time-consuming, admin-wise. 'Restricted check-in days' is the next useful option button – I find that cleaning agencies can struggle to clean on Sundays due to shortages of staff, so I always restrict Sunday check-ins. If you have a flexible cleaner or are happy to clean on a Sunday yourself, then you may find that you secure quite a few extra bookings by offering Sunday check-ins, as guests may struggle to find anywhere else that offers this. Calendar Sync allows you to synchronise your Airbnb calendar with calendars from other listing sites. Sometimes I choose not to import and export to listing sites which charge higher commission and even block certain dates on those sites to encourage guests to book elsewhere - obviously I do not want my other calendars replicating these blocks, hence why I do not always synchronise all of my calendars. Each listing site will have an option, usually on their calendar page, to import and export their calendar to other sites. You can do it one-way, or multi-way, to make sure nothing slips through the net. There will be a link that you copy and paste on this section, and you can do it on the linked websites as well, if you wish. Every time you receive a booking, the calendars on the other listing sites will automatically be updated. It avoids the likelihood of forgetting to manually update the other calendars and getting a double booking, which can incur penalties. The calendars should update at least once a day, sometimes every few hours, so occasionally you may get a double booking despite having this system set up. In this case you need to message or call customer service straight away to explain what has happened. You can usually press the small 'refresh' icon next to linked calendars which should prompt them to export and import straight away, although you will usually need to refresh your calendar page afterwards and wait a minute or so. Be careful not to accidentally press the delete icon which is annoyingly close to the refresh button. Sometimes I update calendars manually even though I know that blocks/bookings will be imported at some point, as some of the listing sites can be quite harsh with their penalties for accidental double-bookings. If you use an i-Cal calendar system on your own website and allow guests to book directly with you, you can also link this here. Any calendar which uses the i-Cal system can be synchronised with Airbnb and the other major listing sites' calendars.

'Sharing settings' allows you to choose from three options in terms of keeping an eye on your competition – Airbnb will give you feedback on other properties in your area, in terms of bookings, whether guests looked at your listing and booked somewhere else, and how much guests are typically paying. In return, your information will also be sent to other hosts. The three settings dictate how much you wish to share, and in return, how much information you will receive. This can be a useful tool in the early days of setting up your business.

Policies and rules

Cancellation policy

Airbnb offers a variety of cancellation policy types, and these can vary from host to host. They are all very self-explanatory. I find that this is something that changes with time – in the early days of a listing, a flexible cancellation policy can entice wary guests to book with you, despite not having many, or any, reviews. I find that once I've established a reputation with my listing and have good feedback that I tend to make the policy a little stricter, as I do get fed up with time wasters booking and then cancelling. A lot of people use booking sites like online shopping – they will secure a place and then change their mind the next day, or a few weeks later. They like to have the option of holidaying at your rental with no penalty for cancelling. This is understandable, and I think guests have been wary of being stung since Covid, with some holidaymakers having lost thousands of pounds through cancelled holidays or illness. During the pandemic, I relaxed my policy a lot to encourage bookings, but with things back to normal I currently have a 'firm' cancellation policy selected which allows full refunds up to 30 days before check-in, then a 50% refund up to seven days before arrival, with no refund under seven days before arrival. It also allows the guest to cancel penalty-free within 48 hours of booking, at least 14 days before arrival. I could probably secure more bookings with a more flexible policy – you can even select the 'flexible' policy which offers guests a full refund if they cancel one day before arrival, making your listing very competitive with budget hotel chains such as Premier Inn, but generally this does not work for larger homes or family holidays which are usually booked months in advance and can be very difficult to fill at the last minute. I have found this out the hard way – never rely on a guest's goodwill or honesty as they will think nothing of cancelling, penalty-free, at very short notice if they are able to. Do not underestimate the cost of your time – each booking requires some administration, from filling out your calendar, sending a written response to the guest, informing your cleaning company and updating any other calendars. You tend to end up with a page of crossings-out on your paper calendar as well, and it can be messy keeping track with lots of cancellations from the window-shopper type of booker. It is usually a case of testing the water and altering your policy as you go along to get a sense of how much of your time is wasted, or if you are attracting enough bookers. There are also long-stay cancellation policy options which are aimed at stays of more than 28 days.

Instant book

'Instant book' is a function very much encouraged by Airbnb. It allows any guest to book immediately, without the need for the host to check their availability and calendar first. Guests are more likely to book with you if they can use 'instant book', but you need to be confident that your calendar will be up to date in this case. If you are more relaxed about your number of bookings and want to personally check out your potential guest and ask them any questions before accepting their booking, then do not choose this option. With 'instant book' you have the option to specify that you will only accept instant bookings from guests with good track records and existing feedback. Airbnb allows hosts to rate their guests, as well as guests to rate hosts, so this will prevent anyone from booking with you who has particularly poor feedback and specifically someone who has previously received the ticked box 'I would not host this guest again' from a host, post-stay. However, it will still allow guests with mixed or average feedback to book, assuming they did not receive the 'won't host this guest again' tick from a previous host. Some guests can look okay on paper but if they must request to book, it often means that a host in the past has marked them as a 'wouldn't host again' option after their stay, but not necessarily marked them down significantly in a review. This can be explained by the fact that Airbnb shares feedback and scores for reviews between guests and hosts but will not share the fact that a host has banned a guest with the 'would not host again' option. People are very conflict-averse in general on Airbnb, which explains why some properties and guests with good reviews are not always as good in reality, compared to their feedback. I always tick the 'good track record' requirement button for 'instant book', due to some past bad experiences. However, you are ruling out new bookers with no feedback from instantly booking with you, but they can still message you and request to book, and it is up to you whether you are happy to proceed with their booking request. I have done so in the past, and generally it has not been a problem, bar a few slightly messier than average guests. Now that I have established lets with repeat bookers, I am a little choosier and generally turn down new bookers without previous feedback just in case they are trouble or a fake account, or someone who has received previous bad feedback and set up a new account. If guests without Airbnb feedback, then choose to book directly with me instead, I am happy to accept their booking, as I take a security deposit from private guests and can control my feedback and any issues better this way. You may find that you have to risk letting the newbie Airbnb guest book instantly with you when you are first establishing your let online, just to get stays and reviews in. It is personal choice, and hopefully the risk of a nightmare guest is diminishing with Airbnb's tightening of guest screening and their AirCover program which includes $1 million USD in host liability insurance and $3 USD in host damage protection, which covers art, valuables and vehicles etc.

House rules

This follows on from the booking option section and is a straightforward tick-box exercise. It is worth setting 'quiet hours' if you are renting out a flat or a home that is semi-detached or terraced, especially in a city setting which is more likely to attract partygoers and clubbers, or if you have a home with close neighbours who could be disturbed, especially by socialising in gardens during the evening. Do bear your neighbours in mind when completing this section.

You also choose your check-in and check-out times. If you are using a cleaning company, I advise that you check their preferences first or have them look at your property to estimate a required cleaning time and if they have a preferred start time. If you have a singular private cleaner, or are doing it yourself, it is worth having a run-through, including changing all the beds, as it can be surprisingly time-consuming – private cleaners often prefer to arrive earlier rather than later if it is a big clean, especially if it is a week-day clean and many often need to get back for school pickups around 3pm. An agency will generally use two or even three cleaners for a larger home and plan to spend less time there, and usually have other properties to clean on the same day. I have had agencies specify that they like to have the option to clean until 4pm – they might push for even later, but I think a 5pm or later check-in is unfair on guests and would strongly advise against this, if possible, although it did become more common during Covid, due to more careful cleaning and disinfecting. In my experience, cleaning agencies prefer flexibility and as big a time window as possible between check in and check out, especially if they typically have several homes to clean on one day, but you can let your preferences be known and encourage them to accept your check in and check out times. Guests' preferred times tend to be 11am check out and 3pm check in, and this would be more in line with what hotels typically offer, but this is not always easy for a cleaner or agency to agree to, especially for larger homes. If you are doing your own cleaning, then of course it's completely up to you, just make sure you allow enough time. I typically put 10am check out and 4pm check in for larger homes, or 10am check out and 3pm check in for smaller lets. Having a key safe on your property allows guests to check themselves in at any time, however late and is very useful. I would try to avoid being reliant on a meet-and-greet type of service, as occasionally guests will arrive in the small hours. Some hosts who insist on meet-and-greet and personally letting guests in, will have a cut-off time for check-in or a limit on how early guests can check-out if they have keys to return, but generally this is very impractical and very unpopular with guests.

Additional house rules

You can also type up any additional house rules below the obvious tick-box ones. I tend to add here that I would like guests to throw any rubbish away, remove all food from the fridge and freezer and put out any recycling, sorted into the correct boxes. As I have removed cleaning fees, I also now ask guests to ensure all kitchenware is washed up, dried and put away before departure and that the dishwasher is left empty. My cleaners' biggest bugbear is guests who leave all the washing up, or even all the drying-up. They have a great deal to do without this. Also, I find that often the dishwasher is not switched on and everything has to be washed up by hand in any case, or the dishwasher cycle is too slow and has to be switched off by the cleaners mid-cycle, all of which uses up valuable cleaning time. If dishwashers are frequently opened mid-cycle or very soon after they the cycle has finished when they are at the steaming, drying stage, you have the added downside of kitchen units being warped by steam over time – I have had kitchen units expand around the dishwasher so that the door would no longer shut partly because of this. Other rules to consider here are; replacing lids on hot tubs, or any important health and safety related guidelines relating to hot tubs, play equipment, ponds, pools or facilities with the potential for harm. I also ask guests to leave the home clean and tidy or to at least return equipment, furniture and furnishings to their original places. A lot of time is lost for cleaners in putting things back where they belong. If you have a wood burner, specify that only logs are to be used, if it is not multi-fuel, as a guest will invariably drag a big dirty sack of coal through your house otherwise. If you allow pets, then I strongly recommend that you do not allow them upstairs, on beds or on sofas and ask guests to pick up after them outside. By making what should be basic decent behaviour into 'rules' you hopefully formalise your expectations from guests.

I do not ask guests to strip beds and advise other hosts against it, especially for high-end lets. A hotel does not expect guests to do this, and it takes away the 'luxury' element of a holiday in my mind. It became a trend during Covid, partly due to a viral video of a holiday let cleaner claiming that removing bedding risked catching the virus, but I do not think it is necessary. If your cleaning agency tries to implement this, I would strongly resist it. It makes their lives easier, but your guests are a lot more likely to complain or mark you down in their review as a result. Also, if your pillow and mattress protectors underneath are anything less than spotless, your guests will have additional cause for complaint. I launder mine monthly – very few laundries and cleaning companies will bother or be geared up for changing and cleaning them at all. It is one of the holiday let and hotel industry's dirtiest secrets in my opinion and many holiday let cottages rarely, if ever, change them. Quite a few do not have any protectors at all, so all the dust mites and sweat simply soak into pillows and mattresses. You will very quickly end up with stained pillows and mattresses as well. However, even with regular laundering, I do not want my guests looking at the mattress and pillow protectors. There is also a risk that the protectors get removed from the beds as well, along with all the regular bedding and get sent to the laundry, never to be seen again (most laundries provide linen for holiday cottages, but rarely provide protectors, and private linen is invariably lost if it enters their system).

You have the option to request a guest photo as part of your rules, but I do not tick this box – I dislike giving photos, especially for something like booking a holiday, and it would deter me from booking. Hosts are encouraged to add a photo of themselves to their profile - it can encourage confidence in potential bookers and studies have shown that people respond well to a 'face' when dealing with a business. However, you are not obliged to, and if you wish to be a low-key or private host, you can use any kind of image - some hosts use a landscape image instead.

You must agree to 'local laws and regulations' on this part of the listing. It is very vague, but the gist is that you should be aware of your local laws regarding holiday lets, as some cities and areas, especially in other countries, do not allow them.

Info for guests

In the pre-booking section, you state your check-in and check-out times and provide an online guidebook, if you wish to. You also state how much interaction guests can expect from you - whether you will be around or readily available, or whether you will be available to contact by the app if you do not live close by. You can also state whether you want to socialise and interact with guests.

Guidebook

I highly recommend providing an online guidebook as it can save you a lot of time answering general queries from guests about the area, visitor attractions, grocery shopping, restaurants and pubs if you have it all stored in one handy online guidebook. Some guests will still ask about these things, but you can usually point them in the direction of the guidebook. I always tell guests in the first message after they've just booked that all local information can be found in the online guidebook. You will find that many businesses are already 'set up' on the guidebook database – if you type in their name or search the nearby area, they will have a ready-made business profile ready for you to link to. It's a useful tool.

You also let guests know whether they will have any interaction with you in this section, whether you will be available in person, or not. I always add that I will be available by email, and by phone in an emergency. I added the note about contacting me by email in the first instance when I was being phoned regularly by guests about the tiniest details and realised that I did not want to be constantly disturbed like this – if you have another job then you need to make this quite clear. Quite often guests would be asking something covered in the house manual in any case. I find that if they have to email you, they are more likely to read the manual or work out the problem for themselves. I notice that lets and B&Bs with on-site owners tend to get more glowing reviews. I am always super friendly towards guests in my communications, but nothing beats face-to-face contact (if it's friendly and polite), and reviews often reflect this. It is much harder to write a mean review about a business when its owner has been kind and attentive towards you as it feels a lot more personal. This is where local lets, annexes and single room lets come into their own – your secret ingredient will lie in your interaction with your guests and the little extra things you can offer if you happen to live on-site or close by.

Post-booking details

In Post-booking details you put the full address of your holiday let and directions. Make your directions as clear as possible, preferably with routes from major motorways and A roads nearby, up to the door or car parking area, with any local landmarks included. Most people have Satnav, but I find that guests expect very detailed instructions all the same. Some hosts include a photo in the main photo gallery of any hard-to-find access roads, parking areas or the location of the lock box if it's not overly obvious. It is not possible to change the location details and address once you are accepting bookings without contacting customer service (probably to deter fraud).

House manual

This is followed by a House manual where you can advise your guests on any basic important things, such as controlling the heating and hot water, or where the thermostat is located, for example. As I include a physical printed manual at my holiday lets as well, I also advise guests to read this on arrival.

Arrival details

You then put the check-in details – where guests should go on arrival, or who they should phone or what the key safe code is, where it is located and from what time they can let themselves in. Although Airbnb states that these details are available 'after booking' I have found that sometimes guests can only access things like the full address, key box codes and check-in details 24 hours before arrival. As guests like to plan ahead and some will want to pre-book things such as grocery deliveries which usually need a few weeks' notice, I tend to give them address details at the time of booking and email them full check-in details via messaging a few days before arrival. If you do not do this, you will receive more messages asking for check-in details as people start to panic that they are not available, although it will state on their listing that this information will be ready 24 hours before check-in.

You can also add WIFI details here, but I tend to have these displayed at the home and don't bother, as I might forget to change the listing if I ever change service provider or password.

You can also add check-out instructions here - i.e. any tasks that guests should complete before departure such as washing up, putting rubbish out etc. Guests do not respond well to long lists of tasks, and as I have said, I would not recommend asking them to strip beds.

Finally, don't forget to add your bank account details for receiving payments!

And there you have it; your listing is set up! You can check out how your listing appears to potential guests any time by clicking on the 'preview listing' button on the top right-hand side of the screen. I strongly recommend doing this before you set your listing to 'live' and then a few times a year in case anything changes or upgrades. Now it's time to tweak your calendar prices.

Using your Airbnb calendar

If you click on 'Calendar' on the listings page at the top, this will take you to a monthly calendar schedule which can be edited on screen. It will have been initially filled out with your 'base' prices that you set up in your listing, but it is easy to change them in the calendar mode. Generally, you will want to raise prices during summer months, school holidays and public holidays and reduce them during low season, which I find tends to last from November to February (excluding Christmas), and sometimes into March. If you click on any date, a box will appear on the right which will show the price for that night and whether the date is open or closed for booking. There is a 'custom settings box' which allows you to change length of stay requirements during the selected date(s) whilst in calendar mode. The custom settings box is a useful tool for little awkward gaps in your calendar or those with restrictions that you want to change once they become apparent on your calendar – Airbnb will sometimes advise you on the calendar if a date range is not bookable for some reason and you can quickly change it or remove the restriction on the custom settings box whilst still on the calendar.

To select more than one consecutive day simply click on a date and hold down the left mouse button whilst dragging the mouse across the additional dates. (On the mobile app you simply press the dates individually). You can then change the price of several nights in one go by typing the new price in the box on the right-hand side. To block dates, highlight them and then click on 'availability' on the right-hand side box, then 'edit' and switch the dates to 'closed' by pressing the cross button. To re-open them simply press the tick button. Bear in mind that blocks on this calendar, as well as bookings, will be exported to any other synchronised calendars you may have on other listing sites. If you synchronise your calendar with other listing site calendars, they will export once or more per day and any bookings on other sites will show as blocks shaded in grey on your Airbnb calendar with the name of the site of the imported booking on top.

Airbnb will show suggested pricing for your property which can be helpful in the early days if you are unsure how to price your let, but you will find in time that it becomes increasingly more intuitive and you will tweak prices more frequently in response to the sense of the market and demand, especially for last minute stays. I avoid lowering pricing for future dates too soon, as it is worth waiting to see if they book for a higher price before you panic and give them away at too low a price – it is sometimes a case of holding your nerve. Increasingly, I find that guests prefer to book more last minute, especially if you have a firm or strict cancellation policy. If you choose a more flexible policy then you will find that you book-up dates further into the future, but there is a much higher chance of these guests cancelling on you. I always start at the lower end of the scale, pricewise, in the early days of a listing, as it is harder to fill dates when you have no previous feedback or reviews and you do need to work harder to entice guests to book at this stage. I usually start to raise my prices and reduce weekly discounts and so on after a few months, or once I have a few good reviews.

By pressing the 'price and availability' setting button (referred to as 'global settings' on the mobile app) on the top right-hand corner of the screen on your calendar page, you can add more specific stay requirements and restrictions on this part of your listing, and it takes you away from the calendar page whilst you do this. As previously mentioned, I add school holidays for larger properties under 'custom length trips' on this page, usually with a Saturday check-in requirement and minimum of a seven day stay and specify that Bank holiday weekends need to begin on a Friday and increase the price of the Friday, Saturday and Sunday on the calendar.

Check-in day preferences were traditionally set in 'custom length trips' but this has been removed - hopefully only temporarily, as it is part of Airbnb's shake up of the calendar system which is still being tweaked and honed throughout 2023. If you find that you cannot set check-in dates here, please refer to the section, 'Airbnb professional hosting calendar', further on in this chapter.

For flats or smaller properties aimed at couples I slightly increase the stay requirements during summer months and public holidays, although you can try for a week minimum stay during Christmas, Easter and the summer holidays, although I do find these types of properties tend to get more short-term and weekend bookings. You can start with a week minimum required for certain dates and if they do not book at all then look at reducing the stay requirement closer to the start date and see what happens.

If the school holidays are only a month or two away when you first set up your listing for a larger home, then you will probably want to offer either a good weekly discount and/or a reduced stay requirement just to get the ball rolling on bookings. I find that families tend to book their main holidays quite far in advance, although you might get lucky with a last-minute weekly booking. Be wary of massively under-selling your home for the sake of early bookings and reviews, as I often find that guests looking for an absolute bargain, or those cheeky enough to barter you down on the price, will often be the guests who leave your holiday let in the worst state.

You can also set 'promotions' via the 'pricing and availability' button - you select a date range and apply a discount. The bigger the discount, the more your listing will be promoted on the site. Be careful here, as Airbnb will refer to older pricing from your calendar to avoid hosts simply raising their prices and then immediately applying a 'promotion' for greater visibility. Check the listed price carefully on the promotions text box before applying it - you can always cancel promotions if you want to. As I've said previously, the ability to set a preferred check-in day has been recently removed from the pricing and availability/custom trip length button - there is a chance that it will be reinstated, as the lack of it here seems illogical, but if it is not then you will need to use the 'professional hosting tools' - more on this later.

To set promotions and stay requirements on the mobile app, press the three small dots on the top right-hand side of your calendar screen and a box with 'promotions' and 'settings' will appear. 'Settings' will take you to a screen where you can change base prices, settings, fees and discounts on the 'pricing' tab. If you click on the 'availability' tab you can change base trip length rules and availability and add and view your custom trip lengths. Again, the ability to select check-in date rules for specific dates appears to have been recently disabled here.

If you end up with a little gap between stays, say of two nights, when your base or main custom settings specify three nights minimum, then Airbnb will automatically block those days out with the word 'minimum' visible on the affected dates – you can now press 'edit' when highlighting these non-bookable dates and a little box, 'custom setting' will appear where you can choose to override the current rule from your custom settings page for the selected dates and change the minimum stay and/or check-in day requirement for them in order to allow guests to book. It's a useful tool when you want to squeeze some extra occupancy out of your calendar or have small gaps you want to try to fill but do not want to have to change lots of your longer-term custom trip settings outside of the calendar page. Obviously, it's only worth offering short stays if you price them at a point where you will make a reasonable profit, once the changeover and running costs are factored in. Generally, I always select three nights minimum off-peak, but I will offer occasional two-night stays if I have gaps to fill on my calendar, or last-minute availability, but generally I will increase the nightly rate in this case to off-set the changeover costs which can make it uneconomical otherwise.

You will find that you gain confidence and a sense of the 'right' pricing with your calendar over time – it is very much a case of 'try and see' until your business is established. If dates are booking up very quickly and you are not making a decent enough profit, then try to raise your prices. If you are struggling to fill dates, then reduce the nightly rates and your occupancy requirements, weekly prices and/or increase any weekly discounts. By clicking on one particular date Airbnb will always suggest a price – these are dynamic prices and supposedly respond to current demands and market trends, although they sometimes pitch a little low in my experience, especially if you are pricing dates some time in the future. It can be a useful guide when getting started though, and for filling last-minute dates which are proving difficult to shift as it encourages you to price very competitively.

Be aware that when you set custom length stays for specific date runs, that these rules will only apply to the *arrival date* when guests come to book and will not be applied to the subsequent days. I have been caught out in the past by a guest booking a three day stay, for example, starting one or two days before the calendar swaps to a minimum stay of four nights or more. To avoid this, ensure that you set restrictions on check-out days on a week which requires longer stays, following on directly from a week with shorter stay rules. Sometimes it's difficult to foresee every possibility, as guests may be staying for a longer period during an official short-stay calendar period yet wish to check-out in the middle of an official long-stay week. Generally, it isn't something worth worrying about too much, but do make sure you protect your school holiday periods if you own a family-sized let and try to control bank holiday and public holiday periods for all properties by restricting check-in and check-out days. Check-in and check-out restrictions are now set via the professional hosting calendar - hopefully Airbnb will reintroduce this function to the regular calendar, as it is a very useful one.

Airbnb professional hosting tools

Airbnb has recently updated all of its calendar tools. It appears to have removed some functions from the regular calendar and listing set-up, but there is a good chance that they will be reintroduced, as the inability to set check-in days for specific dates on the regular calendar and listing seems unhelpful. However, if you find that you cannot set check-in day preferences for specific dates on the regular calendar or via custom length trips, you may need to start using Airbnb's 'professional hosting tools'. This is basically a fancier calendar with additional functions. It allows you to choose and restrict check-in and check-out days and add rules and tailored discounts for specific date runs. It is one of the biggest additions and changes Airbnb has made to its calendar format since its inception. The tools appear to officially be aimed at hosts with more than one listing, but looking on online forums, it seems that all hosts, including those with single listings, can access them if they wish to. Please note; if you choose to use the professional tools, your regular calendar will change appearance and will change to a long horizontal type of scroll-through calendar. At the moment, you have the option to swap back to the regular calendar at any time. By clicking on the 'calendar' button on the top toolbar you can swap between the professional and regular calendar. Alternatively, you can swap from the professional calendar to the regular one by clicking on the property name on the left-hand side of the calendar. These functions were added in June 2023 for some existing hosts, with the plan to roll them out further over the course of the year once feedback had been received. The new calendar functions and 'professional tools' are likely to be further honed and edited as a result. They may not initially be visible to all hosts.

    To select professional hosting tools, click on your round profile button on the top right-hand side of the screen and press 'account'. Then select 'professional hosting tools' and fill out your business information and select to use the tools. Then return to your calendar. It will appear different, and you will need to scroll horizontally to move through the months. If you have more than one property, they will be stacked on top of each other so that you can view bookings and availability for all properties at the same time. The Airbnb mobile app does not currently appear to have access to the professional hosting tools.

    To select a date range on the calendar, click and drag to highlight dates. You can block, change prices and minimum stay requirements all on the calendar setting. The best thing about the 'professional' calendar mode is the ability to set custom stays, check-in day rules and tailored discounts all on one calendar. If you highlight a date, a box pops up on the right-hand side with these different options on it. To select tailored discounts, trip lengths and check-in rules for specific dates, highlight the dates which you wish to edit and then click on the 'rule-sets' box which appears on the table of editing tools on the right hand side and then from the pull-down menu, select 'add rule-set'. Previous 'rules' which you have chosen to save will also appear here on the drop-down menu. Here you can change the minimum or maximum stay requirements for your specified dates, add any last-minute discounts, early bird discounts, preferred check-in dates and tailored length of stay discounts. You will need to give these rules a 'name' at the top and the press 'save' once you have set it up. You can colour-code your new rules and save them as a type of discount or rule which can then be added to the 'rule-sets' box drop down menu, meaning that it can be quickly applied to other dates in the future. I tend to use the rule-set section for popular holiday dates, selecting minimum stay lengths and preferred check-in days on it - I will name these date runs things like 'summer holidays', 'Easter holidays', 'bank holiday' or by the type of discount I'm offering, especially for hard to fill or quiet periods - e.g. '10% off 4+ nights', '15% off 6+ nights' and so on. By saving your new rule set as a template, you can quickly apply these rules to similar dates in the future. It can also be a useful tool if you want to set larger discounts for longer-term stays as well - you can select any kind of discount for 5, 6, 8, 10 and 12 week stays here. The best thing about the professional calendar mode is this ability to set tailored discounts, stay requirements and check-in rules.

    Ensure that you always set restrictions on any calendar dates when you do not want guests arriving - I usually have a base rule that restricts Sunday check-ins, but I also restrict check-ins on bank holiday Mondays, Easter Monday, Christmas Eve, Boxing Day, New Year's Eve and New Year's Day, as my cleaners generally prefer not to work on these days. I sometimes allow check-outs on New Year's Day, but arrange for my cleaners to do the changeover the day after. I do allow check-outs on bank holiday Mondays and try to make Bank holiday stays Friday to Monday - I usually book my cleaners in for the Tuesday. I often restrict check-ins for Sunday to Friday during school holidays, and select seven nights minimum on family sized homes, to ensure that guests book Saturday to Saturday.

The professional hosting tools do not currently appear on the mobile app, but this could change. I generally prefer setting more complex rules and discounts on a PC rather than mobile in any case, as it's easier to make mistakes on a small screen.

Messaging on Airbnb

If you click 'inbox' you can see messages from guests and reply here. You will be notified of any new messages via the email you supply to Airbnb when you set up your listing, but you will not be allowed to share your email address with guests or message them directly, although you will be given guests' phone numbers. Messages are automatically scanned for any email or website links in order to prevent hosts encouraging guests to book elsewhere or directly with the host. If you click on the three horizontal black bars on the left hand of the screen to the left of 'all messages' you can bring up messaging settings including 'quick replies' which allows you to create templates and automatic replies for various instances. This will save you a lot of time and hopefully ensure that guests always receive all the relevant information at the right moments. I have three main quick replies set up for:

- Contacting a guest for the first time after receiving a booking (I title this message 'after booking').
- Contacting guests a couple of days before arrival to give them check in details and directions ('pre-arrival').
- A message to guests the day before they leave to check everything is okay and thank them again for booking ('day before departure').

These messages can also be automated on the settings tab so that they will be sent at a designated time of your choosing – you will need to insert the 'short codes' from the pull-down menu within the message box which allows Airbnb to automatically fill in guest names and dates on your behalf. I do not always use the automatic message sending function as sometimes there are slight differences in booking types and whether I am offering an earlier check in or later check out depending on other bookings. Also, if you have guests staying for work or a funeral, you don't want to automatically message them telling them you hope they had a 'wonderful holiday', for example, so generally it is better to have the automatic replies set up and to use them but with the option to edit them before sending them. Airbnb will generally send you reminders the day before a guest arrives, but do not rely on this. You will need to keep an eye on your calendar from week to week so that you do not ever forget to send the relevant information in time. To send a message, go to 'inbox' and click on a guest's previous message or their booking confirmation which brings up the conversation thread. There will be small icons at the bottom of the message screen and if you click on the small speech bubble to the left-hand side of the message box, you can bring up these pre-written message templates or 'quick replies'. If you select one, it will appear in the message box. You can edit it further before pressing 'send'. To edit any of your 'quick replies' simply select 'quick replies' then press 'manage' on the top right-hand side of the list of templates and make your changes before saving again.

Sending a message to guests the day before departure reduces the chance for misunderstandings or late check-outs – I have had guests mix up their dates in the past and not realise that they are meant to be checking out on a particular day, for example, and then holding up the cleaners whilst they quickly have to pack everything up. You can also remind them of your check-out time and anything that should be done before departure such as emptying bins or washing up. It also allows you to ask if everything has been okay for guests and resolve any problems and complaints, instead of guests rushing home and potentially leaving you a poor review without any prior communication. Although all relevant house information is on my listings, in my virtual guidebook and in a guest information folder at the home, I always included a few 'key' pieces of information on the email I send a few days before arrival as a lot of people do not bother to read the manual provided and you will keep receiving emails about the same few things each time otherwise.

Message template examples:

1. After receiving a booking confirmation from a guest:

Dear [guest first name],

Thank you very much for booking Buttercup Cottage, I hope you all have a wonderful stay. I will send you a message with a key safe code and directions a few days before you arrive so that you can let yourselves into the cottage any time after 4pm. Please do not hesitate to contact me if you have any questions about your stay in the meantime. Local information, including grocery shopping, restaurants and pubs and local tourist sites etc. can be found in our virtual guidebook on our listing here. We strongly recommend booking meals and activities in advance where possible. The full address is; Buttercup Cottage, Field Lane, Little Village AY3 8JJ.

With best wishes,

Host (your first name)

If you do not supply a virtual guidebook, then share some tips and recommendations for some of your favourite or nearest pubs, restaurants and cafes, along with information on grocery shopping and any local sites of interest in this message so guests can book meals and activities in advance. I also share the full address here, as sometimes this remains hidden to guests until 24 hours before arrival, and some guests like to plan ahead with things such as online grocery deliveries, for example.

2. A few days before arrival (I usually send this at least three days before arrival otherwise guests will start to message me to enquire about access):

Dear [guest first name],

The key safe code for Saturday is 1234 and the safe is next to the kitchen door. Please remember to re-scramble the numbers on the keypad after collecting and returning your keys. There is a padlock key if you have bikes which you wish to store in the shed behind the house. The cottage will be ready from 4pm and check out is 10am.

The postcode is ***** and the cottage is in the centre of Little Village, opposite the church, on Field Lane, with a wooden sign by the roadside which points towards a parking area marked for the cottage. We ask that guests read the house manual located in the living room on arrival.

Local information, including grocery shopping, restaurants, pubs and local tourist attractions can be found in our virtual guidebook on our listing here and we also supply further information at the cottage.

If you have any questions or problems during your stay please don't hesitate to contact me via Airbnb or email. In an emergency I can be contacted by phone on 07*****.

Thank you very much for booking Buttercup Cottage, I hope you all have a wonderful time,

with best wishes,

Host (your first name)

You may wish to give more detailed directions to your property in this message, outlining any major roads or routes from different parts of the UK, prior to more local directions, as not everyone uses Satnav. If you live in a town or city, consider including public transport information as well.

3. One day before departure:

Dear [guest first name],

Thank you again for booking Buttercup Cottage, I hope you have all enjoyed your stay and that everything was to your satisfaction? Any problems, comments or feedback, please do not hesitate to get in touch.

Before departure we ask that guests remove any rubbish and recycling to the main bin and boxes by the front gates and ensure that all kitchenware is washed and dried up. Please return the keys to the key safe, code 1234. Check out is 10am. Thank you so much!

Thank you again for booking the cottage, I hope you have a safe journey onwards tomorrow.

With best wishes,

Host (your first name)

If you opt into the new feature of automatically notifying guests of check-out tasks, then you may want to edit or remove this message.

I find that a very friendly and polite tone goes a long way with guests – it is generally better to be too friendly rather than be too formal or distant-sounding. My main customer mantra is to 'kill with kindness'. Always be as friendly and helpful in your communications as possible, even in the face of unreasonable, critical or silly questions or comments. Guests are so much more likely to find fault or complain if they sense the slightest hint of impatience or unfriendliness from you. Most guests will respond in a friendly tone. Some hosts are very jovial, relaxed and familiar sounding in their communications and do seem to get a very good response from guests, although I prefer a slightly more, but not too, formal approach. If you create a sense of openness and kindness with your guests, they are much more likely to start their holiday in a better mood and think twice before leaving poor feedback. It also allows you to make your expectations of guests very clear and to answer commonly asked questions in advance. I find that guests rarely read the small print on the listing itself or the information provided at the holiday let, so I now cover a few commonly asked questions in these messages to reduce unnecessary admin. You will soon learn which things are most frequently asked or requested and can update your message templates accordingly over time.

Airbnb payments

Payments from guests will generally be released to your bank a few days after check-in. I often have guests asking questions about payment and accounts before arrival, but I just point them in the direction of Airbnb in this case as they deal with the financial side of things. If you go to your listings information page and then click on 'menu' on the top right-hand side, you can view all reservations and transactions. Always check your bank account each month to ensure that payments are going through. It's worth making a note of the amount, after commission, that you'll be paid on your own paper calendar as it makes tracking your account much easier and quicker to do. I always advise setting up a business-specific bank account, even if you view yourself as a casual host. It makes tracking and making payments and keeping accounts much easier.

Airbnb reviews

The review system is Airbnb's strength, but it can also be a nightmare for hosts. I find most guests are very friendly, fair and reasonable if you are trying your best as a host, but you will get one or two bad guests per year who will leave you a bad or mixed review without good reason. Some guests have been known to blackmail hosts with poor feedback in return for partial refunds, but I would immediately flag this up with Airbnb if this happens. Airbnb is very reluctant to remove poor reviews, however much evidence you have to show that they were unfair. It can be tempting to answer angrily to a bad review, but it is so much better to sleep on it for at least a night and then reply calmly and professionally – if your guest was unreasonable and untruthful then you can gently refute any claims and refer to their behaviour, if it was unusually poor. A bad review early on can be a death-knell for a new listing, as you do not have the good reviews to fall back on. In this case I would consider removing and re-adding your listing and starting again, assuming that the issues that caused the poor review were not your fault or were something you fixed after they'd been pointed out. A poor review in a sea of good ones will generally not do too much damage, however, as everyone is aware of the problem of online review trolls these days, and will read between the lines of your, hopefully, diplomatic reply to their accusations.

If I am not at the holiday let on the day of departure, I always ask my cleaning company how the property was left so that I can fairly review the guest as well. You do not have to review your guest if you do not wish to. You only see your guests' review of their holiday once you submit one for them. If you do not review them, then their review becomes visible around 14 days later. You still have the right to respond to their review even if you have not reviewed them. Most guests will leave a bit of a mess and very few will do the suggested washing up or bin/food disposal that you may ask them to. However, do not be too angry, for every five guests that leave things a little messy or dirty, there will be one or two who leave it immaculate, and it tends to balance out in the end. Unless your home has been left in a terrible state, I would not voice any disappointment to your guests after their departure, as you are simply increasing the chance of a poor review from them – it is unfair, but that is the way it works unfortunately. You can click on any Airbnb guest and check out what hosts have said about them. There are some subtle tricks you can use to 'warn' other hosts about less than perfect guests, such as not mentioning anything about how the house was left, but just stating the dates the guest stayed, or using phrases which suggest an issue with a guest without outrightly criticising them. For example, a guest who would not stop phoning or messaging you could be described as 'very communicative', or a guest who left a bit of a mess could be described as 'having made very good use of all the facilities', noisy guests could be described as 'exuberant', and so on. There are website communities dedicated to writing clever come-backs or secretly coded warnings to other hosts in these situations which are sometimes worth a look – they can be very entertaining. I do think you have a duty to let other hosts know if a guest is a little problematic, but it is a fine balancing act of not wanting to appear like a critical host either. Hosts and guests are often reluctant to express their true or full feelings about certain things they were not happy with in reviews, because comments and scores are shared between both. I notice that European guests and hosts are a little more forthright in their reviews – I do think that the British often struggle with feedback and criticism. That is why it is always a good idea to ask guests to contact you with any feedback or suggestions, as sometimes problems with your let can remain hidden for a while if no one likes to flag them up.

Airbnb have recently claimed that they now give hosts the opportunity to flag up any 'retaliatory' negative reviews from guests and potentially have them removed. It can still be a slow process however, and you are not guaranteed that the negative review will be removed as it is very much guest and host both claiming different things usually. If you have strong evidence to refute a guest's negative review, then you might have a chance of having it removed.

You have the choice to mark a tick-box at the end of your guest review on whether you would host the guest again. If you tick 'no' then the guest will not be able to instantly book with other hosts but will have to request to book each time for future stays. If you receive a booking request from a guest who has stayed at other properties, then be aware that this might be the reason why they cannot instantly book with you. Hosts can be very reluctant to write an outwardly critical review of bad guests, but they can mark them out, anonymously, through this option. If you decide to accept a booking from a guest with slightly less than perfect feedback or who has been marked down for cleanliness by other hosts in the past, then it is probably worth a gentle reminder on the day before checkout that things should be tidied away and washed up etc., along with wishing them a safe onward journey and thanking them again for booking your home. I always recommend that hosts email guests the day before check-out in any case to make sure everything was okay for them as it will encourage them to let you know about any issues or problems. You have the opportunity to then apologise if necessary. If the issue was serious enough to affect the guests' holiday, then you might consider offering a partial refund or discount off future stays. Guests are a lot less likely to leave negative reviews in this case, in my experience. They are also more likely to let you know if something is broken or requires attention or replacing and you then have time to sort it before the next guests arrive. It is worth replying to all reviews, if you have time, including good reviews, as it shows you to be a committed and friendly host.

Airbnb can be quite a hard taskmaster and will sometimes threaten hosts with removal from the site if they consistently underperform. Some hosts have complained that they have received warnings from the site after receiving several consecutive four out of five star reviews. I do not know of any hosts who have been removed from the site for this reason and can only assume that Airbnb believes this sort of pressure keeps up standards and profits. It is a good idea to build your business through listing websites initially, but over time encourage direct bookings via your own website to free yourself from the tyranny of listing site expectations and the threat of bad guest reviews. More on how to do this later. Airbnb is still a very good starting point for new holiday let hosts regardless of these annoyances. If you only plan to list on one site and want to maximise your occupancy, then I would strongly advise that you choose Airbnb.

Bad guests, damage and theft

I never like to leave a holiday home empty for more than 24 hours after a guest has checked out. Sometimes there will be a break between check out and your cleaners arriving. If possible, it is best to view the home soon after check-out, even if you do not plan to have it cleaned immediately, just in case of any taps or lights being left on etc., and to check the state that the let has been left in. Some hosts like to visit the guests shortly before check-out and will inspect the home whilst guests are still there, but having been the guest in this situation, I found it deeply uncomfortable and inconvenient as we were waiting on the host to show up for the check over before we could leave, and I did feel somewhat 'on trial'. I would strongly recommend that you do not do this.

You need to notify Airbnb as soon as possible if there is significant damage or strong evidence that house rules have been broken. You will need to take photos or ask your cleaning company to do so in the case of this happening, as Airbnb will request evidence. Airbnb insures hosts for damage, so it is definitely worth doing this if you are unlucky enough to have this happen to your holiday let. You should also have your own full holiday let insurance which covers you for damage and loss. If you have specified no smoking, pets or large gatherings at your home and it becomes clear that one or more of these rules has been ignored, leading to damage or excessive cleaning being required, then contact Airbnb straight away with photographic evidence. Likewise, if there is general damage or excessive cleaning required, you will need to photograph and report it to Airbnb. I would not contact the guest in the first instance as they may rush to give a false account to Airbnb and/or write you a terrible review in the meantime. Things do get broken and go missing and you do have to expect a certain amount of wear and tear in your let, so I generally ignore small breakages or missing items and factor these things into my business as running costs. Most guests are reasonable and will notify you if something has been broken. They will rarely admit to being the cause of something being broken or not working, and it is generally not worth the argument or poor feedback that arguing over something like this can cause. Sometimes guests offer to replace things, but I usually tell them not to worry, if it's a relatively small value item, and this creates a certain amount of goodwill and a good review which is usually more valuable to your business in the long run.

If significant damage has been done and it is clear that the guest has caused it, then you will probably want to take steps to recoup your losses; remain polite and civil at all times in your communications if you do speak to guests about the matter. If you are not one hundred percent sure that it was the most recent guests that caused the damage or were staying at your home when something went missing, then you cannot pursue the matter. Cleaners will not always notice damage straight away and even missing objects can be overlooked for a few changeovers, by cleaners, and by you. It is very difficult to prove when something happened if you have a lot of guests going in and out of your property. Do not have high value, easy-to-steal items in your home as sooner or later someone will take them, and it is often the unlikeliest guests that surprise you with this behaviour. I have had Bluetooth speakers, pans, hairdryers and even lamps go missing over the years. I view it as running costs, but I would not have state-of-the-art portable technology or high value items in my home for this reason. I find it is usually fairly low-cost items which disappear most frequently in any case, and it is often accidental. It is easy for guests to accidentally pack away hairdryers from drawers, hangers from wardrobes and take Tupperware, walking books or umbrellas back home in the car. These costs can add up and I now label as many things as possible to try to minimise this issue and no longer supply certain items that kept disappearing – namely Tupperware, picnic equipment and umbrellas. They are very useful for guests, but I got fed up with replacing them.

Make sure you supply clear rules and terms and conditions on your listing and at your home, including clear terms and conditions in your guest information folder. Make it clear that if things are missing or broken through miss-use or excessive force, that you reserve the right to bill guests for any costs. Provide clear instructions for the correct use of appliances and utilities, so there can then be little excuse for guests breaking items by accident or through using them incorrectly. You soon discover your home's 'weak' points in terms of wear and tear or breakages, and you may wish to add a laminated note on the wall close to any fixtures or appliances which are not overly obvious in their operation, just to reduce the likelihood of any problems recurring. I found one property with a macerator toilet and shower was frequently blocked by guests flushing wipes down it, but additional notes above the loo and on the door, including an illustrated sticker warning for non-English speaking guests soon stopped this happening.

Bear in mind that holiday lets will suffer a great deal of wear and tear. People are on holiday and want to enjoy themselves and can be careless with someone else's home or not want to spend time cleaning up after themselves. People are more likely to break appliances and fixtures that they're unfamiliar with. You should only contact Airbnb to make a claim if the issue is significant.

Airbnb rankings

Airbnb is quite secretive about its ranking order, in terms of how you make your listing appear higher up in guest searches. Good reviews certainly help, as does a fully completed listing – it is worth checking from time to time in case Airbnb has added more sections which require completion. I find that tweaking prices, descriptions and adding photos on most listing sites often leads to a flurry of bookings, so I can only think that it's a good idea to edit your property regularly, perhaps weekly, even if it's just a small change. It shows that you are active on the site to guests, who can see the date of the latest update, but it also appears to have a positive effect on booking activity and rankings in my experience. Hosts who have been on the site for longer periods of time also seem to be rewarded with a good position in the listings, as does having the 'Superhost' badge which is earned annually by good performance – i.e. positive reviews and no booking cancellations. Guests can search exclusively for 'Superhost' properties so it will give you better visibility for this reason too. Avoiding the need to cancel guests and getting some good reviews should be your focus in order to climb the Airbnb rankings. Applying promotions, whereby you simply apply a percentage discount to a selected date range, will also highlight these dates to potential bookers - the bigger the discounts, the more your listing will be highlighted. Cancellations are very much frowned upon by all listing sites as it reflects badly on them and doing so will usually incur some kind of ranking or financial penalty, (unless there are good extenuating circumstances which you will need to inform them of), so keeping your calendar up to date is very important.

Other website features

'Insights' allows you to check your progress and performance on the site and you can view graphs which compare your listing with other similar listings. Airbnb will suggest ways in which you can increase bookings, such as additional facilities or items you could add, further discounts or a more flexible cancellation policy. There is an option to remove the guest service fee and have it deducted from your earnings instead, meaning that you pay 15% commission, and the guest pays zero additional fees. Most of the suggestions will involve you paying out more in fees and reducing your income via discounts and making your cancellation policy more flexible, meaning that you will find yourself dealing with more last-minute cancellations. Allowing longer stays will also be encouraged. These suggestions are for your consideration, and will almost certainly increase bookings, but you may not wish to implement them if the numbers do not stack up financially. Guest fees are certainly unpopular with guests, so you could consider removing them and paying additional commission, but you must ensure that your nightly price is still financially viable, after costs. 'Insights' is a useful tool in terms of viewing your progress, however, and you can see your earnings and stats to give you a sense of how many people are viewing your listing, how many carry on to book with you, how many people have added you to their 'wish list' and so on. It will also flag up any issues with your listing.

Airbnb is increasingly honing its 'community' atmosphere. You can now create 'teams' which allows you to add more people to help run your listing - before you would have simply shared a password with another person who has access to your listing, but you can now invite them to be part of your 'team'. It is a useful feature if you co-run your business with other people or have your property managed by someone else but want to have the option to dip in and out of your listing. You can create 'tasks' on the listing which everyone on 'teams' can view, which is useful if you do not have time to carry out the administration tasks yourself, but want to highlight them for someone else to complete. I do wonder if some of these features are aimed at larger businesses who are looking to run multiple properties.

There are also various schemes in which you can contact and even meet up with other hosts, including those in your local area. You can join local notice boards where local issues as well as Airbnb issues and updates can be discussed on an open forum. You can also access 'hosting resources' which has a number of articles on different ways of improving your listing and business.

There is a 'help' centre if you have any questions or problems. Most answers to questions can be found here, but if you need to speak to a customer service agent regarding something specific which requires action, you will need to contact Airbnb directly. I have previously been passed over to an Airbnb community agent when I have had issues on the site - some of these are not actually employees of Airbnb, but rather other hosts or individuals who can advise and help. They do not have the authority to make changes, communicate with your guests or deal with specific cancellation problems etc., so you will need to message or speak to an Airbnb support agent in these cases. If you attain 'Superhost' status, Airbnb makes it quicker and easier to contact them directly.

Key points

- With low commission to pay and an easy-to-use website and mobile app, along with being the largest international and best-known site for holiday rentals, Airbnb is currently one of the best sites to list on for holiday let owners. It typically charges hosts around 3% commission and guests around 14% commission. Always carefully check the terms and conditions, including commission, when signing up, in case they change.
- Airbnb is suited to formal holiday lets plus individual rooms within private homes and many other types of accommodation.
- Set your listing up on a laptop or PC initially if possible – download the mobile app afterwards (not necessary, but useful for when you're travelling or not at home).
- You can have multiple properties listed under one account.
- It is a good idea to give your property a name.
- Talk up your property's key attributes in the listing and descriptions – use superlatives and let guests know about any special features or favourite facilities.
- Good photography is essential.
- Provide as much information as possible to save yourself answering lots of emails and phone calls from guests. Fill out the online guidebook and include information on local pubs, cafes, restaurants, places of interest and grocery shopping.
- Set up base nightly and weekend prices on the 'settings' page but tweak individual dates on the actual calendar. Consider adding discounts for longer stays.

- Airbnb will suggest nightly rates for you - you do not have to accept their suggestions. I advise against using 'smart pricing'.
- Check out your competition on the website and on other listing sites to get a sense of potential revenue and pricing.
- Custom length of stay is useful for specifying longer stay requirements during public and school holidays.
- Generally, it is best to specify three nights minimum stay all year round, bar school holidays and summer months. Two-night stays are most popular for city breaks but ensure your nightly price and any additional fees allow for profit after changeover costs. Fridays and Saturdays are the most popular dates.
- Consider using Airbnb's 'professional hosting tools' in order to set more tailored check-in day and stay requirements, along with tailored discounts, for specific dates. The ability to choose check-in days for specific dates appears to have been removed from the regular calendar - hopefully it will be re-added.
- Remember to set restrictions on days when you do not want guests arriving.
- Recent studies show that additional fees are very off-putting to guests. Try to avoid them and build any cleaning and laundering costs into your nightly price instead. Any fees should generally not exceed 10% of the overall cost of the accommodation.
- Flat rates are usually simpler and better to deal with for pricing, and holiday cleaning agencies will usually charge you a flat rate.
- You can usually choose from a range of cancellation policies. A more flexible policy will encourage more bookings but be prepared for cancellations.

- Allowing 'instant book' will encourage more bookings. If you allow instant book, then it is worth specifying that you will only accept instant bookings from guests who have not been banned by other hosts. New guests with no previous stays through Airbnb will have to request to book. Guests who have been banned by previous hosts can still request to book but you will not be able to see that they have been banned by other hosts. You can see see their previous feedback though.
- Make sure you set up a minimum notice period to receive bookings, especially if you use instant book. You can still accept last minute booking requests, even if you do not use instant book or have a longer required notice period.
- Message templates are worth setting up in the messaging section of the site and will save you a lot of time. Be wary of using the automatic template scheduler as not all guests and stays will be the same.
- Guests and hosts can review each other on Airbnb – reviews will not be shared until both parties have shared them or until 14 days after check-out.
- Time spent on the site, applying promotions (discounts), receiving good reviews, obtaining 'Superhost' status, not cancelling guests and regular editing of your prices and listing details can all help to raise your business profile within the listing rankings.

Chapter Five
A brief guide to setting up listings on other sites

Much of the information and tips provided in the previous chapter will be applicable to most listing sites. However, I will go through some hints and tips for setting up listings on the other large independent listing sites that I use, as each site is a little different and has its own quirks.

Setting up a listing on Booking.com

I list on Booking.com as it is one of the largest, most international free listing sites for holiday lets, along with Airbnb. It used to be more hotels-based but has taken steps in recent years to become more holiday home friendly too, but some of the calendar settings still reflect the hotel model and can initially be a little confusing. Booking.com currently charges a higher commission for hosts than some of its competitors, at a typical average of around 15% of the total stay price. Guests like it for its lack of guest fees and transparent costs. Your listing may also appear on its sister site, Booking.net, and the listing will almost be identical, although I notice that some of my listing details are not correctly transferred across on to this site and there seem to be mixed opinions on the sister site from hosts and guests alike. Hopefully this will improve in time.

You can have more than one property set up on your account, each with its own ID number and calendar.

Booking.com is slower to make payments, the quickest payment time seems to be two weeks after guests check out, but it can typically take a month for the money to transfer. Make sure that they have your account details as a lot of hosts initially think they have added them and then realise they have not been paid for several months – Booking.com don't seem in a hurry to let hosts know that they haven't been able to pay them, so keep a close eye on your accounts at the start. Most hosts get Booking.com to deal with payments, but you do also have the option to take payments directly yourself at the property and be invoiced by Booking.com for the commission. Beware – Booking.com will usually still send you 'invoices' for commission even if it is automatically deducted from your payout if they handle payments for you – so just ignore these and treat them as financial records.

Booking.com offers hosts to opt in for 'business' stays. This means that you may need to email guests an invoice and/or receipt for their stay outlining their payments, even if Booking.com has dealt with the payment. Booking.com does not provide guests with official invoices and receipts as it views itself as a referral service to holiday let hosts. If you are confident in generating an invoice (preferably in a PDF format as most people will be able to view and download these files), then it is worth opting in to encourage business travellers who often need to provide official invoices and billing for their company. The invoices can be very basic, with just your details, including address, the dates of the stay, the guest's name and address and the details of the payment. I always add the details of the commission amount that Booking.com takes from my payment as well and show the total price that the guest pays.

Booking.com does not offer hosts any general home insurance, although they do offer hosts insurance against third-party lawsuits and liability claims (see below). There is a 'guest misconduct tool' which allows you to report any serious issues, but it is probably questionable how interested they will be in any problems. You have the option to set up your own damage deposit, although they advise against it due to a resulting drop in bookings. Booking.com will not handle the damage deposit payments so you would have to arrange it directly with your guest which is not very convenient, and guests are usually very wary of making additional payments outside of the official payment scheme.

Again, I strongly recommend setting your listing up on a PC or laptop and downloading the owners' app (avoid downloading the holiday makers one by accident) onto your phone once your listing is up and running.

Setting up a listing on Booking.com is straightforward and you will be assisted by an automated step-by-step system, as is the case with Airbnb. In the past it was harder to get listed on Booking.com compared to some of the other listing sites and I have had to wait for a site visit to establish my identity in the past, although it seems that the business is learning from Airbnb and becoming more user-friendly over time for hosts and this verification step appears to have been removed for most hosts. Booking.com was always more geared towards hotels and guesthouses in the past, and there are still some quirks on their website and calendar system which reflect this, but they are improving the system for holiday let owners over time. You have the option to enrol in their Partner Liability Insurance program when you register your home which protects you against third-party lawsuits and liability claims, so I would strongly recommend you tick the 'yes' box for this.

All editing of your listing is done on the Booking.com extranet - it is a website for hosts which is distinct from the regular Booking.com site which is aimed at guests. It is very straightforward. Your property is assigned an ID number and most of the information that you provide is basic. There is less scope for flowery descriptions than on Airbnb – you will find yourself mainly ticking boxes regarding facilities, room types and so on. Booking.com will then generate their own very basic description of your property on their website, which can be rather strange in my opinion, although maybe useful to an international traveller with little knowledge about the area your holiday home is located in. It will give distances to the nearest airport and some somewhat unselective points of interest, (not always particularly close by!), and mention a few key facilities that you offer, which I assume it thinks to be particularly attractive to guests, although these can also seem rather random. You certainly do not get a sense of your individuality as a holiday let provider from the generated description, although all relevant information can be found by potential guests by clicking on the various information tabs on your listing.

You do have the opportunity to describe your property in 'About the property', but this is less prominent and obvious on the actual listing, but it is still certainly worth filling out. You can also write about yourself in the 'About the Host' section, although I tend to also add a few more details about the property here as well. The more tick boxes you complete and the more in-depth information you provide, the higher your listing score will be, and this apparently translates into a higher position in the listing rankings, so it is worth completing the different information sections as fully as possible, and they can be quite long and tedious to fill in.

You can have multiple properties or rooms listed on one account on Booking.com, but they will have their own listing number, descriptions and calendar. You have the option to use different bank accounts for different properties.

The calendar on Booking.com is not quite as user-friendly as the one on Airbnb in my view, although it does have some additional useful features. I strongly recommend that you always use 'monthly view' for the calendar – you can switch between 'list' view and 'monthly' view on the calendar by pressing a menu on the top right-hand side of the calendar page. List view seems to be aimed at more of a hotel/guesthouse system with multiple rooms or 'units' for sale - a holiday let counts as a single 'unit'. Monthly view seems much better suited to holiday lets and is easier to use. List view is useful if you have a calendar 'rule' or promotion which you want to apply long-term and permanently through the 'bulk edit' function – i.e. book six nights and receive the seventh free, or a long-term weekly discount and so on. You can apply promotions and discounts for specific dates using the monthly calendar as well though and generally I find it much easier to use compared to list view. For long-term calendar settings, restrictions or discounts, go to 'List view' and then 'bulk edit', highlighted in blue on the calendar and this will bring up lots of self-explanatory options which you can apply to a set number of dates, or continually for years into the future.

In 'monthly' view on the calendar you simply left-click dates to edit prices and stay requirements, and click and drag to select several consecutive nights (the same as the Airbnb calendar). A box on the right-hand side will appear and it is here that you can alter nightly prices, minimum stay requirements or check-in and check-out day restrictions. The 'no departures' and 'no arrivals' button on the 'advanced restrictions' tab here is very useful, although sometimes it is not visible to new hosts – I have had to contact Booking.com in the past to request that this feature is added to the main calendar for new listings. You can also apply rules and restrictions via the 'bulk edit' function on the 'list view' calendar if you do not have the restricted check-in and check-out button option on the monthly calendar. If you do have the advanced option buttons to restrict check-in and check-out dates, then you need to apply them to each date of a particular date run in order to set up a changeover day; you will select 'no check-in' for Mondays, Tuesdays, Wednesdays, Thursdays, Fridays and Sundays if you want a Saturday check-in, and click 'check-in allowed' on the Saturday, for example. Be mindful that occupancy and check-in rules that overlap another set of rules can take precedence if they precede the other dates - e.g. you have four days minimum stay selected the week before a Saturday to Saturday seven day minimum holiday, but guests could check-in on the Friday and check-out on the Tuesday of your main holiday seven day week if you have not selected the 'no check-in' option on that day, even if the Tuesday states a minimum stay of seven nights for that week. I have been caught out by this on several occasions, especially before I had the easy access to check-in and check-out restrictions on the calendar.

You can also choose how much notice you require before a guest arrives. Be careful here as the calendar does have an annoying tendency to revert to 'no notice' required and quite often puts a one-night minimum requirement on dates, particularly after you have edited something else. I think it is a known glitch as Booking.com have been quite understanding when a guest has booked something they shouldn't have been able to due to this happening to me and hopefully it is being dealt with. I have not had it happen recently, so I think their programmers have probably sorted out the issue already. However, I find Booking.com can be quite inflexible at times and they will threaten to charge you as a result of any mistakes or demand that you find alternative accommodation for a guest that you can no longer host even if you immediately notify them of a double booking or inability to host for some reason, even if the stay is months away. If you need to cancel guests due to unforeseen circumstances which are not your fault, such as a broken-down boiler etc., then they will allow this, penalty-free. Try to speak to a customer service agent as soon as possible if you need to cancel.

For weekly discounts or any kind or promotion or discount you want to set up click on the 'promotions' tab above the calendar. Here you have a lot of flexibility to offer very tailored discounts, which is one of the site's strong points. Booking.com will suggest some weekly discounts as well as suggested percentage discounts, but you can alter these accordingly. It is a useful tool when trying to entice guests with last minute deals, but do not forget that you have set them up and *then* lower your nightly price too much as well, as you could end up out of pocket. Promotions can push you up the rankings and your discounted dates will be flagged to potential guests. Dates with promotions applied to them have a little price-tag symbol on them on the calendar to remind you, but it is not always as clear as it could be – there will be a basic reference to the type of promotion if you click on the date in question on the monthly calendar, but it does not give full details unless you click on to your full list of promotions. Longer term promotions set up in 'list view' bulk edit such as weekly discounts or free nights will also be represented by a little tag symbol on your calendar. I find weekly discounts a little more fiddly to set up on the monthly calendar view, and I do not want them applied all year round, so I tend to offer a 'book six nights and get the seventh free' instead via list view bulk editing as a long-term promotion for some properties, which seems to go down quite well with a lot of guests and encourages them to book longer stays. You can select shorter-term promotions and discounts of any kind. I find the 'basic' promotion type the easiest to use. It's very useful if you are trying to fill last minute availability and allows you to offer shorter stays, say of two nights, at a higher rate, but you can then offer a good discount to entice guests to book three nights or more, for example, at what would be a more regular rate. I find it easier to book out shorter, two-night stays as last-minute stays, but I do have to raise my prices to make it profitable. Quite often, it's the stay requirement, rather than the price, which puts people off booking. It's rare that I have someone book a longer stay at short notice. Be careful when setting the dates within your promotion to add the minimum stay requirements that the discounts can be applied to, otherwise it will automatically apply it to stays of one night or more. Also watch for the calendar jumping forward by a month or two, which it seems to do, if you are setting up an individual date run of a few days or weeks. I use promotions a lot if I am trying to fill last minute availability. I raise the nightly price on the calendar and drop the stay requirements to two nights to try to encourage short bookings without being out of pocket, but then specify a 'basic' promotion whereby there is a 10 or 20% nightly discount if guests book three nights or more to encourage longer stays.

If you click on 'calendar connections' on the top right-hand side above your calendar, this will take you to a page where you can copy and paste links to other listing site calendars or import their bookings or blocks, if they also use the i-Cal calendar format. I import calendars from Airbnb, Trip Advisor and Vrbo here.

I noticed with Booking.com that my property sometimes shows up as unavailable when this was not the case and realised that guests must enter the correct number of bedrooms to their search, not just the correct guest number – i.e. if you enter six guests in the search bar, but do not specify the number of bedrooms, it sometimes reverted to one bedroom, and my three bedroom property would not show up as available. I think this is due to the fact that Booking.com was traditionally a hotel listing site. I then added a note to the listing for guests to make sure their search criteria included bedroom numbers as well. The search function is perhaps not the strongest feature on Booking.com, but hopefully they will improve it.

Booking.com has various additional membership types and schemes for hosts under the 'opportunities' tab, most of which involve hosts paying higher commission. There is a ten percent discount offer for guests who are members of the 'Genius' scheme, if you also join the scheme. In return for reducing your prices by 10% for these guests, Booking.com raises the profile of your listing and you appear higher up in rankings. I have generally avoided these schemes, including the 'increased visibility' scheme, as I already find the 15% commission I am charged per booking high enough. Guests get to automatically join the Genius scheme after booking a few stays through Booking.com. You must have an overall average score of 7.5 or higher in order to qualify for the scheme, so you would only be able to join the scheme once you have a few good reviews under your belt.

Under 'calendar and pricing' you also have the option to offer different types of rate plans with different cancellation terms and pricing, but again I find this confuses things. There is also the option to offer a discount for those booking on their mobiles. I do feel that Booking.com is constantly offering ways for the guest to pay less but seems to forget that all these extra reductions and increased commissions for hosts add up and it quickly becomes unviable to offer them. If you have relatively cheap running costs and changeover costs and are looking for a large number of stays, then some of the schemes might be worth a try, but do not forget that many of them add further commission to the base commission of around 15%.

All messaging between guests and you and Booking.com can be found in 'Inbox' and, like Airbnb, you have the option to create message templates and to schedule them. 'Analytics' has various tools which highlight your performance and suggest things you can do to improve it or allow you to compare your data with that of local competitors. Like Airbnb, you have a choice of cancellation policy types.

Like Airbnb, there are various cancellation policy options. I tend to make mine quite strict as I do receive a lot of cancellations otherwise. There is a button on the main monthly calendar page which allows you to mark individual dates as 'non-refundable'. I do not use it as I have a strict cancellation policy in any case, but it could be useful if you have a different policy or want to make it clear to guests that no refund will be offered whatever their reasons are for cancelling. Booking.com will sometimes ask you to consider refunding a guest for cancelling their stay, but you are not obliged to if you have a strict cancellation policy in place - this will always take precedence. Booking.com will sometimes offer refundable or free cancellation on your behalf and will be prepared to take the financial hit if the guest cancels and they cannot re-book the dates. I think they only offer this when their analytics suggest to them that it is an easy to fill date with little risk involved for them.

Booking.com does feel somewhat weighted towards the guest in my experience. They can be quite strict and threaten more serious penalties for cancellations and seem more likely to side with guests when there is a problem. They only allow guests to leave reviews for properties and, unlike most independent listing sites, do not allow hosts to review guests. You can reply to reviews though. In my view, the overall atmosphere is not as friendly as Airbnb, and it seems more detached and business-like. Some of my more negative experiences with guests have been through Booking.com. I sometimes think this is because my prices are higher on the site to allow for the higher commission, although guests do not pay any additional guest fees like some other listing sites, so it should balance out a little. I think there is also less fear of reprisals for guests who leave a mess as hosts cannot review guests and although Booking.com will email guests on your behalf if there are issues or damage during a stay, they do not seem to have much power or inclination in this area. However, international travellers and especially US visitors seem to like using the site and it has a large reach. Some people much prefer it to Airbnb and feel that it protects them better, as guests, but all of this is very subjective. Booking.com is competitive mostly due to its lack of guest fees, so bear this in mind with your pricing as well.

It is worth having the Booking.com owner mobile app, 'Pulse'. To view the calendar, click on 'availability', then select your listing. To select a date run, click on the start date and then click on the end date - this brings up a box below of editing options. You can then set the dates to 'open' or 'closed'. Always select '1' room available - it is misleading, but this means one listing for a single property - multiple room options are for hotels. If you click more than one, you make your listing available to book several times over on one date. Sometimes if this box becomes unticked (a possible glitch on the system), then you will need to put it back to '1' to make it bookable. You can also set the price, minimum stay and minimum notice ('advance reservation') on this page. To clear date selections and select new ones, press 'clear'. You can edit property details, view bookings and access your messages via the other buttons on the bottom of the screen. All other settings and functions can be found under the 'more' button. At the moment it does not seem possible to set check-in and check-out day rules on the mobile app, so I do this on my laptop instead.

Bear in mind that Booking.com sometimes lists your property on Google Maps so that guests searching here are automatically redirected to their website if they are interested in booking. You will not be able to add your property to Google Maps if they get there first. Ensure that you list your property on Google Maps before setting up a listing on Booking.com.

Setting up a listing on Vrbo / Expedia

Vrbo (previously known as 'Home Away' and 'Owners Direct') replicates its holiday let listings in Expedia and both are companies with a large international reach, so I find it helpful to list my properties here as well. The commission charged to hosts is typically around eight percent of the full booking price, so it is a little more competitive than Booking.com. The company was set up in the US and is currently increasing its holiday let marketing campaigns and seems to be taking cues from Airbnb's business model. I do not currently get very many bookings through Vrbo, but this could change. It certainly does not hurt to be on several listing sites, as long as you remember to update your prices from time to time. Vrbo has recently had a large overhaul of its website for owners and the calendar is well thought out, although can initially be a little confusing for newbies, given its many functions. Again, I recommend setting up your listing on a PC or laptop and downloading the mobile phone app afterwards.

Vrbo allows you to list more than one property per account and each will have its own calendar and details. Go to www.vrbo.com, select the UK listing site and click 'list your property'. By entering your property's details, Vrbo will estimate your potential revenue and suggest pricing to you, although you are not obliged to go with this. I prefer to set my own pricing, although it is helpful to have a base line suggestion. You also have the option to use Vrbo's 'fast start team' to help you set up your listing quickly if you are already on other listing sites. Vrbo offers hosts primary liability insurance up to $1 million USD, but you will still need your own property/contents home insurance in addition to this and Vrbo specifies that you need to have this in place in order to list with them. You also have the option to set a 'damage protection' amount in the calendar setting whereby guests will pay you up to a stated maximum price for any damage they cause. Guests tend to dislike these clauses, so generally I do not request this, and your own insurance should cover potential large damage costs in any case. Proving that a guest caused damage or took items is difficult and you would have to prove this to Vrbo and share receipts and so forth in the case of raising a claim.

Vrbo will automatically help you set up your listing, step-by-step, and is an easy site to use. It is worth watching the videos on calendar use, as it is a little more complex than some other platforms. Vrbo seems to increasingly offer only one listing plan which is pay-per-booking (typically around 8% commission for hosts), although it has offered an annual fee with a lower commission in the past, but this seems to be being phased out.

'Property editor' allows you to edit any of your listing's details at any time and is very thorough. There are a range of cancellation policies to choose from along with house rules and you have the option of uploading your own set of terms and conditions on 'rental agreement' which guests must agree to prior to arrival, but you do not have to provide this. As with all listing sites, the more flexible the cancellation policy, the more bookings you will generally receive – especially from early bookers. However, you will also receive more last-minute cancellations with a flexible cancellation policy as some guests will book on a whim or to simply reserve a choice of several properties from which they select one nearer to the time of their holiday. I usually select the 'moderate' policy – one which allows charge-free cancellations for a set period, but not too close to the start date of the holiday, so that I have a chance to re-book dates.

You have the option to offer 'instant book' to guests or to screen each booking request before accepting. Listings with instant book tend to rent more frequently and easily, but you must make sure that your calendar is always up to date if you select this. If you decide you need or want to cancel a booking, go to 'inbox' and click on the reservation message and press 'cancel' – there will be a list of reasons for cancelling. Some of these will allow you to cancel, penalty-free (usually for unforeseen circumstances or if the home has become inhabitable due to damage etc.), but other reasons can affect your ranking metrics meaning that you will appear lower down in the listings, as a penalty for cancelling without good reason. It is usually a good idea to contact customer support if you need to cancel for an emergency reason at late notice.

Vrbo also has a 'welcome guide' option which allows guests to access all relevant information shortly before their arrival, including directions, access information and key safe codes along with useful house information. It will save you time answering queries if you fill out this section, and although guests should have all relevant information at their fingertips before arrival at your home via this section of your listing, I still send an email a couple of days before arrival with directions and access instructions in case they have not accessed this.

Be aware when uploading photos that Vrbo requires relatively high-definition photos and will not accept photos where the pixel dimensions are not large enough – the site will not accept smaller mobile phone photos.

Guests are invited to review your property post-stay and you can also rate your guest with a basic scoring system. You have up to a year to leave a review, but as soon as a guest or host leaves a review, then the other party has fourteen days to submit theirs. Reviews are not shown to either party until both have submitted them. Guests will not be shown hosts' scores of them, but they will be able to see their average score once they have more than one rating. The guest's score is not public, but hosts will be able to see it if a guest books or requests to book with them. If they have a poor score then you may want to consider cancelling or refusing the booking, in my opinion. It is not possible to leave a detailed, public review of your guest as with Airbnb.

Vrbo's calendar is very user-friendly once you get used to it. Like other listing sites you click on dates to select them - to select a date run, click one date, release your mouse, and then click the end date. A box on the right-hand side will pop up showing the selected dates and from there you can edit the nightly price, minimum stay requirement, any weekly or monthly discounts, block dates and restrict check in and check out dates. I like this aspect of Vrbo's calendar as it means that all this information is to-hand on the actual calendar. Vrbo also allows you to edit multiple dates here with different prices set for different days of the week, or a flat rate for all days, which is helpful when filling out large chunks of the calendar.

Tabs above the calendar will allow you to set a general base rate and base weekly discounts, along with setting a minimum notice window for bookings and a base minimum stay requirement – this means that if you do not edit your main calendar these 'base' prices and settings will automatically be applied. If you are happy to offer a low minimum notice of one day, for example, you will be more likely to get last-minute bookings, but if your cleaning company requires some notice you will want to increase this. These are useful tools for automatically filling your calendar, especially when you are first setting it up and it will fill future dates automatically as they appear each month, as well. You also select how far in advance you are willing to accept bookings on 'booking window' through these tabs – I usually select twelve months, but you can choose anything from six to 24 months. You can also choose any additional fees, such as for cleaning or laundry via the top tabs. There is a tax collection tab and Vrbo leaves it to hosts to make sure they are applying any necessary local taxes here. Some overseas cities and areas have local taxes which need to be paid on holiday listings, but currently the UK does not have any schemes like this. On 'payment terms' you can select what percentage the holiday maker pays upon booking and when the balance is due. I generally ask for around 25% at the time of reservation with the rest due 28 days before check in. This encourages holidaymakers to book as people are usually reticent to pay for an entire holiday up-front, but it also allows sufficient time to re-book the dates if the guest decides they do not want to pay the balance for any reason, or decides to cancel at this point – it also filters out window shopping guests who are likely to cancel, although if you have a flexible cancellation policy this still may not deter them. There is an 'export and import' tab above the calendar where you can import and export data from your other listings calendars, such as Airbnb, Booking.com and Trip

Advisor, or any calendar which uses the i-Cal application. The main calendar mode is useful for making changes for specific dates such as raising prices for weekends and holidays and specifying minimum stays and check-in days for certain dates.

Market maker on the left-hand menu of the calendar will show you suggested pricing and compare your let to local ones. Like most listing sites, Vrbo will encourage you to lower your prices as much as possible, but you will need to factor in your changeover, running and commission costs when deciding these. It can be a helpful tool for getting a sense of the most competitive pricing, or for filling last minute availability. If you find you are getting booked up without too much difficulty, you should be wary of dropping your prices too much, especially for dates many months away, or for summer months and public holidays. You can become a 'Premier Host' on Vrbo (similar to Airbnb's 'Superhost') which can improve your ranking metrics and gives you a type of badge of honour which guests can see. This involves hosting a certain number of stays and receiving several positive reviews, along with avoiding cancellations. Payment history and reservation information can be found via the 'Reservation Manager' left hand menu. Like other listing sites, you can set up message templates in your inbox. In addition to this you can also provide attachable files for messaging, such as directions or local information, which is very useful.

Vrbo has a mobile owner app which is worth downloading. It is very easy to use and prompts you automatically on how to use it when you open it. You simply click dates to edit them and click one, then a second, to select a consecutive run of dates. You then press 'manage these dates' to set rates, discounts, minimum stay requirements and check-in and check-out rules on the box that pops up. You can also message guests and edit your listing through the other options on the bottom toolbar. It is all very self-explanatory.

Setting up a listing on Trip Advisor / holidaylettings.co.uk

Trip Advisor is another large independent listing site with a large international customer base, so I find it helpful to list here. It has a main sister site in the UK, holidaylettings.co.uk, where your listing and prices will be replicated, along with other affiliated sites including FlipKey. You can choose to set up your listing on either site and the steps required are almost identical on both – I will explain the process for Trip Advisor, as this is where I set up my listings. The typical, low 3% commission fees are another attraction for hosts, although guests will be charged fees of around 8-16%. I do not get many direct bookings from Trip Advisor, as the company seems to be more geared towards a referral type service these days. They display your prices on other listing sites, including Vrbo and Booking.com, and show your more competitive prices from different websites. It is, however, possible to book with Trip Advisor directly as well. Properties listed on several sites will usually show a variety of prices from the different listing sites which can be instantly compared with a button to click to take you through to your preferred site. You can manage multiple properties through one account on Trip Advisor and each one will have a unique ID number and its own calendar and settings. Trip Advisor will collect and manage payments and will release your payout 24 hours after guests check in, although it can take a few extra days to reach your bank account. Guests are offered 'payment protection' by Trip Advisor and can book by credit card. It is easier to set up the listing on a PC or laptop initially, but it is useful to download the host app to your phone as well once you have done this. It is important to note that Trip Advisor does not offer hosts any kind of insurance, including liability insurance, so make sure you are covered for everything by your own insurance before listing on the site.

Trip Advisor will help you set up your listing, step-by-step, with useful tips and information along the way. Once you have filled out the essential information and they have verified your identity, you can start to edit your calendar and other settings. I have had trouble with my Trip Advisor listing when using the Google Chrome browser in the past, so I tend to open it on a different browser, such as Microsoft Edge. On the home page you will have tabs along the top screen. The big difference with Trip Advisor is that I do not tend to use the calendar function very much. It will show bookings, dates and synchronised calendars, but it is not aimed at setting prices and restrictions. To do this I click on the 'Listing' tab at the top of the home page, then 'Prices'. Here you can set a base daily price, along with weekend, weekly and monthly base prices which will be applied to your calendar automatically when you set it up and as each month becomes available to book. Below this you can choose different pricing and settings for specific dates under 'seasonal prices'. I tend to offer cheaper rates for quiet times of year (November, January and February in particular) in this section and request longer stays and higher prices for school holidays, summer months and public holidays. You can specify preferred changeover days which is useful if you are looking to book up your calendar with back-to-back weekly stays during school holidays, for example. You can also set different weekend, weekly and monthly prices here which will override your base prices and any base discounts. If you do not set a weekly price in seasonal prices, then the base weekly discount will be applied to your chosen nightly price for stays of one week or more.

'Taxes and fees' can be accessed at the base of the seasonal prices list and you list any relevant additional taxes, cleaning and/or laundry fees here.

Most of your property editing will be via the top 'listings' tab. Here you will set your descriptions, policies, photos, location, prices and message templates. There is also a 'welcome pack' option here which allows you to set up check-in information which is automatically shared with guests shortly before their arrival. I always message guests as well a couple of days before arrival in case they miss this. Do not forget to update this information if you change any key safe codes as some guests will rely on this automated information.

Guests will be automatically invited to leave a review after their stay, and you can also remind them by opening an automated 'request review' action through the 'review' tab at the top of the screen. Hosts can review guests within fourteen days of check-out, but the feedback is not public - only the guest can see it. Guests have up to two years to leave a review and this is public, although hosts have a right of reply. Trip Advisor used to have a fool-safe system meaning that only guests who had officially booked with hosts could leave a review, but this seems to have changed meaning that anyone can leave a review for your holiday let even if they have not stayed there, which obviously allows hosts to abuse the system by reviewing themselves or for malicious or false reviews to be left. If you think this has happened, then contact Trip Advisor straight away.

Trip Advisor also has a mobile phone app for owners, but I do not use this. It has quite mixed reviews and as I receive very few bookings via this site, I have not downloaded it.

Final note

I recommend previewing your listing on all sites after it is fully set up – all of them have a preview function. This way you can see what potential guests see and check everything is appearing correctly. Do this a few times a year as sometimes there can be glitches or changes in the listing site's software which alters things. Also test the listing from time to time and ensure that the property is fully bookable - sometimes it is easiest to do this by going to the website in incognito mode.

Key points

Booking.com key points:

- Booking.com is one of the largest international listing sites for holiday lets, after Airbnb, so worth listing on. Higher commission, stricter penalties for cancelling, the inability to review guests, (although they can review you), and some occasionally glitchy calendar software which seems aimed at hotel listings are some of the downsides of using the website.
- Monthly view is the easiest way to edit your calendar. 'List view' is more complicated.
- Ask Booking.com to add the 'advanced options' buttons to your calendar if you do not have them as you can restrict check-in and check-out days very easily this way. Alternatively, set these through the 'list view' calendar on 'bulk edit'.
- Be wary of the calendar reverting to minimum notice for bookings and minimum stays of one night during

editing – it is a glitch in my view that will hopefully disappear soon.
- 'List view' is useful for bulk editing and long-term base discounts. Tailored discounts can be set up in 'promotions' – 'basic deal' is the easiest type of offer to set up.
- Do not feel pressured into joining additional schemes on the website as they nearly all involve paying more commission or lowering your prices.
- Bear in mind the higher commission when setting nightly rates and any additional fees.
- If Booking.com handles your payments, ignore any invoices that arrive for commission, as this is already taken from your payout. You do have the option to take payment at the property and you would then need to pay commission separately.
- Booking.com offers insurance against third party lawsuits and liability claims but not general home insurance.
- Commission is typically around 15% for hosts, guests are not charged any booking fees.
- Check that nights are definitely available to book as sometimes you need to tick the box '1 unit available' in order to make it bookable. Do not put more than '1' room available on the mobile app when in calendar mode - it is misleading, but this is for hotel type businesses. You are providing '1' unit of accommodation per night - i.e. one home per night, not multiple homes.
- It is worth signing up to the 'business friendly' scheme to encourage people travelling for work to stay at your property. You may be asked to provide guests with an invoice.

- The 'Promotions' tab is a very useful way of setting tailored discounts and can help promote your listing in searches – it is a good way to try to fill last minute availability.
- Ensure you state the minimum number of days that must be booked in order for a promotion (discount) to be applicable and check that the dates are correct as the calendar sometimes jumps forward when setting promotions.
- If you plan to list your property on Google Maps do this before setting up a Booking.com listing as they will sometimes list it there themselves and link it to their own website.

Vrbo key points:

- Vrbo is another large international listing site, linked to Expedia. Currently expanding its marketing and profile.
- Host commission is a little lower than Booking.com, typically around 8%. Guests pay a fee as well.
- The site usually requires higher definition photos compared to other listing sites.
- You can set weekly and monthly discounts and restrict check-in and check-out dates.
- Vrbo offers liability insurance, but you will need your own home insurance in place before you can list with them.
- It is worth filling out the 'welcome guide' pages which guests have automatic access to a few days before arrival. I recommend that hosts still send an email with the access information as well in case guests miss this.

- You select how much a guest pays to book and when you want the balance paid.
- Guests can review hosts and vice versa although hosts can only fill out a basic point scoring system visible just to other hosts or potential hosts without the option to add any comments.

Trip Advisor key points:

- Trip Advisor links to Holidaylettings.co.uk and seems to be moving towards a referral type service, but guests can book directly through them as well.
- Low host commission of typically around 3%. Guests pay a fee.
- Guest searches will potentially show your property available to rent on several sites and will show the varying prices. I get very few bookings through Trip Advisor but still list on it as I think some guests find us here and book elsewhere.
- I do not use the calendar function very much and set my prices on the 'pricing' page instead.
- The reviews system is open to abuse by guests and hosts as they do not always appear to be verified or dependent on proof of having stayed at the holiday let. Hosts cannot publicly review guests although they can pass on comments.
- Trip Advisor does not offer any insurance for hosts.

Chapter Six
Selling direct – setting up your own website and calendar

I would always recommend that holiday homeowners have their own website. You may have a lot to deal with initially if you are renovating a house or flat and getting it ready for guests, along with maybe setting up an Airbnb account, so it might be something you look into once things are calmer and you have a clearer vision for your business. You should aim to steer as many potential guests or return guests towards booking directly with you as possible over time. I find that at least three-quarters of my guests now book directly with me.

Direct bookings are the best type of booking in my experience. You no longer have the threat of a bad review, you have no commission to pay, you communicate directly with your guests and set your own terms and conditions, along with having the option to take a damage deposit. Direct bookings and return guests should hopefully increase in number over time – partly by you becoming a trusted online business with a proven track record and partly due to guests who previously booked with other listing sites choosing to return and book directly with you next time, plus by word of mouth and recommendations between friends and families. Any additional marketing that you can do will also increase the number of direct bookings. I am always so happy when guests tell me that they will be recommending my holiday home to their friends and families. It is important to have high standards right from the start of your holiday let journey, as this will certainly encourage more direct and return bookers.

I do not take a damage deposit for smaller and cheaper lets, as I think it deters too many potential guests, but it is certainly worth considering for a larger property where there is more scope for problems and damage expense, chiefly via guests arranging parties or large gatherings, although judging by all the online horror stories this can happen with bookings made on listing sites as well from time to time. I have never personally experienced one of these awful guest party stays (touch wood!), but I have heard of it happening to other hosts via a cleaning company. The worst one I was told about was a booking made through a high-end holiday agency, so you cannot assume that taking bookings through agencies will protect you from this worst-case scenario. However, these occurrences are thankfully relatively rare. It is another reason to make sure you are properly insured though. I do not take a large damage deposit, it typically ranges from £100 to £200, as a lot of guests would be put off by a higher amount than this, but it encourages guests to respect the property and to abide by the house rules – something that can be harder to enforce with private bookings. Although you can set damage deposit limits on the listing sites, they do not usually take them as part of the prepayment, and it is usually stated as a potential after-payment if damage is caused during the guests' stay. I imagine it is difficult to enforce in any case. I think that sometimes guests have a greater sense of accountability when booking through a larger company, especially those which allow hosts to review guests, so a damage deposit for private bookings can help encourage better behaviour. You should also ensure that any serious damage or theft is covered by your insurance policy and not rely on a damage deposit covering all potential issues. Without additional guest fees or commission to pay for either party you can price your nights very competitively, so an additional £100 or so damage deposit generally will not bother most guests, as they are usually making excellent savings by booking direct in any case. With holiday let sites there is often an element of protection for guests and hosts and the reviews can be helpful in giving both parties confidence for bookings. However, with private bookings involving unknown guests, there can be more sense of risk for hosts and guests, and you will have to work harder to entice guests to book directly with you in the early days. It is very important to make sure your booking policy is robust and allows for as many eventualities as possible and that house rules are made very clear to guests at the time of booking, whilst remaining as friendly as possible in your communications. You also need to make your website and communications as professional as possible in order to garner confidence in your guests and to encourage bookings, especially if you only accept bank transfers by way of payment.

Setting up a website

A professional-looking website is very important in my experience of direct sales. It is probably worth the expense of having one created for you, especially if you want them to work equally well on PC screens as well as being mobile-friendly, which I strongly recommend. However, if your budget does not stretch to this there are plenty of free website creator programs out there – e.g. Wix, GoDaddy, Canva and Weebly, to name a few. If you or anyone you know has the skills to create a website then that makes things easier, but always offer to pay, even if it's a family member, as website hosting and edits do cost time and money. If you outsource the job to a professional company then ensure your website is as robust as possible in terms of not requiring frequent modification – i.e. avoid stating prices and minimum stays in any of your terms or descriptions, as these are the things that change most often and you do not want to be constantly paying and/or pestering for updates and changes to your website. Ensure you choose terms and conditions and a cancellation policy that you are happy with for the foreseeable future.

A professional company can discuss calendar and booking options with you and may advise using the i-Cal application which can link to some of the major listing sites' calendars. I would avoid a system that requires anyone updating your availability for you, as this needs to be done as soon as possible to avoid double bookings. I use professionally produced websites but ask that the calendar and booking system is one that I can control myself, separate from the website. There are various free online calendar applications that can be incorporated into websites – they will often take you away to a different site where you can edit your prices and availability at any time. My preferred one is freetobook.com. You can link it to your holiday let website via a 'booking' tab and generate invoices automatically, control reviews and create a large array of different pricing, types of discounts and offers (known as 'specials'). It is incredibly flexible. It can be fiddly to begin with learning the calendar system, but there are lots of tutorials to talk you through it. You can upgrade your account with them for a fee, but I just use the basic free model – an upgraded account allows you to link to other calendars on other listing sites and take card payments plus other special features. If you start to get a lot of direct bookings, then it is certainly worth considering. Guests are invited to review their stay with you, but you can choose to share their feedback publicly or not at all. Guests can book automatically and check pricing and availability and invoices are automatically generated, but I manage my own payments. You may decide that you want to offer over-the-phone or in-person card payments via a card reader, but again this will involve additional site and bank fees. I have only had an occasional guest object to pre-payment via bank transfer, but most people seem to have no problem with it in any case. The longer you are trading for, the more sites you are on and the more reviews you have, the more confidence people will have in booking direct and paying by bank transfer. I always include my own home address and contact details, including a landline phone number, on invoices and this also helps build trust in guests. International and UK guests often like using the big listing sites due to payment protection or the ability to pay by credit card, but competitive pricing can usually override this in terms of giving direct booking the edge. I now use Wise.com to take payments from overseas guests as there are no additional fees for them to pay this way and very minimal fees for me as well, and it is an internationally recognised company, although there are others to choose from also offering this service. International bank transfers and Paypal payments can be very costly for hosts and guests. If you use a different non i-Cal calendar application for your website calendar then you must remember to update any other listing calendars manually as well every time you receive a direct booking and vice versa.

It is worth setting up a specific business email for your let, preferably one that sounds professional and incorporates your holiday let name and links to your website – i.e. 'info@buttercupcottage.com' if your website is www.buttercupcottage.com. A more original property name will be less likely to exist already or require a large payment to buy the domain name if it is already held by someone else. Make sure that your holiday let has a 'name', not just an address, as this will also make your let more memorable and easier to find. Always try to use .com instead of .co.uk, as it gives your website more reach and strength. Alternatively, Gmail or similar are very easy to set up and are very convenient, although may deter some guests in the early days as they are more generic and less typically used for professional businesses. Make sure all business emails are automatically forwarded to your personal email as you are less likely to miss any inquiries or bookings this way.

If you really do not want an interactive calendar on your website, then you can simply give an indication of typical prices for high and low seasons, or even a list of prices, week by week and ask guests to email you regarding availability and final cost – quite a few small businesses do this. This will deter some guests who like to book instantly, and you will have a lot more admin to deal with, but it might be a solution for the short term if you do not initially have a very complex website.

I advise that you have professional photography taken for your website photos. If this is not possible, then a good camera should suffice if you want to take your own or even use a mobile phone if it has a good quality camera built in – make sure you set your camera for large, high-resolution photos as many listing sites will not accept small images and they will not look great on your website either. On the homepage I have a gallery of photos which can be browsed through which showcase all the bedrooms and main living spaces, along with any bathrooms, the kitchen and any outdoor spaces. It is worth taking photos on the brightest, sunniest days, and rooms usually look best with lamps switched on – avoid switching on ceiling lights unless it is necessary as this type of lighting can be very unflattering. Summer photos of outdoor spaces are preferential, although you can include photos of the outdoors in other seasons too but have them lower down the list. I usually edit my own photos on my laptop – a lot of photography editing programs will have auto settings to improve lighting and colour or you can usually change these individually, along with increasing the intensity of colour and contrast as well. Most PCs come with free photo editing software, but there are lots of different free photo editing programs that can be downloaded. You will usually want to do some straightening and cropping of your own photos too. Professional photographers will usually edit and enhance their photos before giving you the files. Some room-set photos can work well – dining tables laid for dinner, lit candles (if you allow them), trays with afternoon tea laid out in the living room or on top of a garden table, lit fires or wood burners and a throw draped across a sofa, vases of flowers and so on. These items certainly make your property look very appealing, although you should be careful not to set false expectations in terms of what sundries are included in guests' stays. The most important thing is to take as good a photo as possible of each main room and showcase its best features. Take several external photos of your property too, it is always good to give guests a true sense of the home they will be renting. I always add some photos of local interest and scenery too at the end of the photograph reel – it can be the surrounding area that appeals most to your potential guests, so make sure you show it off sufficiently.

It is worth having a brief, concise summary of what your property offers on the home page – i.e. how many people the let sleeps, how many bedrooms and bed sizes, whether you're pet friendly, how close you are to any famous landmarks, towns, cities, rural or coastal areas, and so on. Specify any parking provided and whether it is free, whether you provide WIFI, a hot tub, barbecue, and specify what type of property it is. It is also incredibly useful to have a small location map on the home page pinpointing your property's exact location, along with contact information which includes an email and phone number. I also include a large booking button to take guests to an external calendar with prices, availability and the option to reserve dates. Along the top of the page, I have tabs for; property details (provide more detailed and appealing descriptions here including facilities and appliances and any interesting information/unique aspects of your property), prices and booking (takes you to an external booking site and calendar in my case), local information/places of interest and terms and conditions.

Setting up terms and conditions

Make sure you have a clear Terms and Conditions section on your website. If you are using an extension calendar website such as Freetobook for your calendar management on your website, then you must ensure that the booking terms on this match your official website terms and conditions. You can find various templates and suggestions for terms and conditions online, but I often find that I end up adding my own extra ones, usually through experience, once the let is up and running. Make it clear that guests are agreeing to your terms and conditions when they proceed to book. I also add a note on invoices stating that guests are agreeing to my terms and conditions on the website when they proceed to book. It is worth including a hard copy of your terms inside the manual at the holiday let as well. I also save them as a PDF file so that they can easily be emailed and uploaded on other sites or via email. Here are a list of terms and conditions that I find useful. For some I have simply given examples to help with wording, but obviously you will edit these depending on what kind of let you have and your specific house rules.

Sample terms and conditions:

- Mention some of the most important house rules; state any guest age restrictions – i.e. no under 21s, no pets, no smoking, no parties/large gatherings, no stag or hen parties etc. It is worth specifying the minimum age of the 'chief booker' if you want to allow children and teenagers of families to stay as well. It is good to state that if there is evidence of pets or smoking in the house (if you do not allow either) that guests will be billed for any necessary additional cleaning costs.
- 'The period of let shall be from 3pm on the day of arrival to 10am on the day of departure. Late departures will incur a fee.' (You would be surprised at how many guests routinely ignore check-out times by an hour or two.)
- Information on booking and payment terms – i.e. how much guests pay at the time of booking (deposit), when a balance payment will be due, plus any other additional fees, including a damage deposit. Let guests know how soon they will receive a refund of their damage deposit subject to conditions having been met. Give a timescale for payments – eg. payments should be made within 48 hours of booking (also state this clearly on your guest invoice as chasing up payments is time consuming). State what type of payments you accept – bank transfer, Paypal, card payments over the phone etc., plus any excluded card types. Include payment information for overseas guests. I use Wise.com for payments in foreign currencies, as it is free to set up and there are minimal conversion and transfer fees to pay for the host and none for the guest.

- Any key Health and Safety requirements – i.e. If you have a pond, a hot tub, a barbecue, an accessible fire escape, a trampoline, climbing frame or any open boundaries or unstable structures in the grounds that should not be climbed upon (particularly dry-stone walls), then you should note them here and specify that guests are responsible for supervising children accordingly and state that guests use equipment at their own risk.
- 'The hirer must personally stay at the accommodation throughout the holiday and is solely responsible for the whole party. Sub-tenants are prohibited. No more than the stated number may stay at the property'. Clearly state how many people your let sleeps – this discourages people subletting or inviting additional guests.
- 'The hirer undertakes to take all reasonable care in the use of the property and its contents, including the security of the property. The hirer will report any damages, losses or breakages as soon as they occur. We understand that breakages and accidents happen from time to time, but reserve the right to charge for repairs, losses or replacements if they are deemed to be more severe than everyday wear and tear.''
- 'Guests should conduct themselves in such a way as to cause no undue noise, annoyance or disturbance to neighbouring properties. We reserve the right to evict any guests who are disruptive, abusive, or cause disturbance and damage to the house.'
- You can include your cancellation policy here or have it stated on your booking page or calendar extension and tell guests that they agree to any cancellation policy terms when they proceed to

book. I usually add that I strongly recommend guests take out holiday insurance in case of illness or in case they are unable to travel to the property for any reason.

- 'The hirer undertakes to leave the accommodation tidy and return furniture and items to their original places before departure. We reserve the right to make a charge for extra cleaning if the property is not left in a satisfactory condition.' You would be surprised at how many guests like to rearrange all the furniture and furnishings and leave them in their new (and usually strange) positions. State any tasks that should be carried out before departure here.
- 'The description of the property is as accurate as possible. However, we reserve the right to alter or remove any of the furnishings without notice. We cannot be held responsible for the breakdown of any appliance or service at the property. We will do our best to arrange for any repairs or replacements as soon as possible but cannot guarantee that this will be completed during your stay.' This is an important clause as it will deter guests from demanding compensation if an appliance breaks or if there is something missing at the property.
- 'As far as the law allows, we take no responsibility for loss, damage or injury to the hirer or any of the party. The hirer will indemnify us against loss, damage or injury sustained to the property or guests.' Full holiday let insurance should cover you for most instances of damage or injury for you, your property, or guests, but it is still worth including this in your terms as well.

- 'The owner reserves the right to enter the property at any reasonable time.'
- 'Every effort has been made to ensure an enjoyable and comfortable stay. If there is any cause for complaint, we ask that guests contact us so that any problems can be quickly resolved. We ask that guests inform us of any broken or missing items as soon as possible so that they can be fixed or replaced for current and subsequent guests.'
- Guests often let you know about a broken appliance or fitting on the day of departure, which is not always sufficient time to fix it, especially on a same-day changeover.
- 'We offer free WIFI to guests. WIFI is provided on the understanding that the loading of illegal or copyrighted material is strictly prohibited. Guests must have their own virus protection and children must be supervised at all times when using the WIFI.'
- Mention any parking requirements or restrictions, especially if access and parking for neighbours could be impacted by inconsiderate parking by guests. State how many vehicles can be accommodated or if there are any size restrictions – I have had a car towing a caravan try to squeeze into a single parking space before now.
- Consider including a minimum charge for the cost of posting back forgotten items to guests. One of my biggest annoyances is guests expecting me to wrap and post items back to them - it is time-consuming, and the costs add up if you do not bill guests for it. I find that stating a minimum charge of £20 or so ensures that guests are a little more careful to pack up everything on departure day or that they do not

expect me to return a small, relatively low-value item to them. I have returned items without charge in the past, and guests have not even acknowledged it, let alone thank me. I no longer do this.

Website cancellation policy

Have your cancellation policy clearly stated on your website's terms and conditions and on any calendar booking software you might be using, such as Freetobook, and make sure they are the same on all sources. Also print out a copy and leave it at the property in your information file. You may want to make your policy similar to those that you are using on the listing sites or be more flexible in order to encourage guests to book directly. Some hosts add a small administration fee for early cancellation to dissuade window shopper guests from booking then cancelling soon afterwards – bookings can be quite time consuming, admin-wise, as you will be raising invoices and taking payments unlike on listing sites where they do this for you. It is worth adding; 'we strongly recommend that guests take out holiday insurance in case of illness or travel difficulties. We offer no compensation or flexibility to the cancellation terms if you are unable to travel to the property for any reason, including poor weather.' If there was a terrible storm or extreme weather event I would most likely refund guests in any case, but this discourages guests from expecting last minute refunds for real or fictional problems including illness or travel difficulties that they could potentially have insured themselves against. Even if you have a very clear-cut cancellation policy, people will still invariably ask if you can make exceptions for them if they decide they need to cancel at the last minute. That is why I always recommend guests take out holiday insurance – if they do not do this, that is their mistake, and it is not for you to take the financial hit for them. If guests are polite and seem genuine then I will sometimes offer to try to re-book the dates and refund them for any re-filled dates, although this is still likely to be for less than they paid and/or for a shorter stay, as last-minute availability usually needs to be priced down or occupancy requirements reduced to sell dates quickly. I have worked hard to compensate guests in this way in the past, and for little thanks, so generally I am a lot more inflexible with my cancellation terms these days. If you have charged a cleaning and linen fee you may want to offer to refund this, even if the guests are not entitled to a refund, although theoretically you should probably offer it to your cleaner if it is a last-minute cancellation as they will end up out of pocket and will lose out on business as well. Typically, I ask for the balance to be paid 31 days before arrival and will give full refunds if stays are cancelled 31 or more days in advance of arrival, sometimes minus a reasonable and modest administration charge to deter window shoppers. I will refund half of the paid balance between 15 and 30 days before arrival if guests cancel then and if they cancel within 14 days of the holiday starting, they receive no refund. It really is up to you what you choose to do and is often a case of trial and error in terms of how many cancellations you receive and how much of your time it wastes. You will get more bookers with a flexible policy, but more cancellations as well.

Additional marketing tips

It is a very good idea to have your business listed on Google Maps as this will also link to your website and contact details. Guests can also leave reviews and potential bookers can see how long you have had a presence on the site - an official listing on Google Maps also encourages guests to book directly with you as it shows your business to be real and legitimate. I really recommend adding your business to Google Maps in general – guests will find you when searching visitor attractions and other landmarks nearby, and it is free advertising. If you plan to list with Booking.com, secure your Google Map listing as soon as possible as sometimes Booking.com will list your business for you on there and route potential guests to their website – it is very annoying, and you cannot do anything about it if you agreed to their terms when you signed up to their site. The only downside to Google Maps is that anyone can leave a review, however spurious, and I have never known Google to agree to removing one even when there is proof that it was written by someone who has never stayed at the holiday property. If you receive an absolute stinker of a review early on it would probably be worth removing the listing and then re-adding it. I have a surprisingly large volume of website visits via Google Maps and their analytics are very useful as you can see how many people viewed your listing each month and how many views led to website visits, calls or a request for directions. You can increase your visibility on Google by signing up to their 'advertising' scheme for an additional fee, although due to the high costs I have not ever done so. I still receive a surprisingly high number of views and website clicks from Google Maps though. It is worth uploading photos and information to the listing. Google Maps will compare your data, via a graph, to your local competitors' performance as well.

    I strongly advise having business cards printed to leave at your holiday let. These are very popular with guests, and it always surprises me how quickly they disappear. It encourages those who booked with one of the larger listing sites to book privately next time. Have your business name, one good photo, along with contact details and the phrase 'book direct for best prices' or similar included on the card. I find Vistaprint very user-friendly and reasonable for this. It can be useful to leave cards in businesses in your local area (if they allow them), and in the holiday let area if you do not live there.

Look into further advertising, especially via magazines and local newsletters. Some tourist information centres will also list your property online for a fee. This can get very expensive, so I would advise that you avoid trying some of these suggestions unless you have a large marketing budget or offer a very high-end, luxurious type of holiday let and want to maximise your exposure to get the ball rolling in the early days.

If your home is particularly interesting, unique or historic, then it is definitely worth trying to get a feature spread in one of the homes and interiors type magazines. You can often add rental details at the end of the article. Having worked for a magazine in the past, it is best to email the editor and sub editor with some good photos and interesting facts about your property – the clearer and simpler the better.

Instagram and Facebook are useful tools for marketing via social media as well. It is worth setting up accounts on both with your property's name and contact details. By adding hashtags, you help other people to stumble upon your posts, including those who might be interested in things that your property or area offers. I often tag local activities, famous local beauty spots and places of interest, including place names under my social media photos along with holiday let specific tags. People love interior photos and décor so include lots of these, along with beautiful and dynamic shots of your local surroundings. House renovations are incredibly popular on Instagram – some of these accounts have huge followings. If you renovate your let as part of the journey, then try to photograph every stage as people love a 'before and after'.

You can pay extra to elevate your account and widen its reach or to promote individual posts. I have experimented with this over the years but have not had much noticeable success with it. People like to connect with real people on Instagram so if you are prepared to open up about yourself and your journey with the holiday let, including photos and videos of yourself, you will find that you get a better and bigger response from your target audience than from a more detached, anonymous account, although you may also attract some negativity and may need to limit interactions on your posts – holiday let owners are not universally popular in the current climate. I notice that some holiday homeowners manage to increase positivity through sharing and promoting other local businesses and by highlighting ways in which they support the local community and by trying to be as sustainable and inclusive as possible. Buying sundries such as tea, coffee, biscuits, soap and so on from local businesses is another way to do this, although it generally works out more expensive than buying in bulk from larger national online companies.

Instagram actively promotes videos above photos these days, so you might want to consider short videos to raise your profile – just a few seconds of a room with a lit fireplace or a tour of a few rooms can suffice. Reviews can be left for your business on Facebook, but they are often anonymous, and this allows for an abuse of the system. You can choose to turn off reviews and commenting if you wish. I find that the highest number of followers on my Instagram account are other holiday let owners and I have subsequently noticed that some of my furnishing ideas and approaches have been replicated by some of them, so be wary of sharing too many of your trade secrets in this case if it is a competitive market in your area. It can be inspiring and instructional to see how a similar local business operates and encourages you to keep on your toes in terms of standards and services. Following similar businesses has helped me at times and I even found a cleaning company through another account's shout-out recommendation when I was really struggling to find one.

Some holiday let owners create competitions where a hamper or short stay can be won by followers sharing your post and tagging friends. Again, I'm not sure how successful these types of schemes are, but it could be worth a try. A smart or stylish business logo can also be very helpful and can be used on your website, stationery, emails and on sundries at the let. It gives your business a polished professional-looking edge. You could design this yourself or create a 'drawn' impression of your property using photograph editing software which can convert photos into many different types of images, including ones that look like a pen drawing. Alternatively have one designed by a graphic designer – there are plenty to be found online. 'Fiverr' website is a great resource as you can find designers here who will create various projects for you at a very reasonable cost – they also offer website design.

Some holiday homeowners gift free stays to well-known influencers, friends or acquaintances with a degree of fame or public visibility in return for a feature on their social media accounts or blog. Be very wary though, as some influencers may not treat your property with respect - some can be very entitled in their attitudes, looking at some of the horror stories online. Just because something is free, does not mean that it will be treated respectfully or with gratitude. It must be someone trustworthy or a friend who is comfortable with a transactional type of favour. Not everyone will be open to the idea. However, if you are lucky to know someone with a degree of fame who is keen to visit your let and enjoy a free holiday in return for sharing details about their visit online, you could find yourself inundated with new bookings shortly afterwards.

Repeat bookers are the best type of guest of all – they have chosen to re-visit you due to a previously good holiday at your let and will be confident in booking privately and will be glad of the savings made by booking privately. Depending on your budget there are lots of little ways to market your home to guests whilst they are staying there – i.e. postcards or bookmarks featuring your property or any kind of personalised stationery, sundries or extras. Some hosts send Christmas card emails to previous guests to jolt their memories. It is worth keeping a database or email list of direct bookers and you can send out group emails regarding last-minute availability or special offers as well, preferably using an email marketing platform such as Mailchimp or similar. These types of communications are very effective at generating extra interest and bookings. Always ensure any marketing communications are GDPR compliant – you can find more information online for these guidelines.

Useful administration practices and tips

I find it very helpful to keep a binder file with an A4 month-by-month calendar print-out inside. I set up a table in a Word document with at least 31 numbered boxes on it (usually 5 rows with 7 columns, so there will be spare boxes for some months) and write the month as a header and the days along the top. It is much more convenient to have one generic template which can be adapted for each month and printed out in bulk than twelve different files. I also make a note of the year and property on each calendar page (if you have more than one), as I keep all my paper calendars filed so that I have an easy-to-use record of my number of stays and booked dates which is important due to legal occupancy requirements (more in chapter seven). I tend to fill these out up to a year in advance. I find it helpful to mark school and public holidays on the calendars as well, so I do not forget to update my calendars online. I mark each booking and its duration on the sheet with a note of the site it was booked through, guest name, and price.

I also keep a cleaning spreadsheet which I email to my cleaning company to notify them of new cleans. I mark existing cleans by filling the date box in yellow, and new cleans are marked out in red. I also have a column in which to note anything else they need to know – i.e. early or late check-in or check-out, same-day changeovers and whether fresh milk is required (only applicable for guests arriving within the next few days). I update my cleaning spreadsheet as soon as I get a new booking and double check that all cleans are booked in at the start of each new week. Once I've emailed the latest updated spreadsheet to the cleaners, I change any new red cleans to yellow on the spreadsheet ready for the next update. You can simply email or message your cleaners with each new booking, but this system seems to work best in terms of any miscommunications and avoiding missed updates. I find that individual cleaners are a lot more likely to forget cleans or keep checking with me if I don't provide a full monthly spreadsheet. Even if you do not share the spreadsheet with your cleaner, it is still useful to keep your own record and check that your cleaners are up to date at the start of each week. I also mark dates for cleans on my main booking paper calendar, as they will not always necessarily happen on the date of a guest's check-out, and it further reduces the chance of forgetting about it. Always notify your cleaners of any cancellations straight away and make a note of this on the spreadsheet, in another colour.

It is useful to set up an invoice template for your business for invoicing direct bookings. You can find templates for free online or simply create your own. Always export any Word documents as PDFs before sending them to guests as other file types might not be readable to them. I put the date, holiday let address, my home address and contact information at the top. I have a table in the centre which specifies the dates of the stay, including year, on the left-hand side. The given dates are always arrival and departure dates. I always specify the number of nights being booked, just to be absolutely clear, as guests can be confused whether an end date refers to a final night's stay or a departure date. I include the total price, specifying any additional cleaning or damage deposit fees and then put the 'due' amount on the right-hand side. If the invoice is for a deposit payment, then specify this, and likewise do the same if it's a balance payment. For deposit payments note that you will contact the guest X number of weeks before arrival for the balance and how much this will be. For balance invoices note that X deposit has already been received, with thanks. Do not allow for any confusion. You can also add or note VAT if you charge it in this box (more on VAT in chapter seven). Even if you do not charge VAT it is worth stating this – just list VAT and show it as £0.00. Guests sometimes insist on having your VAT details if they are using the let for business reasons. Always let guests know that you have received their payments – it helps you keep track as well, as you can refer to emails if you need to check, rather than scouring through your bank account later on. Generally, I do not bother with receipts anymore, as it is extra admin, but you can if you wish, or if your guest insists upon it. I always make a note on my paper calendar of due dates for balance payments as it is easy to forget otherwise. Alternatively, keep an electronic calendar for all of the above with alerts set for payment reminders and guests' arrivals and departures.

I use message templates to save time. I have these for booking confirmation emails, welcome emails with access instructions sent a couple of days before guests' arrival and one that I send the day before departure. I have PDF files for directions and local information which I attach to the welcome email. The local information file includes tourist attractions and activities nearby, with approximate distances and/or travelling times, the nearest shops and supermarkets, restaurants, pubs, garage, cashpoint, doctors, hospital and dentist. I also send the local information PDF with the initial booking confirmation to give guests the opportunity to book meals and activities in advance – I also recommend that they do this, as guests can be very put-out if all the local restaurants and activities are booked up. It saves a lot of time answering queries as well. The most commonly asked question is 'do you have a local pub or restaurant you recommend for dinner?', followed by 'where is the nearest supermarket or food shop?' It is worth specifying what kind of restaurant or pub each one is on your list, and to give an indication of cost or if a place is particularly pricey, to avoid your guest getting a nasty shock if they book without checking it out first. The more information you provide, the happier your guests will be and the fewer emails you will receive.

It is usually worth emailing guests the night before departure (especially if it has been a longer stay) to ask if everything has been okay for them at the let and to remind them of any pre-departure requests such as putting out the rubbish and washing up etc. I wish them a safe onward journey for the following day and tell them to contact me if they have any feedback or concerns. This encourages guests to let you know about any problems or shortage of supplies which you can hopefully remedy in time for the next guests.

With all messaging, I always recommend being as friendly and positive as possible. Always address guests with 'Dear' and use their first name. I like to sign off with 'best wishes' or similar. 'Kind regards' is fine, but sometimes sounds a little formal. Do not ever address guests by their first names, with no salutation, and do not sign off with any kind of abbreviation such as 'best' or similar – it is more typical with guests from the US, but it does not go down well with most British and European guests. It can feel repetitive, but it is usually worth reiterating that you hope your guests have a 'wonderful holiday' and to 'not hesitate to contact me if you have any questions' in your confirmation and pre-arrival messages. Even if your guest is rather cool or off-hand in their communications with you, do not let it alter your friendly, positive tone. 'Kill with kindness' is my mantra for all my dealings and communications with guests – it will protect your business from poor reviews or negative feedback more than anything else.

Key points

- Direct bookings are always preferable due to lack of commission and lower risk of bad reviews.
- Taking a damage deposit is advisable, especially for larger properties – no more than £100 to £200, as guests will be put off booking otherwise. You will still need home insurance.
- A professional looking website will greatly increase direct bookings and confidence in your business.
- Consider having a booking page or calendar which you can control on your website. Freetobook is very easy to use and can also manage payments, including card payments, for you for an additional fee.

- Some guests are wary of bank transfer payments, but it is the most cost-effective way to take payment. A good online presence and a professional website will engender confidence in your potential guests.
- Consider a payment system for overseas guests, such as Wise.com, as international bank transfers and Paypal payments will incur higher fees.
- Consider professional photography for your website or using a good camera. Include photographs of well-lit rooms and outdoor spaces along with photographs or any local scenery or attractions of note.
- It is a very good idea to list your business on Google Maps. It is free to do, and you can include your website and contact details. If you plan to list on Booking.com then do this straight away as sometimes they list your property for you on Google and it will then only link to their website.
- Have a memorable property name and incorporate it into your email address – always use a professional website-linked email address if possible.
- Get business cards printed and leave at the property and at any other local businesses that allow them.
- Have thorough and clear terms and conditions on your website. Ensure your cancellation policy is replicated exactly on any external booking websites. Include a hard copy of your terms and conditions in the house manual at the property. Make it clear that guests agree to your terms and conditions when they proceed to book your property.

- Consider having social media accounts – Instagram and Facebook are easy to use. Renovation stories and photos are very popular.
- Keep a paper calendar file and a cleaning spreadsheet.
- Create an invoice template and messaging templates to save time.
- Use as friendly and positive a tone as possible in your communications. Always check if everything was okay for guests the day before departure as it will flag up any issues that need to be fixed before the next guests arrive.
- Create a local information PDF file and email it to guests at the time of booking and just before they arrive – it will save you a lot of time answering queries.

Chapter Seven
Legals and finance

UK legal holiday let requirements and legislation (incorporating health and safety)

Always check current local council and government legislation before proceeding with a holiday let or the renovation/conversion of a residential home or private room into a holiday let. Central and local governments are increasingly adding new legislation and changing rules on holiday and short-term lets. I would advise you to tread very carefully if you are considering a property in Scotland or Wales as recent changes to legislation here suggest that it is going to become increasingly difficult to qualify as a holiday let in these countries and that there will be greater costs to pay and more criteria to fulfil. You need to be prepared to potentially pay tax as a second homeowner, if certain occupancy thresholds are not met, so always check what these rates are likely to be. In Wales the local government has significantly increased the required period of time that a property has to be available to rent and actually rented out. Scotland has introduced mandatory holiday let licences for all owners of Scottish lets and as well as controlled zones where planning permission must be sought to open a holiday let. Proceed with caution. Wales has also given powers to local authorities to greatly increase tax on second homes. The information provided below is true as of June 2023, shortly after a lot of the new legislation for holiday lets was announced, particularly for Scotland and Wales, but I would always recommend that you carefully research the current rules in your part of the country before proceeding and allow for the fact that occupancy rates and tax rules can change at any time. There is currently talk of introducing licences and greater controls in England as well. Holiday let owners are likely to feel the squeeze from further regulations in the coming years, but with increasing taxes on second homes and more legislation for buy-to-lets, holiday lets will still be preferable, from an economic view, for many second homeowners.

Health and safety legal requirements for UK holiday lets:

- Furniture and furnishings should comply with the Fire Safety Regulations from 1988 (amended in 1989, 1993 and 2010) and applies to all upholstered furniture, beds, headboards, mattresses, sofa beds, cushions and pillows. It is not applicable to antique furniture or furniture made before 1950. Most modern soft furnishings and fabrics will be fire retardant in some way, but if they are not you will need to change them or have furniture reupholstered in a suitable fabric (assuming the furniture is not antique). Be wary of vintage soft furnishings and furniture in particular due to this law. You should look to buy new mattresses, pillows and cushion pads for your holiday let in any case.
- Holiday lets must comply with the Regulatory Reform (Fire Safety) Order 2005 (England & Wales) and under part 3 of the Fire (Scotland) Act, supported by the Fire Safety (Scotland) Regulations 2006 that came into effect in October 2007. You should carry out a fire risk assessment either using a professional body or by yourself, by referring to the guidelines. Ultimately,

ensure that you have adequate measures in place in case of fire, preferably with a fire blanket and a fire extinguisher provided and clearly marked. Have accessible fire escapes. Clear fire safety instructions and a well-marked fire escape should be provided for guests. Smoke and carbon monoxide alarms are mandatory and should be regularly tested. Smoke detectors should have an interlinked automatic detection and fire warning system and must be loud enough to wake anyone sleeping.

- Ensure all gas appliances are safe and conform to the current safety standards. The Gas Safety Regulations of 1998 require annual testing of gas appliances (including gas and LPG boilers) by a Gas Safe registered installer. Records should be kept for two years. A valid certificate should be displayed in the holiday accommodation.
- As of 1st October 2015, it is law for private residential landlords to have carbon monoxide alarms installed in all rooms containing a solid fuel burning appliance – i.e. an open fire, gas fire, wood burner etc. Appliances should be tested annually by a Gas Safe registered engineer. Any working chimneys should be swept annually as well – this is often a condition of your holiday let house insurance. Carbon monoxide poisoning can be fatal so you should regularly test alarms. I would recommend that you also place a carbon monoxide alarm in the same room as your boiler.
- Although not enforced by many listing sites, the Disability Discrimination Act 2005 requires your property to have a written Accessibility Statement which provides detailed, accurate information on the facilities and services at your property. Most listing

sites will have a section dedicated to guests with disabilities and will ask you a number of questions in order to ascertain if your home is suitable for those with disabilities. Many older and listed homes have quirks which make them difficult to adapt for those with mobility issues, so if applicable you should make it clear in your listing or on your website that your property is not suitable for those with certain disabilities and explain why. If you are looking to create a holiday home specifically tailored to those with mobility restrictions and disabilities, then you will want to research this further and ensure that you fulfil as many criteria as possible. I would recommend making your home as accessible as possible if it is a single storey home as an ageing population and guests with mobility restrictions will specifically be looking for this kind of accommodation. Ramps, wider doorways, accessible bathrooms with raised toilets, walk in showers and support rails, accessible light switches and sockets will all help to make your home as user-friendly as possible for everyone.

- There are no specific regulations relating to swimming pools and gym safety, but you do need to comply with general health and safety legislation as laid out in the Health and Safety at Work Act of 1974 and the Management of Health and Safety at Work Regulations of 1999. A thorough risk assessment should be carried out.
- If your property has a private water supply then you have a duty in law to ensure that the water, along with the filter system, is safe and tested in accordance with regulations. Your local council will be able to advise you on these requirements.

- If you plan to build, extend, renovate, or change a regular residential property into a holiday let then it is best to contact your local planning department in the first instance for guidance. This is particularly pertinent for Scotland now that licences must be applied for to trade as a let, and due to the fact that controlled zones in Scotland now require a change of use planning agreement if the property is currently a residential home.

UK Holiday let legislation

To qualify as a furnished holiday let **(FHL)** in the UK, the government stipulates that the property needs to be:

- In the UK or in the European Economic Area **(EEA)** which includes Iceland, Liechtenstein and Norway.
- Furnished with sufficient furniture provided and available for use for normal occupation.
- Commercially let with the intention of making a profit. If you let the property out of season to cover costs but didn't make a profit, then your let will still be treated as a commercial let.
- Available to rent for 210 days a year. If your property is in Wales, it will need to be available for at least 252 days.
- Let for at least 105 days a year (you cannot count any days when you let the property to friends or relatives at reduced rates). In Wales it will need to be let for at least 182 days per year. If the availability and stay thresholds listed above are not met, then the property will potentially be classed as a second home and taxed as such. In Wales local authorities can increase council tax

premiums on second homes and long-term empty properties by up to 300%.

If you own more than one furnished holiday let in the UK, they are taxed as a single UK furnished holiday let business and all furnished holiday lets in other EEA states are taxed as a single EEA furnished holiday let business.

Applying and meeting occupancy conditions:

For a continuing let, apply the tests to the tax year – e.g. from 6th April one year, to 5th April the next year. For a new let, apply the tests to the first 12 months from when the letting began. When your letting stops, apply the tests to the 12 months up to when the letting finished.

If the total of all lettings that exceed 31 continuous days is more than 155 days during the year, then your property will not be classed as a furnished holiday let that year. Do not count any days when you, family or friends are staying in the property, towards your annual occupancy, even if it is at reduced rates. HMRC does not consider the property to be available for letting while you're staying there. Do not count longer-term lets of more than 31 days towards your occupancy threshold, unless the 31 days is exceeded because something unforeseen happens, such as a guest being delayed due to illness or a delayed flight etc.

If you do not let your property for the required occupancy over the course of the year, you have two options (known as elections) that can help you reach the occupancy threshold. These are the averaging election (applicable if you own more than one holiday let), and a period of grace election – if your property reaches the occupancy threshold in some years but not in others. These are outlined below;

Averaging election:

If you let more than one holiday let and one or more of these properties does not meet the occupancy requirements, you can average the total number of stays between your properties. An averaging election divides the total number of occupied days between the number of holiday let properties to ensure that they all qualify if one or more has underperformed. You can only average across properties in a single furnished holiday let business and you cannot combine UK and EEA properties together. You make an averaging election up to one year after 31 January following the end of the tax year.

Period of grace election:

You may genuinely intend to meet the letting condition but were unable to. If this happens, you may be able to make a period of grace election that allows the property to qualify as a furnished holiday let as long as the pattern of occupation and availability conditions were met. To make an election, you must be able to show that you had a genuine intention to let the property in the year. For example, where you have marketed a property to the same or a greater level than in successful years, or where the lettings are cancelled due to unforeseen circumstances, including extreme weather. You can make an election where the property met the letting condition in the year before the first year you wish to make a period of grace election (either on its own or because of an averaging election). If your property again does not meet the letting condition in the following year, you can make a second period of grace election (as long as you made an election in the previous year). If your property does not reach the threshold by the fourth year, after two consecutive periods of grace elections, it will no longer qualify as a furnished holiday letting.

Other rules:

- If your property is only used as a furnished holiday let and is closed for part of the year due to a lack of customers and bookings, you can deduct all the expenses, such as insurance and loan interest, for the whole year, provided you do not live in the property.
- If you let part of the property as a furnished holiday letting, or where you use the property privately for part of the year, you need to apportion your receipts and expenses on a reasonable basis.
- Your property will no longer be a furnished holiday let if the property is sold or used for private occupation or if occupancy requirements are not met, even with the averaging and period of grace elections.
- If your property does not qualify as a furnished holiday let, the special tax treatment will no longer apply. You'll need to work out any balancing allowance or balancing charge for capital allowances.
- If your UK furnished holiday let business makes a loss, you can set the loss against your UK furnished holiday let profits of later years. Similarly, if your EEA furnished holiday let business makes a loss, you can set the loss against your EEA furnished holiday let profits of later years. You cannot set the losses of one furnished holiday let business against the profits of the other if you have a UK and an EEA business.

There are special tax rules for rental income from properties that qualify as furnished holiday lettings:

- You can claim Capital Gains Tax reliefs for traders (Business Asset Rollover Relief, relief for gifts of business assets and relief for loans to traders).

- You are entitled to plant and machinery capital allowances for items such as furniture, equipment and fixtures.
- The profits count as earnings for pension purposes.

To benefit from these rules, you need to work out the profit or loss from your furnished holiday lets separately from any other rental business.

Scotland

If you are looking at setting up a holiday let in Scotland, always check the government and local councils' latest rules as legislation has recently been changed and made stricter and is likely to be subject to further changes and rules over the coming months and years. Edinburgh is currently looking like a problematic area to set up a let, now being in a 'control zone'. Currently if your property is available to let for 140 days or more a year contact your local assessor - this is because your property, or part of it, might be liable for business rates. The assessor will apply a price per bed space on each property, based on its type, size and location, to produce its rateable value. Single bed space is the term used to describe how many people can sleep in the property. Renting out part or all of your home to private tenants is not normally considered business use.

Scotland has also recently stepped up its legal requirements for holiday lets, and electrical safety certificates are now required. New hosts are required to apply for a short-term let licence before accepting bookings or receiving guests. The short-term lets licensing scheme is mandatory for all short-term let accommodation across Scotland. Applications for a short-term let licence are made to the local authority. Further information on the types of licence, exclusions and how to apply can be found on the Scottish government website.

Local authorities have been given powers to designate control areas, in order to deal with areas affected by high levels of short-term lets, especially where there is a shortage of housing or long-term rental homes. Within a control area, the change of use of a property which is not a host's only or main home, to one providing short-term lets will always require planning permission and a licence can't be obtained without it. Each planning application will be determined on its individual merits. On 5th September 2022 Edinburgh became Scotland's first designated short-term let control area.

Holiday let insurance

Holiday let insurance is a specialist form of cover that is required for holiday let properties. It is often a requirement of mortgage lenders that you have specific cover in place. It is recommended that you take out a policy that is designed specifically for your property. Holiday let insurance covers you for many things that regular home insurance would not protect you against.

Holiday let building and contents cover:

Having insurance is meant to protect you and your holiday let, so it is important to know what it should cover and that you have the right policy in place. Your holiday property must have adequate building and contents insurance. This is to cover against accidents, damage and loss of earnings.

Public liability insurance for holiday lets:

Public liability insurance for a holiday let host is essential. Having public liability cover for £2 million is essential. It protects you from compensation claims in the event of someone being injured or having an accident at your property.

Employers' liability insurance:

If you employ any individual in your holiday home, it is a legal requirement to have employers' liability insurance. It covers you if an employee has an accident and claims for injuries. The minimum legal requirement for employers' liability insurance is £5 million, but a lot of insurers provide cover of £10 million as standard.

Holiday let mortgages, renting out your own home or part of your home plus change of use and planning permission

Any property being used purely as a holiday let will require a specialist holiday let mortgage, assuming you require one to finance the let. Holiday let mortgages can be harder to find and tend to have higher rates of interest. Whether you are letting out a room, annex, or part of your own home long-term or short-term, you will need to talk to your mortgage lender. Not all mortgage lenders will allow you to do short-term lets of six months or less due to the increased risk of damage to the property posed by renting it out to other people. If your lender does not permit the let, it may be worth talking to a mortgage broker to find a suitable holiday let mortgage to switch to. Often smaller mortgage lenders and building societies are more flexible.

If you are looking to change your home into a holiday let you will not usually require planning permission. Please note that this is no longer the case in Scotland where a change of use from a residential property into a holiday let will now require planning permission. I always recommend checking local planning rules with your council in advance. If you plan to make big changes to your home to change its use over to a holiday let then it is more likely that you will need planning permission, especially if it changes the character of the home or could impact neighbours in some way. If your council does require planning permission, bear in mind that it can be harder to get approval if your property is part of a greenbelt, in a heritage site or located in a site of outstanding natural beauty. Bear in mind that if you require planning for your home to become a holiday let and then decide that you or others wish to stay there for extended periods, or to move back there, then you may need to change its use back to residential via the local planning department again.

Financial responsibilities

It is compulsory to keep accurate documentation and accounts which record income and expenditure for tax purposes. You must declare all earnings from your holiday let business when filing your annual return to HMRC. Understanding the tax rules and allowances is important to make sure that you are compliant with the government tax system. Hiring an accountant to manage your finances can be helpful in ensuring that you are paying the correct tax as well as making the most of the allowances provided by the government. See the government website for further advice.

Business rates

Most holiday let owners declare their trading and accounts on their personal annual tax returns. However, a furnished holiday let property is considered a business/commercial premises rather than a residential premises. Therefore, it is important to contact your local council tax/business rates department and inform them that your property is a self-catering property. Outside of Scotland, a business is a self-catering property if it is available for 140 nights and rented for 70 nights. In this case, the valuation office will determine what business rates are applicable. There can be small business rates relief of up to 100% meaning you may find that you have nothing to pay. For Scottish property, check the local situation carefully.

If you are registered for business rates, then your property is no longer classed as a residential property. Some residential services, such as bin and recycling collection will no longer be offered to you as you won't be paying council tax. In this case you will need to find a private waste removal contractor. Occasionally in very rural areas it can be difficult to find a private waste collection service. If you cannot find a private contractor to provide you with bins and to empty them, then you will usually have to provide proof of this to your local council, via copies of emails or correspondence, who then have a duty to provide you with a bin collection service, although it will be at cost.

VAT

If your revenue exceeds £85,000 (at the time of writing) then you will have to register for VAT. This means you will have to charge your guests the prevailing VAT rate on top of your normal price (20%, again, at the time of writing). This 20%, you must collect and pay to HMRC via quarterly VAT returns which you can complete online. You can offset the amount by reclaiming any VAT that you are charged in the supply of your holiday let service. For instance, if you are charged VAT by your laundry company or cleaning company, this can be deducted from the amount owed to HMRC.

The £85,000 threshold is contentious because it creates a cliff-edge. Note that if you need to VAT register, 20% is due to the government on your *total revenue* and not just any excess above £85,000. In other words, if your revenue is £85,001, you must register for VAT and you will owe HMRC £17,000 and 20 pence (i.e. 20% of £85,001). However, if your revenue is £84,999, you need not register and you will owe nothing. Clearly, this creates an extremely strong incentive for any business whose revenue is close to this threshold to avoid overstepping it. It is not unknown for bed and breakfast businesses to shut up shop as soon as they are close to the limit and avoid further trading. This is why the threshold is controversial, insofar as it encourages businesses to reduce their economic activity.

If you have a collection of properties and you are confident you will surpass the threshold, you may choose to add the 20% to your pricing from the outset. Obviously, this may make your pricing uncompetitive versus lets that are not having to add VAT. The end result may be that you end up 'swallowing' the 20% tax yourself to keep your pricing in line with the market. If your holiday let is unlikely to reach the £85,000 revenue threshold, you need not be concerned by this. If it looks like it might be close, you would be well advised to consider the implication of exceeding the threshold and take action accordingly. Professional financial advice is worth seeking if you are unsure. Any VAT charged must be shown on invoices. If you are going to report VAT, keep good records and receipts. Remember that all your UK furnished holiday lets are treated as a single business from a tax perspective, so it is the collective revenue that matters, not whether any single let will pass the £85,000 threshold.

Financial returns

The expected returns for running a holiday let in the UK can vary depending on several factors, including location, property type, demand, seasonality, and the quality of your marketing and guest experience. While it is challenging to provide specific figures as returns are influenced by numerous variables, here are some general considerations which may help you as you put together a business plan:

1. Occupancy Rate: the occupancy rate, or the percentage of time your holiday let is occupied, is a crucial factor in determining returns. A higher occupancy rate typically leads to increased revenue. The average occupancy rate for holiday lets in the UK typically range from 50% to 80%, but it can vary significantly depending on the location and popularity of your property, and of course the rate you charge.

2. Rental Income: the rental income you can expect to generate from a holiday let depends on factors such as location, nightly rate, occupancy, property size, amenities, and market demand. Properties in popular tourist destinations or areas with high demand may command higher rental rates. It is important to research the local market and assess comparable properties to estimate rental income. Estimate a high and low season rate and multiply by your expected occupancy rate to forecast your projected annual rental income. Divide

the expected rental income by the property value and you have the gross yield for the property.

3. Seasonality: the seasonality of your property's location can impact returns. Popular holiday destinations may experience peak seasons where demand and rental rates are higher, while quieter periods may have lower occupancy and rates. Take into account seasonal fluctuations when estimating returns.

4. Costs and Expenses: operating a holiday let involves various expenses, including property maintenance, cleaning fees, utility bills, insurance, marketing costs, and potential management fees. These costs should be factored into your calculations to determine net returns. Distinguish between overheads (fixed costs, paid monthly, quarterly or annually) and variable costs (those which vary with the number of stays, such as cleaning and laundry).

5. Market Competition: the level of competition in your area can affect occupancy rates and rental rates. Research the local market to understand pricing trends and ensure your property stands out from the competition through unique features, excellent amenities, and outstanding guest experiences.

6. It is advisable to conduct a thorough financial analysis, considering both potential revenue and expenses, to estimate expected returns for your specific holiday let. Local market research, speaking with other holiday let owners in the area, and consulting with professionals such as accountants or property management experts can provide valuable insights and help you make informed decisions.

Chapter Eight
Housekeeping

Cleaning and laundry

Cleaning will be one of your biggest running costs and potentially your biggest headache in terms of setting up your let. It is worth looking into local companies in terms of availability and pricing before you even start looking for a holiday let or undertaking any other work towards setting one up. Always get several cleaning quotes first to get a sense of these costs in advance of purchasing a holiday home. You may decide to hire an individual private cleaner, but for me, reliability has always been an issue. It will usually be a little more cost effective to book a private individual cleaner, but there is nothing more stressful than being let down on a same day changeover, and I promise you that this *will* happen, even if your cleaner promises that they have a backup or will not let you down. If you live locally, then at least you have the option to do it yourself, if necessary, in an emergency, or you may prefer to do your own cleaning in any case, and this will help you to maximise your profits. If you do hire a private cleaner, then avoid changeovers booked for when you are away or unable to fill in during an emergency – alternatively book a cleaning agency just for those dates.

Laundry costs do add up, but it is the cleaning, along with utilities, that will be one of your biggest costs. If you plan to do your own cleaning, you will save a small fortune, but it is not an easy job, and you will need a strong stomach at times and a keen eye for detail. It is a physically demanding job, as I know well from the times that I have had to do it myself. Few people will clean as well or take as good care of your holiday home as you do. Private cleaners and agency cleaners will often cut corners and do the job as quickly as they think they can get away with. The rural idyll of a home in the middle of nowhere can be very appealing – especially since the Covid pandemic when we all suddenly wished we could escape to the countryside. However, do your research very carefully first in terms of local businesses and services, as you may struggle to find a cleaning and laundry agency if your home is very remote, or they may be reluctant to travel to you, especially in bad weather or on poorly made roads in the winter. Rural cleans and services can end up being more expensive due to a lack of supply and rising demand, so watch out for this and factor it into your property search. If there is only one cleaning agency for a 40-mile radius, they will be able to pick and choose their customers, charge a premium rate, and set all the terms. In short, they hold all the power.

You will find more companies in busier cities and more touristy towns and villages, and this competition can push prices down – in this case you will want to shop around for the best prices and service. Cleaning agencies will be very much geared towards the holiday market in tourist areas, and some will offer to fully manage your let, in terms of cleaning, laundry, maintenance, meet-and-greet, supplies and so on, for an additional cost. Local self-employed cleaners may be very keen to be paid the equivalent £20-40 per hour (per cleaner) that a holiday let clean typically commands but may not always be reliable (and usually aren't, in my experience.) I always use a cleaning agency now – it is usually more expensive and the standard is not always great, (the cleaners only keep a portion of the money you pay), but someone always shows up as they have reserve staff. Most agencies will charge a flat cleaning rate, regardless of how long the clean takes. Sometimes guests will leave the property immaculate, and the cleaners will whizz around and get the clean done in half the time, sometimes guests will have left a big mess and it will take them twice as long, so things usually balance out overall. Be careful to agree clear terms with your cleaner in advance. I once had a cleaner who consistently cut corners and generally did a pretty shoddy job and spent about half the time she should on cleans, but when a guest left the house in a messy state she would demand additional payment for her time – I was not prepared for such an unfair arrangement (and the standard was poor anyway), so let her go. If you have a very casual and part-time business plan with few back-to-back bookings or same-day changeovers, then it might be worth considering the self-employed cleaner, as there will be less time pressure and risk or things going wrong on check-in day. Generally, I would advise against alternating between a private cleaner and a cleaning agency – it might save some money to employ a private cleaner during quieter spells, but the agency may not like this or may not prioritise you in an emergency if they feel you have other loyalties. It is as well for a cleaner or agency to be familiar with a property year-round and this produces a better working relationship. You might want to consider employing an agency just for holiday cover, however, if you will not be able to step in during an emergency if your private cleaner lets you down at short notice. The average cost of a regular cleaner, per hour, these days seems to be around £15, but most holiday let cleaners will charge more than this. I would always agree to a flat rate to clean the property, rather than an hourly rate as the time required to clean will be different each week. You cannot assume that you will pay the equivalent of the hours spent at the property, and it will nearly always work out at a lot more than £15 per hour regardless. You are paying for a high level clean, reliability and beds being made up properly. A good self-employed cleaner is hard to find and will be in high demand, so, again, expect these prices to keep rising.

Cleaning and laundry costs are currently spiralling upwards – it is important to research these in advance. To give an example, it used to cost me £65 to have an agency clean and manage the laundry for a three-bedroom city-centre let around three years ago, but it is more typically £70-£150 now. If you can find a cleaning agency who will take your laundry away for cleaning and return it as and when needed then this will make life a great deal easier for you, as will an individual cleaner who is happy to do the laundry for an extra fee. If you are outsourcing your laundry to a laundry company, then you may need to arrange a pickup and drop-off system or arrange to pay for your cleaner to do this and you will need somewhere to store spare linen as well. Some laundry services will run a collection and drop off service, but again, you will need somewhere to store used and clean linen. Some cleaning agencies which are geared towards the holiday let market will offer full management of your let – i.e. laundry, maintenance, occasional deep cleans, a meet and greet service, all sundries supplied and so on, at an additional cost.

Agencies are more likely to send two or three cleaners to properties with more than two bedrooms and will aim to do it in one and half to three hours at most, usually with other properties to clean afterwards. However a four bedroom house can take an individual cleaner around three to five hours to change over, depending on how thoroughly they clean, hence why it still works out quite expensive – it is a labour intensive experience for an individual cleaner and I do sometimes find that cleaners soon tire of the high workload involved, despite the good pay, and often opt to change to housekeeping hotel jobs with more regular hours. It is not easy to keep a good private cleaner – you will need to entice them with good pay, compensation for cancelled late cleans and a good Christmas and summer bonus (if they have been busy).

I often carry out a clean and bed changeover at the property in the early days and time myself so that I can set out my expectations to a cleaner or agency. However, I find that they rarely take as long as I think they should, and corners are invariably cut. A four-bedroom larger home typically costs anything from £120-£180 per clean in my experience, laundry is typically an additional £40-£60. I find it takes me a minimum of five hours to change a four-bedroom house over, to a high standard, but private cleaners seem to spend about three to four hours at most. For comparison, a one-bedroom cottage or flat tends to typically cost anything from £40 to £80 to clean, and laundry around £20-30. Small properties are not always proportionately cheaper compared to larger ones for changeover costs. I think this is because things still need to be done to a high standard. Bedding, towels and sundries all need replacing and the cleaner still has to travel. Having changed over smaller properties, it is surprising how long it can take, especially if it has been left in a slightly messy state. I have spent nearly three hours on a one-bedroom cottage in the past, mainly due to the state of the kitchen. I find that the smaller properties do not offer such good value for money when an agency cleans them either, probably due to overheads, so you may want to consider a private cleaner for a one-bedroom property as this will usually be more typically around the £40 to £60 price range. A typical two-bedroom property can typically cost between £60 to £130 to clean and a three-bedroom property between £70 and £150. New holiday let homeowners nearly always underestimate cleaning costs. The biggest influencing factor in cleaning costs will be the availability of cleaners in your area.

Sometimes it is easier to find more competitively priced cleaning and laundry in a city. I find that rural lets can be very expensive for cleaning, as there is usually a shortage of cleaners and the local company has the monopoly. I had an agency increase their fees by 20% this year with no notice, but as it is in a very rural area, I had no alternative but to pay up. The holiday let market reflects economic booms and downturns quicker than most other industries. I typically lose at least one night's full revenue to laundry and cleaning costs at my properties, so it can make short stays unviable, especially two-night stays, once other costs are also factored in. If you are looking to have your property fully managed by a holiday let agency, then do not forget that they will be looking to the local area for cleaners and cleaning agencies and will probably add a charge on top of this as well. I sometimes find that some smaller local cleaning agencies get fully booked up by some of the holiday let agencies and prioritise this type of work.

Laundry

One set of linen and towels for a one-bedroom property is typically around £20-£30. For a three-bedroom home it will be around £30-£40 and a four-bedroom house will typically cost around £40-£60. Most holiday homes offer full bed linen and towels. I always provide four pillows for a double or king-size bed, and two for a single bed. I provide each guest with a bath sheet (a sheet is larger than a bath towel – people tend to complain these days if given a bath towel due to its smaller size) and a hand towel. I also put one hand towel in each bathroom and a floor bathmat on each towel radiator. I provide two tea towels per stay in the kitchen. A laundry agency will usually loan you the linen, at cost. Many have a scanning system which counts the laundry automatically and generally fewer mistakes are made this way. I usually have to provide my own mattress and pillow protectors. Some laundries will not launder these, or some will do it for an additional fee, but make sure they are clearly labelled with your property name. I advise cleaning these a *minimum* of once a month, preferably fortnightly if the let is busy, although a lot of holiday homes seem to rarely change them unfortunately.

If you do have a cleaner or laundry service dropping off spare linen and collecting used from your let, then you will need a lockable storage cupboard in your home. This is not always ideal if the laundry company wants to collect or drop when you have guests, but it is useful if your cleaner is dealing with the linen. You can sometimes arrange for linen to be dropped and collected from your cleaning agency if you use one. The best solution is usually to have an outbuilding or weather-proof, locked box for storage, although it should not be too cold or damp as your linen could get mouldy. Again, it is important to consider these practicalities at the start, especially if you are looking to buy somewhere specifically as a holiday let. I would say that a lockable cupboard within the property is essential, and a separate storage building or external lockable unit can be very helpful. I tend to leave sundries with my linen – i.e. tea, coffee, soap, mini shampoos, toilet and kitchen roll, bin bags, dishwasher tablets, cloths, sponges etc. as I provide my own. Some cleaning companies will provide them for you for an additional fee which will save you having to re-stock and store them.

If you or your cleaner do the laundry then ensure everything is washed at 60 degrees minimum, as this kills off bacteria, and will remove any stains more effectively. It is best to use all white linen and towels – coloured or patterned towels and bedding looks very unprofessional. A cotton/polyester mix is best for bedding as it does not get as creased as some pure cottons and linens. If you are storing linen on site then have an enclosed cupboard to put it in, or zip bags at the very least to keep it dust free. I sometimes add a silica gel sachet inside zip bags of linen to ensure they stay mould-free if a property is quiet during the winter months. I have a minimum of four full sets of linen and towels for each property – that way, during busy times, I should never run out. It is surprising how quickly you can run out if your laundry is not collected or returned one week or is late in its return. It is vital to have a minimum of one laundry collection and drop off per week during busy periods, I often have two. It can be worth having your own emergency set of labelled linen as well, even if you are being provided laundry by another company, as sometimes things can go wrong. Always provide pillow and mattress protectors – they are hygienic and will save your mattress and pillows from getting stained or dirty. Ensure you have a full set of spare protectors for when these need laundering. I also provide a waterproof mattress protector underneath a regular one to prevent the mattress getting soiled.

Cleaning

You need to have clear expectations from your cleaner or agency at the outset, in terms of what you pay and what services they provide. You need to agree whether they will supply cleaning tools and products or if you are expected to. I always leave a mop, vacuum cleaner and set of cleaning products at my holiday lets just in case guests want to use them (not usually, in my experience!), even if the company brings its own. I usually ask my cleaner to drop fresh milk as well, although I supply my own sundries such as tea, coffee, biscuits, toilet roll, washing up liquid etc. I leave a laminated checklist for my cleaners so that things are not forgotten or overlooked. Agencies will often send inexperienced or new cleaners to your property, so it is vital that they have a clear list of what needs to be done, along with other helpful information. There is always a surprisingly large number of things to remember to do during a holiday let change-over.

I have had to change cleaners several times in the first year of trading on some properties due to problems which include poor cleaning, over-charging, poor communication, frequently letting me down at the last minute, additional charges which were not previously agreed and a suspiciously fast disappearance of sundries and supplies. If you find a good cleaner or agency then treat them well, as they are hard to find and will make all the difference in terms of your property being successful or not and will save you a great deal of time and work. I would always send them a Christmas bonus and even an end-of-summer bonus if they have been busy and have done a good job. If you are lucky to find a good local housekeeper who is prepared to manage everything at your let, including supplies and general DIY and maintenance, this could save you a lot of time and travelling. It will have to be someone you can trust and who works to a consistently high level - you will need to pay them very well.

Unless I have an exceptionally good cleaner or agency, I find I usually have to visit properties a minimum of once a fortnight to deep clean, fix and replenish items which the cleaners should have done. The most common things that I find get missed are: shower plug filters not being cleaned, supplies and sundries not being replenished, log baskets not filled up fully, wood burner windows are rarely cleaned, cobwebs, dust in corners and on skirting boards, loose toilet seats, smudges on windows, burnt on food or spills in ovens, under beds and sofas rarely vacuumed, crumbs inside kitchen drawers and cupboards, marks on kitchen cupboard doors, dirty dinner place mats, washing machine drawer and drum trim rarely cleaned, vacuum filter rarely cleaned or replaced, hair trapped in vacuum cleaner beater bar. If I let these things slide, then I would very quickly start to receive negative feedback. You can give your cleaner or agency clear instructions on what needs to be done every week, but whether they do it is another matter. Be wary of falling out with agencies or cleaners as it is not always easy to find a replacement quickly or one that is any better. Sometimes you must accept that an 'acceptable' clean is enough and fill in any gaps yourself from time to time. Alternatively, arrange for a separate monthly deep clean, if possible, with a clear and detailed list of tasks.

Suggested cleaning checklist:

- Strip all beds and bag up linen and re-make beds before you start the cleaning – tuck all duvet edges in around beds and replace any stained pillow or mattress protectors. Place pillows on top of the tucked in duvet. Place one bath sheet and hand towel per guest on the end of the bed. Plump cushions and shake out any throws or send them for laundering and replace with spares if necessary.
- Dust all surfaces. Use wood polish sparingly and only occasionally to avoid build-up. Use glass cleaner on glass surfaces including mirrors.
- Vacuum all floors, preferably under furniture where possible as well. Empty the canister afterwards and change and wash the filter if necessary. Sweep or hoover any doormats.

- Mop all hard floors – use a wrung-out mop for any wood or stone floors and make sure you use a specialist stone floor cleaner for natural stone finishes. It is preferable to have two mops – one for bathrooms, and one for kitchens and other hard floors.
- Bathrooms should be sparkling. Use a good antibacterial bathroom cleaner preferably with anti-limescale and antibacterial properties. Scrub baths and shower trays with a cleaning sponge. Remove and clean the shower filter plug if you have one, remove hair from the bath plug. Wipe down and dry tiles and glass shower screens and finish with glass cleaner. Clean shower hoses and heads carefully. Clean toilets with disposable wipes (never flush down the WC) or a cloth reserved purely for this job and put bleach or limescale gel in the bowl and leave. Clean the toilet and basin pedestals, the bin and bath panel (often overlooked). Refill liquid hand soap, if necessary, leave mini shampoo and soaps if you provide them. Empty the bathroom bin and replace the bin liner. Put a bathmat on the edge of the bath or on a towel radiator. Clean any towel radiators with non-abrasive cleaner and cloth. Use glass cleaner on any mirrors. Clean toothbrush holders if provided. Leave a minimum of two toilet rolls per bathroom. Consider leaving more for a long weekend stay, as people do not necessarily want to go to the shops during a short break to buy more – guests use a surprisingly large amount of toilet roll in my experience and one of their biggest bugbears is a lack of loo roll.
- Change all bedroom bins and the kitchen bin and replace the bin liners.
- Clean the kitchen thoroughly, including worktops, kettle and toaster – shake crumbs from the toaster.

Clean inside the oven if necessary as well as the outer door and hob. Consider a specialist cleaning fluid and microfibre cloth for electric and halogen hobs – you may also need an oven scraper tool for burnt-on food but be careful not to scratch the hob surface – these should be used at 45-degree angles and not gouged into the surface too roughly. Ensure any tiles or splashback above the oven are clean. Dust any shelves. Clean the washing up bowl, inside of the sink and draining board and draining rack if you have one. Ensure washing up liquid and dishwasher tablets are topped up and any sundries topped up as necessary such as oil, salt, pepper, oil, foil, tea, coffee, sugar, biscuits, kitchen roll, bin bags etc. Leave a new cloth for surfaces and a scouring sponge or brush for washing up by the sink. Clean inside the fridge and the exterior of the kitchen bin. Ensure the inside of the bin is clean as it can smell very bad if food has leaked - always leave a new bin bag inside the kitchen bin. Remove any food from the fridge and freezer. Clean the coffee machine and inside the microwave if you have one. Leave two tea towels near the sink. Clean marks off cupboard doors and clean any tables and check chairs for crumbs and dust. Ensure pots, pans, cutlery and implements are all clean. Empty the dishwasher if necessary - top up dishwasher salt and rinse aid if necessary. Check all food is removed from cupboards, fridges and freezer. Do not leave half opened packets of food in cupboards as there is a contamination risk. Check the dishwasher filter at least once a month - this is usually located on the base of the dishwasher, and you generally have to twist and lift it out. There are usually two parts - the filter holder and filter. If guests do not rinse food off plates, this will quickly get clogged and make your dishwasher smell. I

add a reminder note nearby to rinse dishes before putting them in the dishwasher as it does save having to carry out this unpleasant task too often.
- Clean all surfaces in the living room, tidy any magazines, games and books, remove the sofa cushions and hoover underneath as crumbs collect here. Clean any marks off sofas. Sweep and empty ash pans on wood burners or fireplaces if necessary. If you have a wood burner, clean the glass - the best way to do this is to get a damp cloth and dip it in any residual ash inside the stove and rub it over the glass. Replenish logs, kindling, firelighters and matches where necessary. Plump cushions. Check any coasters are clean and stacked up. Wipe any marks off the TV. Check the visitor book for any recent comments or feedback about low supplies or missing items.
- If you have a utility room, check the washing machine drum trim and drawer are clean. Ensure the sink is clean and if you have a tumble dryer ensure that the filter is clean and free of lint – this is really important, in terms of removing a fire risk. Replenish laundry pods or detergent if necessary. Providing laundry pods instead of detergent ensures that the detergent drawer stays clean.
- Dining room – check the table is clean and that place mats and coasters are clean and placed in the middle of the table (this ensures they are used as guests will not necessarily look for them inside of cupboards). Cleaners always seem to like to pack them away. Dust chairs and remove any crumbs from seats.
- Bedrooms: shake out and ensure any bed throws or bedspreads are clean, (send to launder if not), plump up any cushions, clean mirrors, replace any dirty pillow or mattress protectors when changing the beds,

ensure all sheets fully tucked in under mattresses and that pillows are arranged on top of a tucked in duvet. Place bath sheets and hand towels on the ends of beds. Push coat hangers to one side inside wardrobes, wrap cords around hairdryers in drawers. Ensure drinks coasters and surfaces are clean. Check all drawers are empty - use a handheld vacuum cleaner to remove dust and debris from inside drawers occasionally.
- Additional cleaning checks: clean any marks off windows, check all drawers and cupboards are empty, check all lightbulbs are working. Tidy any garden furniture. Sweep any steps, paths and patios of debris. Collapse the garden rotary airer if it has been left up. Check supplies and sundries and make a note of any that are running low if necessary.
- Note: it is really important to check all drawers and cupboards as guests sometimes leave medications behind that could be harmful to any subsequent children staying at the property.

Hot tubs

Hot tubs seem to be one of the most popular facilities you can offer guests these days. When I speak to holiday let agencies, one of the first questions they often ask is 'do you have a hot tub?' My answer is 'no' as having researched them: the maintenance and cost is usually prohibitive for a private let, unless you are charging a very high nightly rate, are on site to manage its maintenance yourself, or have on-site staff. This might not be the case in a holiday park or similar with a dedicated maintenance person who services them daily, but otherwise they can be very impractical. Some cleaning agencies will specifically train their staff on how to clean and maintain them and there are formal training programmes available for it, but this will be another significant cost for your business, not to mention the higher energy bills. You then have health and safety to consider – will children be staying at the property, and will they have free access to the tub? Will you trust guests to follow instructions in terms of safety and replacing lids etc. or not altering the temperature and so on? Some hot tubs require daily maintenance, and again this is not always practical for holiday lets, unless you happen to live on site and are happy to do it or have a permanent housekeeper or on-site staff. I suspect a lot of the hot tubs on offer at holiday lets are simply not serviced and maintained as they should be, and you therefore run the risk of various health problems, including the potentially deadly Legionnaires disease, for your guests. However, if you do have staff or are happy to maintain it yourself you will find that a hot tub gives you a significant advantage over your competition as they are extremely popular.

Key points

- Cleaning will be one of your biggest costs. Research the availability and pricing of local companies or cleaners before committing to a holiday let business. Finding cleaning and laundry companies in rural areas can be a real headache.
- Individual private cleaners can work out a little cheaper than using an agency, but reliability is usually an issue. An agency will have back-up staff.
- Agree clear terms and conditions with your cleaner or agency in advance.
- Cleaning and laundry costs are currently rising - it is not always possible to pass on these increased costs to guests.

- A regular cleaner's salary is typically around £15 per hour, but a holiday let cleaner will usually charge much more than this. It is usually best to agree to a flat rate in advance.
- Some typical cleaning costs (individual cleaner or agency); one bedroom property £40 to £80, two-bedroom property; £60 to £130, three-bedroom property; £70 to £150, four-bedroom property £120 to £180 (as of June 2023. Prices will vary depending on the type of property, area and availability of cleaners and cleaning agencies).
- Some typical laundry company costs (for one hand towel, one bath sheet per person, one bathmat, a couple of tea towels, all bed linen including two pillowcases per person); one bedroom property £20 to £30, two-bedroom property; £25 to 35, three-bedroom property; £30 to £40, four-bedroom property; £40 to £60. Prices will vary depending on the area, the service required and availability of laundry companies.
- A lockable cupboard is very useful for linen and supplies storage. An outdoor or separate annex storage room is very useful for linen drop off and collection. Some cleaning agencies can provide linen too.
- Have at least four full sets of linen to allow for delays and shortages, especially during busy periods. Have at least one collection and drop off per week during busy times, preferably two, if using a laundry company.
- Be prepared to visit your holiday let at least once a fortnight or a minimum of once a month to check on things, to make small repairs and to replenish supplies.
- Cleaning agencies and private cleaners will rarely clean to a perfect standard.
- Provide waterproof mattress protectors underneath a regular mattress protector on all beds and put pillow

protectors on all pillows – label them with your property name. Not all laundry companies will launder them. Have a full spare set of them.
- If you are providing your own linen, choose all white linen preferably in a cotton/polyester mix for ease of ironing. Always wash at 60 degrees and label it.
- Provide each guest with one bath sheet and one hand towel. Also provide two pillows per person and one hand towel and one bathmat in each bathroom. Provide at least two kitchen tea towels.
- Provide a full spare set of linen for your cleaners, even if you are using a laundry company's hired linen, in case of a shortage or emergency and ensure it is labelled and kept separately.
- You should launder pillow and mattress protectors regularly, preferably every fortnight or at least once a month. Many holiday homes and hotels do not bother.
- Hot tubs are high maintenance – only install one if you have researched the running costs and have a cleaner or company who can service it regularly. There are serious potential health hazards if they are not properly maintained.
- Always ensure all drawers are checked during changeover cleans in case of medications being left behind.
- Provide a laminated checklist for your cleaners of things that should be carried out during each clean. Consider a monthly deep clean with a checklist if you cannot regularly visit the let.
- If you find a good private cleaner, pay them well and compensate them for last-minute cancelled cleans. Consider giving generous Christmas and summer bonuses.

Chapter Nine
Renovating and furnishing a holiday home

Whether you have a new or old building, annex, room or lodge that you want to let out, it is likely that you will need to carry out some renovation or refurbishment. In this chapter I will provide some guidelines for furnishings and finishes to hopefully help you optimise the aesthetic appeal of your let, whilst making it practical for purpose. Any kind of rental property will need a much sturdier and damage-proof finish than a regular home. The compromise will lie somewhere between making your home look as good as possible whilst ensuring that it can live up to day-to-day heavy wear and tear. People are often more careless with a rental home and will be more likely to break or damage things due to a lack of familiarity with them.

    A lot will be dependent on your budget, but there are ways of making your home look great, whether you are looking to present high-end luxury or something more modest. You will need to factor renovation costs into any house or flat buying process – never underestimate these. Even with a strict and realistic budget for each aspect of a renovation, it usually comes in at least a third more than you expect, in my experience, so always allow for a contingency fund. It might be worth getting quotes from builders or kitchen and bathroom fitters in advance of a purchase. I have fully renovated entire large period properties, city flats, cottages, a bungalow and terraced houses in my time and have learned some important lessons the hard way. Some renovations will be partial – the bones of a property might be good, and you may get away with just updating some aspects such as flooring, décor and tiles for example. If you have DIY skills you will be able to save yourself a small fortune, but if not, you would still be surprised at what you are able to do with off-the-shelf products and some YouTube videos. DIY and online stores stock a vast array of types of paint, flooring, kitchen units and doors, making it easier than ever to renovate existing décor or improve the appearance of your home without ripping everything out. If you need to hire builders, get several quotes, plus references. Since the pandemic there has been a large bottleneck of people waiting on building works which has resulted in long delays and intermittent works for many frustrated customers. However, this is likely to calm down over the next few years. You may still find yourself waiting on building work, however, so you also need to factor this in, especially if you have a mortgage to pay and time is of the essence. If you are not going to be around or on-site, you will need to hire a project manager, which is another large cost. It can be very difficult managing a large renovation remotely and things are likely to go wrong on occasion, even with a project manager, so think carefully if you are buying a home more than an hour away as you will find yourself doing a lot of driving and dealing with a lot of phone calls during building work otherwise. Even if you plan to renovate the home yourself, deliveries of large items and materials will ideally need to be sent to the site and you need to decide if you will be able to be there to accept them. The same applies for furniture deliveries. If you have a van then you can consider having things sent to your main home address and transporting them across to your let over time, or possibly hiring a van to do so. I lost a lot of school holidays due to renovation work and would often have to spend most of them at a semi-finished home with bored children as I would be waiting in for quotes and deliveries. A lot of builders and tradespeople will want to discuss work at the property, in person, so again you will have to be there frequently if dealing with a large renovation. My easiest renovations have been those closest to home and in more modern, smaller properties and those which require less major intervention and work – I would recommend this, at least for your first foray into the holiday let world.

If you are looking to make a good profit from your holiday home, then you will be watching your budget carefully. Builders often have their own wholesale suppliers who can price kitchen, bathroom or joinery at very competitive prices, although they may add a handling fee for this. Alternatively, DIY stores such as Screwfix, B&Q, Homebase and Wickes are good value too and replicate many of the more high-end products at a more wallet-friendly price. Many stores have a paint mixing service and you can have expensive brands of paint approximately matched colour-wise in bulk at a reduced price. I would get a plumber to check out your boiler and plumbing at the start of the project, and an electrician to check the wiring, regardless of your survey results. I find issues often crop up despite having a detailed survey and you do not want to be rewiring or re-plumbing the whole house a few years after having renovated and redecorated it. Heating, plumbing, electrics and the roof are absolutely key, and you really should have these carefully checked over as you cannot take short-cuts on any essential work needed in these areas. I have had some nasty shocks in this regard, especially in older houses, and have had my budget severely dented by having to carry out major remedial works which I had not accounted for initially due to them not being picked up by the survey.

When you first exchange on the property, fit a key safe to the exterior of the property and leave a couple of spare keys in it in case work men need to access it when you are not there, especially if you do not live close by. Keys can sometimes go missing in the chaos of a renovation, so it is as well to always have a couple kept in a key safe. Make a note of the code straight away. After this, take LOTS of photos of the property, inside and out – it is very easy to forget finishes, layouts, and positions of things when you are not based at a property fulltime, and it is a very useful tool during a renovation. Also take as many measurements as possible – a battery powered laser measure is helpful in measuring large spaces and rooms in one go. Always have a tape measure on you during the renovation process. Measure existing fittings, doors and windows and carefully consider any access restrictions – i.e. narrow doors/tight bends that might restrict the sizes of appliances and furniture in terms of getting them into the house. Then make a list of things that must be done, in order of importance with a rough estimate of cost. Make a detailed description of the works you want done as these are useful to give to builders when they are quoting for you. The sooner you decide exactly what you want done and which fittings and appliances you want, the sooner you can get a clear quote. Being decisive will save you money as the sooner you finish the renovation, the sooner you can start letting your property. Get in as many quotes as possible and see if there is any work that you would be able to do if you have time. Keep a renovation spreadsheet to track costs – include the date, company, item, and exact amount. I sometimes put estimates on the spreadsheet in a different colour, alongside paid costs, as it allows me to keep an overall sense of the full cost and encourages me to try to stay within budget.

Be very wary if you are buying a listed property or one in a conservation area as there will be restrictions and rules that must be closely followed. Conservation areas can have strict rules regarding the exterior or the property, although this can extend inside as well. Always check what restrictions or rules are in place before making any changes. With listed buildings you will need to apply for planning permission for any building works, alterations and even some repairs. Repairs usually involve a like-for-like rule, meaning you will usually be allowed to replace something rotten or broken with the same material, but it can be costly and require a specialist company to do the work. If in doubt, speak to your local planning office. They will usually advise you on small queries by email or phone. You can sometimes pay for more detailed queries and reports. It is very unlikely you will be able to extend or put in a loft conversion or reconfigure an internal layout or remove any original features. Some councils will allow you to upgrade single glazed windows to slim-lined timber double glazed windows, if the current ones have no particular age to them, but this varies throughout the country. Very old windows are unlikely to be allowed to be replaced, although secondary internal glazing can be a solution to cold rooms, however it does not always look the prettiest. You will have to apply for planning to replace any rotten windows, doors, to re-point, change any hard flooring or to re-roof, even if the replacement will look the same or will be using the same materials. I know someone who needs to re-roof their collapsing grade II listed cottage roof – they have all the tiles but the beams underneath are rotten. They have to number every single tile and put it back in exactly the same place afterwards. These sorts of rules and restrictions will make any renovation much slower and more costly. There are curtilage rules which restrict you in terms of changes you can make outside the property up to a certain distance, including landscaping, fencing and outbuildings. Tread carefully and check with your local authority planning office if in doubt. A listed property will always cost a great deal more to renovate than a regular home and each planning application will take time and cost money. During the buying process carefully check if any works have been done without permission as theoretically the council could request that you remove additions or changes that did not receive planning, however far back in the past they were made (from the time the property was originally listed). It is very rare for planning departments to come looking for issues, but better safe than sorry. It is usually worth taking out indemnity insurance at the time of purchase for old properties with a chequered history of renovation, as this covers you for any potential costs should any previous works be flagged up as not having suitable planning permission or for any subsequent costs involved in rectifying these issues. Retrospective planning can always be sought if this happens, but you cannot guarantee what the outcome will be with the planning department.

You need to decide at the outset whether you will be project managing any major refurbishments yourself or whether you will pay someone else to do it – quite often the owner of a small building company will do it for an additional fee. Professional architects and private project managers will be very expensive but are worth investigating if you are looking at a high-end refurbishment for a luxury holiday home. Check out references and reviews carefully and get several quotes. If you are looking to save money by managing the renovations yourself and contracting individual trades for each job, then you really need to live close by and have lots of free time on your hands. I would not recommend this route if you do not have much building or refurbishment experience as a lot of the skill is knowing what to do and in which order and there are more likely to be delays when employing a number of different trades as opposed to one main builder. It is usually worth employing a single building company if you have a large refurbishment project to deal with – again, get at least three quotes and check references and reviews carefully. Make sure you get a clear contract in writing and that terms, costs and a timescale and time commitment are clearly laid out before any work commences. Time is money when renovating a holiday home and the longer it takes the bigger the dent will be in your finances – you cannot afford to employ a builder who will not turn up consistently. Building firms seems busier than ever at the moment and can pick and choose the most profitable jobs sometimes on a day-by-day basis – I have heard so many horror stories in recent years of renovations taking much longer than they should for this reason, with builders only attending for a few hours a week or even disappearing for several weeks or months at a time, so tread very carefully if you are considering a large-scale home renovation. For smaller projects where a home just needs a bit of updating then it is usually more cost effective to contract individual jobs to various companies or individual tradespeople. Ensure that your plumber is on the Gas Safe register if they are dealing with your boiler or any gas products. Your electrician should preferably meet NICEIC standards and provide corresponding paperwork for any work. Always check out references and reviews for any tradespeople before employing them. Recommendations from friends and family can be a good starting point. Also check reviews on Yell.com and on Google. Mybuilder.com is another useful site where you can post jobs and receive quotes from a variety of tradespeople or firms who will have feedback and an overall score rating from other customers.

Kitchens

I rarely rip out an entire kitchen unless it is in very poor shape. There are companies who specialise in giving kitchens 'face lifts' and this can be at least a third, if not more, cheaper than replacing it with a new one. This involves changing cupboard doors and handles, changing appliances and tiling but keeping most of the original framework of the kitchen and interior cupboards. They can also change the worktops with new laminate or upgrade them to granite, marble or quartz/Corian hard surfaces, although this will depend on whether the framework of the kitchen is strong enough to support this. There are companies who can wrap a thin granite or quartz layer around an existing worktop, so that could also be worth looking into. Stone or stone composite worktops look more luxurious, and I would advise them for a high-end let, but I am not sure the cost is worth it for a more modest home. There are some very effective wood and stone effect laminates available these days and it could save you thousands of pounds. It is quite common for kitchen companies to offer to line wall surfaces with the same quartz-effect laminate as the work surfaces, for a seamless look, and this usually works out cheaper than tiling. Pale stone and marble type worktops are very fashionable right now, but they stain easily and require special and careful cleaning which guests generally will not do, and your cleaner may forget or use the wrong type of cleaner which can damage them. It would pain me too much to spend thousands on such a worktop as it will rarely look clean, and stains can be tricky to remove. Guests can be very careless, and kitchens get an absolute battering in holiday lets, so everything needs to be as resistant to staining and breakage as possible. If you do go for stone, I would strongly advise a darker coloured one, even though they are not the most fashionable choice right now.

Pale worktops have been fashionable for a few years so their time is limited – day-to-day practicalities often kill off trends and I suspect the difficulty of maintaining pale stone, marble and marble-effect quartz worktops will hasten their demise. Black granite is very much a classic finish and safe option, although citrus can damage it, so remember to seal it. If your kitchen already has a wooden work top then I would advise leaving it in situ, unless it is damaged, but you will need to regularly deep clean and treat it accordingly (usually with specialist wood oil). I would not choose to put a new wooden work surface into a holiday let in general, however, as it will be much harder to maintain and keep it looking smart. Also avoid tiled work surfaces for the same reasons – they are also a bit of a health hazard as the grout can never be fully sanitised.

Be wary of choosing anything too current or fashionable, as it will date quickly. Classic is always safest for longevity. Avoid dark grey, industrial finishes, dark navy or dark green cupboards and brass or copper handles and possibly metro tiles, especially with dark grout, as they are all very 'now'. High gloss cabinets are on the way out, but I would always advise against them anyway as they show up every little scratch and cannot be easily painted over. If your property comes with a solid wooden kitchen then definitely keep it – the fact you can paint and repaint the cabinets is a massive bonus, as they will get scratched and damaged regularly. New hinges, handles and a deep clean can work wonders on old units. Specialist kitchen cupboard paint can make repainting units an easier task, or a strong primer designed for 'difficult' surfaces could be worth considering if your existing cupboards have a high gloss finish. Consider using a microfibre mini roller to apply kitchen cupboard paint, rinsed and dried first to remove any lint, or employ a professional decorator for a really seamless finish.

Kitchen cupboard doors, drawer fronts and worktops can all be bought in most DIY stores and online these days if you want to replace these. They come primed, plain or ready painted. A lick of new paint and updated handles can transform a kitchen, as can new wall tiles or putting in tongue-and-groove panelling instead of tiles, which can look lovely in period homes. Be wary of tile paint and stick-on adhesive tiles as they rarely look convincing and tend to scratch and peel.

If you do need to replace the entire kitchen then check out DIY stores as most supply units, and some will also offer planning and fitting, or will have a list of approved fitters. Howdens and Wickes are certainly worth a look. Ikea sells very reasonably priced kitchens and general builders will usually be happy to work with units you have bought, although you will have to do more of the planning this way. For a modern kitchen I would strongly recommend plain matt white units and doors with minimal decoration – white never goes out of fashion. If you can afford real wood or MDF then you have the option to choose any colour and change it over time, although with the correct preparation and primer you should be able to re-paint cheaper foil-wrapped chipboard type cupboard doors and units as well. For country homes a shaker type or traditional panelled unit is preferable, and these seem to be timeless. I find Wickes very good for wall tiles, although there are plenty of good online stores too. MDF tongue and groove panelling can be bought from most DIY stores and online. Trustpilot is very helpful when checking out kitchen suppliers and fitters, as they can vary a lot in terms of customer satisfaction. Some have very poor reputations so always check the reviews first. If you have a remotely located property you may need to use a smaller local kitchen fitting company, but I find they often give a better and more tailored service and can be very competitively priced, compared to the large national companies. If you want a high-end tailored look then it can be worth getting a quote from a local joiner to make your cupboards and sourcing granite or quartz surfaces from a specialist company. It will still work out a lot cheaper than using one of the luxury national kitchen companies. If price is no object, then check out Mark Wilkinson, John Lewis of Hungerford and Plain English kitchens, which are ideal for luxury and period homes in particular.

Where possible have free-standing appliances. Modern streamlined kitchens tend to have in-built appliances which look very smart, but it can be time-consuming and expensive when they need replacing. If your oven, dishwasher or fridge stops working, you need to be able to replace it as quickly as possible. Companies such as AO.com can often deliver appliances within a day or two if necessary and you can usually pay for them to connect your new appliance and remove your old one. If you do have in-built appliances, then make sure you have their exact measurements to hand in case you need to replace at short notice. I have had problems with built-in appliances in the past, especially with fridges and ovens, and have found myself having to employ a joiner to remove appliances or make room for a new one when it is not possible to source a new appliance of the exact same dimensions as the old one. Even if you do have free-standing appliances then still make a note of the dimensions as you will be able to order new ones immediately without having to measure up. Keep any warranties to hand as most appliances are usually covered for at least a year. Have the contact details for a repair company to hand in case it is an issue that can be fixed. Unfortunately, in my experience, appliances do seem to have shorter and shorter shelf lives and it is not always possible to repair them, or the cost of the repair can be the same or more than the cost of a new appliance. Repair shops are often booked up and you may have to wait a few weeks. Speed is everything in terms of replacing any broken appliances for a holiday let.

Avoid using tiles above a hob unless you have dark grout, as white grout will become stained quickly and you do not want to be scrubbing it every other month or having to re-paint it continuously with grout reviver. A stone, glass or stainless-steel hob splashback is much lower maintenance. For a high-end let I think you need to have good quality floor tiles – preferably natural stone or a high-quality ceramic, preferably with under-floor heating. A lot of guests complain about cold feet when under-floor heating is not provided. Ceramic floor tiles can be preferable to natural stone which can be damaged by the wrong cleaning product or spillages. Always keep several spare wall and floor tiles in case of damage. If your property already has natural stone flooring it will probably need a good clean and re-sealing which can prevent a lot of damage and staining but will need re-doing from time to time. You will also need to find a suitable floor cleaning solution that will not damage it. I would strongly advise against engineered wood or natural wood floorboards as they will get pitted and easily marked. Vinyl and luxury vinyl tiles can be a cost-effective solution and are generally hard-wearing. Some of the luxury vinyl wood and stone-effect tiles can look quite convincing. They will be less cold to walk on and usually require less maintenance (no mucky grout or smear lines), plus dropped crockery and glassware will not always automatically smash to pieces. Try Tapi flooring and Carpet Right. Local companies can also be very competitively priced with better customer service, especially when it comes to fitting and preparation. Be aware that cheaper vinyl flooring can sometimes be marked by vacuum cleaners, especially if the carpet beater is switched on – again, I learned this from bitter experience. Ensure you use the correct type of floor cleaner on luxury vinyl tile flooring (LVT) though, as it could potentially be damaged by certain products and suppliers usually recommend specific cleaning solutions. Some types of rubber, including rug backing and rug grips can stain or discolour LVT flooring over time, so be careful about what you place on top of it. Avoid pale grey laminates as they will date quickly. Consider putting felt pads on chair and table legs to avoid any potential scratching - attach them with superglue as the adhesive they come with is usually inadequate and wears off over time.

Stainless steel sinks are the easiest type of sink to maintain and are preferable for a modern kitchen. Resin and plastic sinks always end up looking tatty. Butler's sinks can look lovely in a period or country home but are more liable to staining and require regular bleaching. They do get chipped over time as well. Double sinks are always preferable, or at least a small secondary rinsing sink. A built-in draining board is advisable.

Spotlights (individually recessed or several on a long bar) are usually desirable for kitchens due to the strong bright light they give off – a lot of older people struggle to see properly in poor lighting. I always advise warm white bulbs to prevent it looking too clinical though. Strip lighting is very old-fashioned and unflattering, so I always recommend removing this if possible. It is good to offer gentler low lighting as well – either through hidden strip lights under cupboards, pendant lights, wall lights or even a tabletop lamp, if you have room.

If you have space for a dining table in the kitchen then definitely provide one, even if you have a separate dining room, as a lot of people prefer to eat in the kitchen for convenience. Choose a glass-topped, granite or easy-to-wipe table though. Zinc topped tables can be great in a modern setting and are very robust. Wood will always get damaged, even if you provide place mats and coasters, although you can choose to top it with toughened glass which can be cut to size by various online companies – make sure you use little clear rubber feet underneath so that the glass does not move around. A lot of holiday home owners choose to buy a cheap table and cover it in a PVC cloth, but these often get stained by tomato or curry sauce and you will forever be changing it. It is also rather unsophisticated looking for non-family groups. Laminate type tables can also be permanently stained by curry and tomato sauce. One large pendant light or two or three smaller hanging pendant lights can look very effective over a dining table and offer more subdued lighting for mealtimes.

Ensure any existing gas appliances are safe - this should be done as part of your landlord's boiler and gas safety annual check-up. Many people prefer to cook on gas, but electric is also fine. Glass electric hobs tend to get easily marked as people often let pans boil over when they are not used to them – ensure you have a specialist glass hob cleaner and scraper to hand in the kitchen. Keep user instructions close by as some electric hobs can be complicated to use – you may want a laminated sign nearby instructing guests how to switch it on and off, preferably with diagrams for non-English speaking guests. A double oven with a grill is preferable, especially if your home sleeps more than four guests. High-end properties will often have several ovens and a separate five or six ring hob or a large multi-oven range with integrated five or six ring hob. Keep a folder of kitchen appliances to hand for guests to refer to and include information on how to clean ovens in the general guest information file as well – some ovens are self-cleaning and cleaning products could damage their linings. Grill operation varies from oven to oven (i.e. grill with door open or shut), so again include clear instructions. If you have an Aga, you will need it serviced annually and to include in-depth user information for guests plus a sign telling them not to adjust it, as they will likely trip the fire valve and switch it off accidentally. You should also add a notice about the surfaces being hot to warn parents of young children who could hurt themselves on it. Agas are a pain in general, and I would advise against putting one into your let or relying on it as the only source of heat, as they can be unreliable and make the kitchen very hot in the summer. They are difficult to clean when switched on – the ovens are self-cleaning as all fat and spillages will turn to ash eventually, but guests rarely clean the lift-up hot plates which get very dirty, and cleaners are reluctant to do it due to the heat. It can be done by lifting the lids up and leaving for 10-20 minutes so they're not so hot, but generally it is easier to do when the Aga is switched off. Ensure your cleaner has silicone gloves provided just for the job of cleaning the Aga so that they do not burn themselves. Soap scouring sponges and an oven scraper are the best way to clean the hot plates and top surface. You can convert older Agas to electric with a more flexible 'on/off' button, although opinions of their efficacy vary from person to person, and they will still take a long time to initially heat up. A powerful air extractor above an oven is essential. Older paper-lined boxy extractors can make a kitchen look very dated, so I would always advise upgrading these to something more modern looking. Always try to vent hob extractors to the outside, if at all possible, as re-circulated air extractors are never as effective.

    I would advise installing as large a fridge and freezer as possible, even if this means moving a freezer to a utility room, for example. Large family gatherings often equate to lots of cooking and food shopping. If you have a high-end let then some kind of additional wine or drinks fridge is highly recommended, as is an American style double fridge freezer with ice maker. I would only provide an under-counter fridge with an integrated freezer for a property that sleeps two people – any more guests than this would expect a full-size fridge and at least an under-counter freezer, ideally. Try to choose frost-free type freezers. I always adjust the feet on my fridges and freezers so that they are slightly higher at the front – I have even added little plastic wedges to do this. So often fridges and freezers are left slightly open by guests or cleaners causing them to frost up or leak, and it can be a nightmare defrosting a freezer on a same day changeover - having the fridge and freezer slightly leaning backwards means that the doors tend to self-close if not pushed fully shut in the first instance. If space is an issue, you can get mini table-top fridges and freezers and free-standing drinks fridges of varying size which do not even have to be placed in the kitchen.

Always provide a dishwasher if possible – slimline versions can be purchased for kitchens with limited space. The only type of accommodation where guests would not expect some type of dishwasher would be glamping pods or caravans. I do not recommend buying an expensive dishwasher as I find them more liable to go wrong, especially those with lots of complex electronics and extra features. They get a battering from guests and will constantly become clogged with food due to people not rinsing kitchenware before putting it in to wash. I find that the more basic models last longer in general.

Most guests expect to have access to a washing machine. I dislike washer-dryers as they are not very effective at drying clothes and sometimes overheat when they automatically go on to a long drying cycle – they can be very expensive to run as they are drying clothes from wet, although guests do like the opportunity to dry clothes. Again, it is not worth buying a top of the range model, but look out for machines with a good energy rating and a large drum, if your house sleeps more than four. I am incredibly wary about providing tumble driers for guests due to the fire risk. The filter should be cleared of lint and fluff after every use ideally, but this never gets done in my experience. You can try adding a very clear note telling guests to do this, or make sure you or your cleaner does this weekly, but if this is not possible then I would advise you not to provide one. Tumble dryers vented to the outside are a lot more effective at drying than condensing dryers. If you have a garden then a rotary drier or retractable line is very much appreciated by guests, although this is only helpful during warmer months. Also provide an indoor clothes airer. A dehumidifier can also help speed up the drying process. You can also buy electric indoor airers, although I don't find them overly effective, and they will increase your electricity bill. Occasionally guests have a little moan about the lack of a tumble dryer in my homes, but as most stays are a week maximum, it generally is not a big problem. If you have a country home with an Aga then consider a Sheila-Maid hanging clothes rack or Aga-top drying rack for clothes drying.

Small appliances that you should include are an electric kettle, toaster (four-slice for groups of four or more) and a microwave. I have had several microwaves blown up by overseas guests in recent years – I can only think that they have mistaken them for table-top ovens. It is worth keeping clear instructions nearby and a diagram illustrating that metal cannot be placed inside for this reason. Guests love a pod-type coffee machine, but they never clean them after use, and very few cleaners do as well. They also require descaling from time to time. I prefer to provide a cafetière for this reason. If you do provide a coffee machine then only provide basic coffee pods as the milky ones such as Lattes, mochas hot chocolate and cappuccino make more mess and require the machine to be cleaned each time.

List of kitchen essential items:

- Minimum of one dining plate per person, preferably two
- Minimum of one side plate per person, preferably two
- Minimum of one cereal bowl per person, preferably two
- Minimum of one pasta bowl per person, preferably two
- Minimum of one glass dessert bowl per person, preferably two
- Minimum of one mug per person, preferably two
- Minimum of one teacup and saucer per person, preferably two (teacups sound rather old fashioned, but some guests will complain if they are not included.)
- One egg cup per person - as above
- I advise buying basic white china for all of these – patterned can look old fashioned and fussy and can be difficult to replace. Avoid supplying any high-quality crockery in general as it will frequently get broken or stolen – I knew a woman who supplied Emma Bridgewater mugs at her holiday home and all of it 'disappeared' within a few months. Ikea, Wilkinsons or supermarkets all have good basic crockery and glassware. Always buy plenty of spares at the time and keep them separate so that chipped and broken can be replaced as and when needed.
- Two tall tumbler drinks glasses minimum per person
- One pint glass minimum per person
- One wine glass minimum per person
- One champagne glass minimum per person
- Cutlery – large knife, fork, dessert spoon and soup spoon – preferably minimum of two per person. I would only consider providing starter/small knives and forks for high-end lets as they get mixed up

together in the drawer. Also provide lots of teaspoons and a couple of large serving spoons. Preferably buy a spare set as sometimes the odd piece gets thrown away by accident. Steak and fish knives are advisable for a high-end let, but most guests do not expect them.

- Kitchen knives – inadequate knives are a big bugbear for many guests. Provide a minimum of four sharp knives of differing sizes, including a carver and bread knife, meat knife and a couple of vegetable knives. Kitchen Devil or similar are good and not too expensive, but I also include a couple of large Japanese style heavy duty knives – these can be very expensive, but you can buy perfectly adequate ones for £10-£20 from discount shops such as TK Maxx and from supermarkets. Serrated knives can be difficult to sharpen, so always have a few non-serrated knives and a knife-sharpener tool and check them occasionally.
- Minimum of four good quality pans of differing sizes – avoid providing very expensive or high-end brands as they will 'vanish'. (One of my friends had her entire pan collection taken). Companies such as Pro Cook are perfectly good and offer robust pans at a mid-range price (around £70 to £120 for a set of three or four). Cheap pans are a false economy as they will soon be damaged beyond use. Avoid non-stick pans too, (apart from frying pans), as they always get scratched. Try to provide an extra-large stock pan (good for boiling lots of vegetables for Christmas), one smaller milk pan, a mid-size pan and a large pan, at the very least. If you have space, try to include a three-tier steaming pan set as guests really like them for healthy steamed veg. I provide at least one large non-stick frying pan and one deeper frying pan with a lid (useful for curries and stews). It is also helpful to provide a smaller frying pan

for one-off eggs and pancakes etc. Tefal are generally very good for frying pans and the supermarkets often have offers on them.
- Kitchenware: minimum of two large baking sheets, one large roasting tray, one medium roasting tray, one muffin tray, one large casserole dish with lid, one large baking dish, one medium baking dish, one small baking dish (ceramic or Pyrex/glass is fine). A large mixing bowl, fruit bowl, large measuring jug, cafetière, teapot, hand whisk, citrus juicer, minimum of two silicone mixing spoons, one silicone fish/egg slice, one silicone or nylon large straining spoon, one nylon potato masher, one nylon ladle spoon, one nylon or silicone pair of tongs, cheese grater, garlic crusher, cork screw, bottle opener, large colander, large sieve, vegetable peeler, one glass worktop saver chopping board and at least one large wooden chopping board, preferably two. I avoid wooden spoons as they are unhygienic and get smelly and stained. I avoid metal kitchen implements where possible due to potential damage to non-stick frying pans. An electric whisk, blender and set of scales are also useful for guests. A slow cooker is also a nice touch, if you have storage room for it, as is an air fryer.
- Plastic draining rack and washing up bowl, preferably in a darker colour.
- Salt and pepper grinders with spare salt and peppercorns provided.
- Plastic cups, plates and cutlery for children, if you allow them, along with an easy-to-clean highchair or booster seat. A booster seat is usually adequate and can be hidden away in a cupboard when not in use.
- Sundries to include; a new sponge scouring sponge for washing up and a jay-cloth for wiping surfaces down

with each changeover, kitchen roll on a holder, foil, baking paper, dishwasher salt, washing up liquid, dishwasher tablets, rinse aid for dishwasher, olive or vegetable oil. A basket with some tea, coffee and sugar sachets (allow for a minimum of one per person, preferably two). I also provide some filter coffee sachets for the cafetière. Alternatively, a jar of coffee bags will also do. If you have a coffee machine then just provide some regular coffee pods – the latte, cappuccino and hot chocolate ones create more mess. I also provide a packet of biscuits, some hot chocolate sachets and two pints of fresh milk in the fridge. Provide UHT milk sticks if the property is going to be empty for any length of time between stays. I find that jars of sugar and coffee get spoiled by wet teaspoons being dipped into them, so I no longer provide these, but a jar of tea bags is often appreciated by guests. Amazon is very competitive although there are lots of online sites selling sachet goods for hotels and holiday homes too. You can create any kind of welcome basket for the kitchen depending on your preferences. A bottle of wine, some local bread and cheese, chutney, jam and crisps are all nice touches, but only if you have storage space or the time and inclination to buy these weekly. I simplified my welcome basket when I found that a lot of the food was being wasted. Biscuits and milk are usually sufficient. A bottle of wine or prosecco is often appreciated by lets aimed at couples as it is a nice kick-start to a romantic weekend. Supermarkets are very competitive with their pricing or buy in bulk from wine merchants online for decent discounts. Provide some laundry detergent or pods for washing machines, plus a basic set of cleaning equipment and a dustpan and brush for the kitchen. Soap scouring sponges are

excellent for cleaning Agas and ovens. I only provide a few laundry pods these days as they are expensive and people frequently take most of them at the end of their stay. Detergent is cheaper but the laundry drawer will need cleaning out more often as a result and is often overlooked. I am more generous with dishwasher tablets as I prefer that people use them rather than leaving a big pile of dirty dishes at the end of their stay, although I avoid the gel ones as they frequently burst or get wet in the bag – solid Finish tablets or supermarket all-in-one tablets are perfectly good. Always provide enough bin bags for your guests' stay as they will invariably put rubbish loose in a bin if they are not supplied.
- A radio in a kitchen is always appreciated by guests – do not buy a very expensive one though as it will get splashed with water, food and oil or possibly stolen.

Bathrooms

If you have a smart white suite, then I would advise against changing it. Although some of the edgier interior designers are re-introducing colour to their sanitary-ware or salvaging older coloured suites, (mint green, baby blue and salmon pink in particular), I would tread carefully here, as it is very niche, and a lot of people have not lost their horror for avocado-coloured suites yet. If you have a very quirky characterful property and a 1940s-70s coloured suite, then this may be an exception, although you will still potentially be deterring a lot of customers. I would always advise a very plain modern white suite for modern homes with very simple tiling. Modern suites can also work in older homes, although I always think a simple Edwardian or Victorian inspired basin and loo suits most older properties. Avoid any fancy or elaborate detailing on your suite and stick to chrome fittings – there is a fashion for brass and black metal fittings, along with black and glass crittal shower doors at the moment, but I imagine they will date quite quickly. White or neutral coloured floor and wall tiles are advisable, and be wary of grey which is on the wane, although it might be worth considering a dark grey or dark taupe grout with white tiling which won't stain as easily as white grout. I would avoid black or very dark reflective tiles if possible as they show up every mark and smear and need to be polished dry every time. Smaller metro brickwork design tiles look good in older homes, although they have been popular for a long time now, but they are very classic. Stronger colours such as blues, greens and yellows can work well in a period bathroom. I would consider a more modern tiling pattern, using larger tiles, for newer homes – simple linear blockwork in square or rectangular tiles or rectangular tiles laid in a brickwork/metro pattern. Avoid mosaic or grout-heavy designs, as they will get dirty and can be hard to clean. White and grey Marble-effect ceramic tiles and laminate are very popular at the moment and look luxurious, but again be wary due to it being fashionable. A laminate type shower or bath wall surround can be quick to install and cost-effective, it also avoids the need for grout which often gets mouldy and dirty – I find few cleaners really give it the good scrub it requires. However, you will need to make sure laminate surrounds are fitted by a reputable firm and that the seals are maintained around the edges as it will warp if moisture gets in behind it. It can provide a very clean, stream-lined look, however. Avoid polished, slippery floor tiles at all costs. Vinyl flooring can be a cost-effective way to update the look of an existing bathroom and can be found in non-slip versions, which is useful and much safer for older guests. Underfloor heating is another consideration, but the wired, dry type can be expensive to run, especially if guests are liable to leave it on, and the hot water pipe type involves a lot more work in terms of installation and may not always be workable with your space. All the DIY stores stock a good range of sanitary-ware, and I find Victorian Plumbing online very good for bathroom fittings too, especially in terms of price. It is worth checking out your local bathroom suppliers as they will often offer a fitting service and can help you design it.

If you can fit a bath in your room, then I strongly advise that you do. If there is not room for a separate shower, then I would recommend fitting a thermostatic shower above the bath. I would avoid cast iron free-standing baths in general, unless you have a lot of space to play with and are looking at a luxury finish – a lot of people find them cold and uncomfortable despite their aesthetic appeal. I would usually place the bath within a corner of the room which allows for a single opening shower screen door – avoid shower curtains at all costs as they ideally should be washed with every guest, but this is not practical and keeping them beyond one changeover would be very unhygienic – it makes a bathroom look and feel a lot less luxurious. If you want a large rainfall type fixed shower head, then I strongly recommend you also have a separate handheld flexible hose shower fitted below it as well – not everyone wants to douse their head for every shower and baths and shower surrounds are very difficult to clean without a flexible shower head. I generally find that a single hose handheld shower is perfectly adequate on its own, just make sure it has a rail so that it is adjustable in height and angle. Do not buy the cheapest tap and shower fittings as they will usually go wrong within the first year or two – look at the midrange instead and taps made by well-known and trusted brands. I have had a lot of trouble with generic branded cheap taps in the past and it is not worth the stress. Avoid single hot and cold taps if possible and choose a mixer tap instead – guests are much less likely to scald themselves this way.

Simple pop-up plug wastes are generally the easiest in terms of guest use and maintenance for basins – they sometimes get stuck or damaged over time, so always have a spare ready for your handyman. A plug with chain is okay for a bath in an older property, but maybe consider a press pop-up waste for a modern bath. Be wary of the pop-up type of bath wastes with a dial which operates it by turning it on the bath as the mechanism is usually hidden under the bath and it can be tricky to fix if it gets broken and usually involves removing the whole bath side panel first. This can be very problematic if you have a tiled bath panel, as I have discovered! I would always avoid tiling bath panels for this reason, along with the potential issue of accessing any leaks or pipework problems under the bath. An acrylic bath panel is always preferable in terms of maintenance and practicality. An MDF or wooden panel can look very nice in a modern or period bathroom, although you need to ensure it's kept dry and that any shower screens don't leak above it as they can swell with moisture and crack over time. It is usually worth giving these an extra coat of moisture repelling varnish on top for this reason.

If you are planning to host families and older people, try to provide a safety rubber bathmat, but make sure it gets cleaned every changeover as they can get very dirty and mouldy otherwise, and are often overlooked by cleaners. Always have an emergency spare in your housekeeping cupboard in case it needs replacing. Also always provide a fabric floor mat for guests to step on from the bath or shower. Most laundry hire companies can supply these.

Avoid buying any cutting-edge designer or unusual sanitary-ware – toilet seats are something I find myself replacing most frequently of all and if you have an unusual shaped toilet you will be very limited in terms of where you can buy replacements and it will work out a lot more expensive over the years. Go for a regular oval shape and then you will find that most universal loo seats will fit. Always buy soft-closing seats as they are practical, quiet and less likely to be accidentally slammed shut, as most people have them at home these days. I have tried providing more expensive heavy seats and wooden type seats, but they often get damaged. Measure the size of the hinge holes of your loo and make a note of their diameter – quite often it is the nuts and bolts or rubber plugs that require updating or replacing on the toilet seat after a few months, rather than the actual seat. I often find the fittings supplied with loo seats inadequate. I now put the rubber bung type fitting through the toilet seat holes as it creates a much stronger vacuum meaning that your loo seat is less likely to move – Ebay and Amazon sell them for a few pounds, but they come in different diameters and lengths, so measure up first. Toilet seats should be easy to tighten just using the screws or butterfly screws provided, but I have found over the years that whilst these should be tightened, you then usually need to hold them still underneath whilst then tightening the screw on the top side of the round hinge – i.e. tighten the top and bottom of the hinge screws at the same time, usually in opposite directions. You will need to remove the silver round hinge cover first. Always keep a spare toilet seat at the property as often a broken seat will only become apparent on a same-day changeover and a handy man might not be able to source the right kind on the same day. Plastic seats often get smashed – I think it is partly heavier guests using the loo as a 'seat' and plonking themselves down on it too suddenly, or possibly even standing on them – it is more likely to happen in cold weather when the plastic can become more brittle as well. Keep disposable gloves to hand as changing seats is not a pleasant job, but it is one that you will find yourself doing regularly. If you are expecting to host a lot of older guests at your property, then consider a toilet with a raised seat – it means guests can sit down and get up more easily. They do not look unusual or different to regular toilets. You may also want to consider a large walk-in shower for this reason as well, as older guests can struggle to climb into a bath. If you have a ground floor home then it is certainly worth considering as you will be able to attract guests of all ages, including those with mobility issues, who are a growing population. If you have a ground-floor or single-storey home and do not have space for a bath and separate shower, then I would definitely choose a walk-in shower as you will appeal to young and old guests. Make sure you provide a toilet brush and ensure it gets deep-cleaned and changed regularly – I personally think they are unhygienic things, but guests do expect them. I usually leave a bottle of bleach near the loo as it encourages guests to keep it clean but consider leaving it out of reach of children if your home is child friendly.

I would avoid fancy technology if possible – i.e. sound systems, bathroom TVs, Bluetooth connectivity on showers and baths, mood lighting etc., as it will be difficult and expensive to fix when it goes wrong and there is more opportunity for guests to get in a muddle with things or to complain if something is not working.

Spotlights are recommended for modern and traditional bathrooms, and it is advisable to have a mirror above your basin and additional wall lights above it or either side of it – guests frequently complain if they can't see themselves closely in the bathroom mirror. A shaving socket and shelf or somewhere to put toothbrushes and toiletries close to the basin is another must. Some bathroom lighting incorporates a shower socket so this can be helpful if space is limited. Do not supply glass or ceramic toothbrush holders or moveable objects as they will be dropped in your bath or sink and could chip them – cleaners usually forget to clean them as well in my experience. If you provide an extra shaving mirror, then ensure it is the type that is fixed to a wall.

A towel heater is usually best for heating and towel drying – consider buying a dual fuel towel radiator – this way it will work off the central heating in the winter, but your guests will be able to switch on the electric element in the summer to dry their towels. Most regular central heating towel rails can be adapted into dual fuel radiators by buying the electrical heating element and a t-bar adaptor for the valve separately. If you have a radiator which you wish to keep, then try to offer hooks or towel shelving above it. Provide as many hooks as possible in general – it is always worth putting at least two on the back of the door. Ensure there is a corner shelf or somewhere to put soap and shampoo bottles in shower cubicles.

For windows, consider a roller-blind or Roman blind– some companies offer them made in wipe-clean fabrics, especially for roller-blinds, which is very useful as regular fabric will tend to get dirty quite quickly. Be wary of wooden or metal venetian blinds as they can warp and rust over time. Some shutter and blind companies make their slats from PVC which would be better suited to a humid/damp environment and will look good in modern and traditional settings. Bathroom curtains are making a comeback in country and period homes so you could consider this – but make sure they're easy to wash. Simple solid panelled shutters also work well in period homes and a local joiner could probably do this for not too big a cost. Alternatively check out Jali.com which makes a whole host of different types of furniture, including shutters, from MDF, made to customers' requirements and sizing.

For sundries in the bathroom, I provide a small travel soap or two and a few mini bottles of shampoo-conditioner.

Amazon and Ebay have lots of different ranges for sale, although I also use guesthotelsupplies.co.uk and Out of Eden. There is a movement away from small disposable plastic bottles, so you might want to consider a wall mounted shampoo and/or shower gel dispenser instead, which can be refilled. I also provide a bottle of liquid hand soap by the basin. I like to buy fancier brands and bottles but often re-fill them with a more basic liquid soap or buy bulk refills which works out cheaper than buying new individual bottles each time – you can get them on Amazon and from the suppliers mentioned above. I avoid supermarket own-branded liquid soap as it always feels a little cheap-looking to me. TK Maxx stocks some very nice soaps and toiletries at reasonable prices and the supermarkets generally stock a good range of mid-range toiletries too. If you are offering high-end accommodation then you will probably want to spend a little more on toiletries, either via hotel suppliers or through buying bulk toiletries from a high-quality supplier. Check out local businesses as well as guests will really appreciate locally made good quality toiletry products and it is good to support the local economy and is usually more environmentally friendly too. Couples on a romantic luxury break do appreciate these additional touches and it will allow you to compete with the hotels. I would not consider offering dressing gowns and slippers unless you are trying to capture the luxury or couples' market. Most laundry companies offer dressing gown hire, and cleaning and hotel suppliers offer disposable slippers for fairly reasonable prices. A lot of hotel sundries are starting to be phased out by some businesses due to their impact on the environment – lots of single use plastic is frowned upon by an increasing number of guests, although hotel supplies companies appear to be adapting to these with more sustainable products being offered all the time. Some listing sites ask you to share ways in which you are reducing your impact on the environment and will ask you to answer questions regarding whether you provide single-use plastic items, although you are not obliged to fill out these parts of the listing. Always provide a new, full toilet roll on the holder plus at least two spares. Consider leaving four spares for short breaks as guests will not want to have to go shopping for more. One of the biggest complaints from holiday makers is a lack of loo roll, especially if they are on a short break and do not want to go shopping. However, do not give your guests full access to any bulk supplies as your costs will rocket, especially for longer stays.

Living room

Provide enough seating for all your guests and ensure it meets modern fire safety standards – older sofas will often not be suitable. Avoid pale fabrics and linens, along with fixed covers, as they will get dirty very quickly. You can buy washable throws and stretchy seat covers in various colours online which might help avoid this happening too quickly. I would advise against spending too much on sofas as they really get a battering from guests and can start looking tired quite quickly. I really like Ikea for sofas as many of them come with removable, washable covers and some come flat-packed which is useful for older homes with smaller doorways or limited access - they are very good value too. There are lots of online companies who make replacement sofa covers for various ranges of Ikea sofa, which means you can change the look of your sofa and have spares for when one set is being laundered. I find Bemz or Sopheria very good for these. You can go for fixed covers if you prefer and there are lots of sofa companies who often have good deals on – but you will need to steam clean them at least once a year, preferably by a professional company, although you could try to do this yourself with a steam cleaner. John Lewis, Marks & Spencer and Next all have good value sofa ranges too. I would avoid leather as it does get damaged quite easily – ink and other stains can be difficult to remove. If you do have a leather sofa, then definitely add a throw or seat cushion covers on top. Try to choose sofas in neutral or traditional colours, preferably without a pattern and try to avoid very light or dark colours as these will show up marks and lint. If you have a high-quality sofa in a period home then a traditional floral or damask type pattern might be suitable but avoid this in a modern home. Always add feather pad scatter cushions – at least two per sofa, with one square one at each end, preferably matching. Synthetic cushion fillings are rather rigid and cheapen the look of the room. An oblong cushion in the middle of a long sofa looks inviting too and helps to add interest. If you have a very plain sofa, you can add pattern and colour through these and it is not a big cost to change them from time to time as fashions change. Ebay, Dunelm Mill, John Lewis and Marks & Spencer are all quite good for cushions, although I also have cushion covers made to size in my own fabrics by a local company as well, if I am struggling to find what I want in the shops.

If space is limited, then avoid providing a coffee table as it will get knocked and will be difficult to clean around – a nest of tables or several smaller side tables is preferable in this instance. If you have room for a coffee table then provide one, plus some smaller side or sofa tables if possible. You might want to consider an upholstered or leather Ottoman or large square stool in lieu of a coffee table as they are very fashionable these days. If you do, then make sure you have a large drinks tray in the kitchen, or even leave it on the stool with a few books or accessories placed on it, as people will put drinks on it. A darker pattern or easy-clean fabric is also advisable. Provide lots of good quality drinks coasters which can easily be wiped-clean (rattan or cork gets dirty, so avoid these). Pale and medium oak furniture is very popular with a lot of holiday cottages – although it is a very generic look. So many holiday homes have oak side tables and two beige checked sofas with a matching Roman blind, an oak TV stand and generic modern chrome lamps. It is a safe, neutral look for a holiday home, and ideal for families and older people, but may put off younger guests. There are lots of oak furniture companies online, often with good deals and sales, and it is a relatively cheap way to coordinate all your furniture. Ikea is worth a look as well – they have some funkier looking pieces and a wider range of finishes including mid and dark wood veneers, vintage and modern styles and a variety of different coloured furniture. I would avoid pale melamine finishes and veneers for side and coffee tables as they do get damaged and stained – you may want to consider buying toughened glass panels for the tops of coffee and side tables, or just buying metal or glass-topped tables. Avoid pale marbles and stone-topped tables as they will get stained. Quite a few of the Ikea sideboards and tables come with glass tops which are very practical. Solid oak can be sanded and re-varnished or sealed. Do not discount your time in terms of putting flat-packed furniture together – a lot of the 'solid oak furniture' companies supply solid furniture with no assembly required. John Lewis, Oak Furniture Land, The Cotswold Company and Marks & Spencer are good for a mid-range budget and provide a variety of styles of furniture plus excellent customer service and an agreed delivery date.

For older or period homes check out your local auction house and Ebay. You can also follow and bid in auctions from around the UK on various websites including the Saleroom.co.uk but will usually need to arrange your own courier to deliver – Shipley and Anyvan.com offer competitive quotes for couriers. 'Brown' (dark wood) furniture is still ridiculously cheap, in my opinion - often cheaper than modern flat-packed furniture, but in the right home can look very classy. Try to match the period of your antique furniture approximately to the date of your home – it does not need to be exact but can look wonderful. For much older homes then I think you can get away with a mish-mash of period furniture styles, as long as none of them are too flamboyant. I would not buy expensive antique furniture as it will get a battering, but I think less than perfect old furniture has a charm to it and it will pain you less if it gets marked or damaged – it can often be sanded, re-waxed, re-varnished or French-polished in any case. The biggest headache with buying auction or antique furniture is usually in terms of arranging delivery and waiting in for couriers. Always check for woodworm and any loose joints first. Modern hardwood furniture made from sheesham and mango wood furniture can work very well in a period setting too and rustic Indian furniture can be effective too. It tends to be very hard-wearing.

You should provide at least one ceiling light in your living room and I strongly recommend that you provide at least two table lamps for soft evening lighting – it is so much more flattering than an overhead light. Always provide a TV, preferably a Smart one. You can convert a regular TV into a Smart TV by adding an Amazon Firestick or similar, although they can be stolen, and I have had this happen. Smart TVs do not have to cost a fortune if they are a basic model, so generally this is better than plugging in any additional devices. Guests appreciate access to Netflix and other streaming services – I usually provide Netflix and tell guests to feel free to sign into their own accounts, as so many people have it these days. I also remind them to sign out again, although eventually this will happen automatically. If you provide an account, you will need to re-sign into it every few weeks as Netflix has tightened up its rules regarding sharing on other devices. I also supply Amazon Video. Advise your guests that your TV is a Smart TV with access to adult content in case children have access to it. I have had guests apply parental locks in the past which have been hard to undo, so I would advise asking guests not to do so in your house information file. A games console can be very popular with groups of friends and families with children or teenagers, but do not spend too much on one, as games and controllers do go missing – Ebay and second-hand gaming shops are worth checking out for these. Always buy a spare remote control for your TV – they can be found on Amazon and Ebay relatively cheaply. They get dropped and damaged quite easily, so it is always good to have another readily available. Also ensure you have spare batteries for it.

I recommend providing good quality curtains or Roman blinds for your sitting room. If privacy (or lack of) is an issue in the home, then definitely also supply Venetian blinds, shutters or cotton voile panels. I advise avoiding floral or polyester net curtains. There are lots of online companies that can make curtains and blinds to your exact measurements. I find Curtainsandblinds4homes and Blinds2go very reasonable and they offer free swatches and a variety of heading types and linings, but there are lots of similar companies to choose from. Alternatively, ready-made curtains and blinds can be bought from shops such as Dunelm, Next, John Lewis, Marks and Spencer and Ikea and can be of good quality and value, although you may need to pay extra to shorten curtains to fit. Dunelm is very good for voile panels, curtain poles and voile tension rods. Polesdirect.com is very good for curtain poles, offering budget and high-end ranges. Jane Clayton is an excellent company for fabric, and they can make curtains, blinds, cushions and headboards in most of their fabrics to your requirements, plus they offer free fabric swatches, although it is generally more expensive – I would recommend this company for luxury lets. I would be wary of using florals in a modern home and advise that people be careful with patterns – small and subtle is usually preferable to large graphic designs and patterns. Older homes seem to lend themselves better to a mix of fabrics and styles. I think it is best to focus on texture, colour and quality of soft furnishings in modern settings rather than pattern.

    Coordinating some of your soft furnishings can give a room cohesion, but I always advise having at least more than one colour or pattern in your rooms. I have seen a lot of rooms with grey carpet, grey walls, grey sofas and grey curtains. It is terribly dull and is already looking dated. Try to use one neutral base colour for walls and/or carpets and add another stronger yet complimentary colour or two for sofas and curtains, then further contrasts of colour and texture through cushions, throws and maybe a rug. You do not want everything matching, or a kaleidoscopic headache of a room – I would say three key colours is ideal with one of them being used for a larger percentage of the room and all of them featuring at least twice in some way through other furnishings, objects or art, with maybe a fourth colour pop used on a couple of small extra items to make it seem less contrived. I would recommend neutral pale walls and flooring with a mid-depth colour sofa and curtains – either the same or complementary in colour. You can make cushions, throws and art reference the colour(s) of your curtains or walls or match the colour of your sofa and curtains. Cushions, lampshades and/or a rug are a very easy way to pull a colour scheme together if your curtains and sofas are different colours. You ideally need to place a flooring sample next to a paint and fabric sample before decorating and furnishing to see if the colours compliment or contrast each other in a pleasing way. Pinterest and Instagram can be very helpful for researching colour schemes and interior design ideas – try following interior designers or holiday let owners whose homes inspire you. I usually make my own renovation Pinterest board as it helps me to keep track of ideas, furniture, colours and objects that I want to incorporate into a scheme – seeing it all together on a board in pictures is very helpful and I tend to arrange it room by room.

Feature walls of block colour are starting to look old fashioned so I would avoid these. A lot of designers are painting their walls, skirting boards, doors, radiators and ceilings in one hue – it's called 'colour washing', but I would only advise this for soothing, subtle colours. Darker colours tend to work well in period homes, just ensure that the effect is not too foreboding as a lot of guests prefer light, bright rooms. A lot of people are currently using large swathes of very dark navy or charcoal black at the moment, especially in period homes, but I don't think this trend is set to last. Get hold of paint colour charts and check them at different times of day within the room to see which colours work best and ideally buy sample pots and paint small areas with them as paints can look very different in situ compared to on a chart.

Many guests expect some kind of sound system or speaker in the living room. I would provide a fairly basic Bluetooth speaker of a decent size if it is a family sized let. Include operating instructions in the holiday let information guide and clearly label the speaker with your holiday let name, preferably on the base, as sometimes equipment like this goes missing or can be taken by accident. I would never leave expensive equipment for this reason. I have had several Bluetooth speakers disappear over the years.

If you have a real fireplace or wood burner then it is worth providing a large basket of logs, a smaller basket of kindling, matches and some firelighters for each stay. I would not recommend having an accessible log store, even with an honesty box, as it will greatly increase your running costs and guests rarely pay for extras like this willingly. Instead provide details for the nearest places that sell logs. I would advise against using coal or allowing guests to, as it creates a lot more dirt and soot in the home. Some wood burners are only suited to logs – leave a clear sign near the fireplace if this is the case. Make sure you have a carbon monoxide and smoke alarm close by. Test that they are working regularly. Ensure your wood burner is checked by a HETAS registered tradesperson before you let your home to ensure it meets current safety requirements. Chimneys and vents should be properly lined and fitted to avoid any carbon monoxide poisoning risks. Be aware that if you have a single opening stove door that it does not open over rugs or carpets as this adds a fire hazard – it should only swing over a hearth or tiles. Generally wood burners with double doors are best for this reason. If you have an open fireplace, then make sure you have a good fire screen available to use for families with children – the same goes for gas fires. You may want to supply one for your wood burner as well as the glass and surround will be extremely hot to touch. I would avoid electric fireplaces as they generally cheapen the look of a room and will send your electricity bill soaring.

    Provide a few local books on the area, some general fiction books, magazines and local walking books or laminated printouts for walks if you are in an area known for hiking trails. Walking books often go missing, so printouts or laminated walking sheets can sometimes be more economical. If you do provide books, then I would recommend labelling them with the property name and address in case guests accidentally take them home. Second-hand walking guides from Ebay are acceptable as guests do not expect walking books to be in pristine condition. Families often appreciate a basket of toys and some board games – they are much appreciated when the weather is poor. I also leave the house manual and local information guide in the living room.

Dining room

If you have a dining room then it is worth providing as large a table as will be required for the maximum number of guests that can stay at your property, but it can be worth adding a few additional chairs, if possible, as sometimes family gatherings invite additional guests for meetups. An extendable table can also be a big bonus for guests for this reason. If you have spare chairs dotted around in bedrooms or other rooms, then guests can utilise these if needed. The dining table will frequently have hot dishes or bake-ware placed directly on it, even if you provide place mats and protectors for this or ask guests not to, so you need a robust tabletop which is preferably heat-resistant and strong or which can be easily sanded back or re-waxed if it does get damaged. Fine polishes or varnished finishes are not advisable. Scrubbed pine, zinc or safety glass are usually best. A regular varnished wooden table with a glass tabletop protector cut to size and mounted with little clear rubber feet can be another practical solution. Ikea sells some very reasonable glass-topped tables. You could use a PVC tablecloth if you are specifically catering for families with young children, but generally I would avoid this as it really stops a room looking sophisticated and inviting for other types of groups and they tend to get stained quickly. I do not provide fabric tablecloths as it is additional laundry to deal with and they often get stained. If you want to provide one, then you will need several and I would recommend choosing darker colours. You will also need a fabric table protector placed underneath to help keep it in situ and help to protect the wood underneath. Always leave a full set of place mats and coasters in the centre of your table – I would recommend solid wood or leather-effect mats as most other types tend to stain and get dirty. I would avoid providing real candles, although they can look lovely, especially in period homes. There are some quite good imitation LED pillar and dinner candles available online instead if you want to provide ambient lighting – you will find yourself changing batteries quite often though.

Again, have a central ceiling light, but also provide side tables with lamps, or a couple of wall lights as well for softer lighting. If you do not have furniture to put lamps on in the dining room then a standard lamp will work fine. Make sure any carpet is stain-resistant and easily cleaned as there are likely to be more spills around and under the table or choose a rug which can be easily cleaned. Ruggable sells rugs which can be machine washed, so might be worth considering.

Avoid buying chairs with fixed fabric seats as they will get stained – if they are a lift-out type of seat then maybe swap the fabric for imitation leather which is much easier to clean. It is easy to change fabrics on older lift-out chair seats and you will only need a pair of scissors and staple gun to do so. If using fabric tie-on seat cushion pads, then ensure that they are fully washable and have a few spares to hand. Do not provide bare hard chairs, otherwise guests will use your sofa cushions instead – people like to sit comfortably at the dinner table. Ikea, M&S, John Lewis, Amazon, Ebay and any of the oak furniture shops are worth checking out for reasonably priced dining furniture, as are salerooms. Beware of buying antique chairs – they can look lovely in a period home, but are often built for smaller, lighter adults. Chairs need to be *very* robust in my experience – any loose joints will fail very quickly after a few months of holiday let use. If you buy flat-packed chairs and tables, bear in mind that the screws will usually need tightening from time to time, especially in the first year. If you are providing a highchair, store it discreetly in a cupboard.

Study

Having a study is a bonus as it will encourage guests who need to work remotely to book. I have found increasing numbers of guests who specify this requirement as part of their holiday. It seems to have changed since the pandemic – the working-from-home phenomenon seems to have changed people's approach to leisure and work and it is not unusual for a family or couple to book a break at a holiday home but still expect to carry out some remote working. If you do not have a dedicated study room, try to create some desk or workspace somewhere in your home if possible. You can buy some great space-saving lift-down or fold out desks and tables these days – avoid putting them in the living room as this will most likely be in use by the rest of the family. Space for a laptop, a lamp and a couple of plug sockets is usually sufficient. If you have an outbuilding or summerhouse, consider insulating it and adding power to create a separate office. If you have super-fast WIFI make sure you advertise this clearly as it will encourage these kinds of guests to book. Good WIFI and a quiet working space will also encourage longer-stay and working guests to book your home.

Bedrooms

It is always worth buying as large a bed as you can fit into a room – even if this reduces the space for other furniture. Increasingly guests book accommodation with the best and biggest bed options. Expectations have changed a lot over the last ten years or so and many people much prefer at least a king-size bed rather than a queen or double. If your home is a tiny quaint cottage then people may be happy to make an exception, but generally bigger is better for most people. Super-kings are better still if you have room. If you have single beds ensure that they are full-size singles, not a child-size single. They should be 190 x 90cms – tall guests often check the size of our single beds before booking.

Bunk beds will allow you to maximise your number of guests but check the dimensions of them carefully as they can be smaller than a regular bed and adults will generally not be happy to sleep on them. I tend to find that they are often cheaply made and regularly require the screws to be tightened. If your home is aimed at families with younger children and you only have two bedrooms including a single, then it may be economical to have the smaller room set up with bunk beds. Some city centre apartments specifically aimed at stag, hen and friendship groups of young people squeeze in as many bunk beds as possible in each room, often with several placed back-to-back along a wall to maximise occupancy, but this is only advisable if you are confident that groups of young friends will mostly likely be your only guests and will fill up your calendar sufficiently.

A sofa bed in a living room can be an option for short stays and additional guests, but generally will not be as comfortable as a regular bed. I generally advise not providing more beds than the home can cater for comfortably as you are much more likely to get complaints and negative feedback – whoever gets the short straw of the sofa bed will be least happy of all. It creates a bit of a student-dig vibe and is more likely to encourage larger groups to gather and your home will suffer more wear and tear as well. If you have a one-bedroom flat then it could be worth considering as it will allow a couple with one child or a couple of young children to stay at your home, or a group of three friends (possibly four at a push if it is a large sofa bed), but do not expect to earn the exact equivalent of a two-bedroom property. You will need a shared bathroom for all guests ideally rather than just one ensuite in this case, which is more typical with one-bedroom flats. A sofa bed will increase bookings though and you should be able to ask a little more per night because of it, although there will be additional laundry and work for you or your cleaners in setting it up and putting it away again. There will be a little more admin involved too as you will have to check with each booking whether guests want additional bedding and towels provided (you may want to add a surcharge for this) and you will have to inform your cleaners for each stay. You must provide adequate numbers of bathrooms, seating and dining space for all of your potential guests even if you expect your sofa bed or top bunk to only be used occasionally. Possibly consider occasional chairs in bedrooms and an extendable dining table to allow for this if space is a little tight.

If you have several bedrooms at your property I would have at least one or two set up as a couple's room with a double or king bed and reserve at least one double room as a twin with two single beds in it – this gives you greater flexibility in the types of guest configurations and groups that you will be able to accept. If you have two double rooms and a single then I would strongly recommend that you configure it as one double, one twin and one single. If the house is large enough to comfortably accommodate more guests, and you are expecting families to stay regularly, then you could consider bunk beds in the twin and/or single room. For four double bedrooms I would provide two doubles and two twins. It amazes me how many holiday homes limit themselves by providing two or even three double/couple room configurations without any twin options – many of my holiday groups are made up of friends or relations who do not want to share a bed but are happy to share a room. Many couples, especially older people, prefer two single beds within the same room too. Divan beds with storage drawers are very useful for situations where storage is limited as you can put spare bedding, duvets or pillows in them. It is quite a modern look, so probably best in newer houses. If you do put one in an older property, then I would recommend adding a linen style valance to soften the look of the surround. A valance is also advisable if you want to hide an older patterned divan bed. I recommend choosing a sprung divan base (some are rigid) as it makes for a much more comfortable night's sleep.

If you have an older home then consider a more characterful bed such as an iron Victorian or Edwardian style bed, or a carved wooden, or even four-poster, bed for older homes. Ensure it is robust and strong though and up to modern mattress sizing standards. Cheaper timber beds will invariably start to squeak over time, even if the construction screws are tightened up. It is not a good idea to scrimp on beds too much. Upholstered headboards are very popular with divan and modern beds now, but I would avoid them if possible as they will get dirty and require frequent steam cleaning. Ikea is excellent for flat-packed good quality basic beds and has some nice wooden and metal models which can be helpful if access is limited. Other shops that are good for beds include Feather & Black (higher end and pricier), John Lewis, The Cotswold Company, Ikea, Marks and Spencer or any of the oak furniture companies. I would avoid very cheap beds as they will not stand up to guest use. Alternatively try Ebay if your budget is limited. Some of the older pine 1980s beds can be very reasonable and can be transformed with a lick of paint. If you buy a flat-pack bed, then remember to tighten the screws from time to time and try lying on the mattress every few months to ensure there are no squeaks from the bed.

Mattresses are one of the most important parts of your set-up – without a good night's sleep, your guests will not be likely to give you a good review or want to return. Do not skimp on mattresses, they are a worthwhile investment – cheap ones always deteriorate quickly, and the springs will be poking through before you know it. You do not need to spend a fortune, however – many shops now provide good quality mattresses at relatively reasonable prices. I like Ikea's pocket-sprung deep mattresses – they are competitively priced and incredibly comfortable, and I always get complimented on them – the Hovag range is particularly good, but choose medium-firm, never firm. People complain most commonly about overly soft or overly firm beds, so choose somewhere in-between. Avoid pure memory-foam type mattresses as they make a lot of people too hot. I always place a waterproof mattress protector on top of my mattresses – accidents will happen so you do not want a ruined mattress to deal with as they are expensive to replace, and you will be found out sooner or later if you provide a stained or dirty one. I launder the waterproof protector once or twice a year as it is not in direct contact with anything. I then top this with a regular mattress protector which is laundered more regularly. I provide synthetic duvets and pillows as a lot of people have allergies to feathers. Do not buy the cheapest bedding as it will deteriorate and go lumpy very quickly and tends not to wash well – Silent Night is generally good for pillows and duvets. Buy medium pillows and provide two per guest (i.e. four pillows on a double or king-size bed, two on a single). Always put pillow protectors on your pillows – they will keep your pillows clean and absorb the dust and sweat from guests and can be regularly laundered. If you are providing your own bed linen, then choose a plain white cotton-polyester mix as it washes and irons well. Avoid colour or patterns – it is easy to replace individual pillowcases and sheets if everything matches. Oxford pillowcases which are edged with a fabric border can elevate the look if you want something more luxurious. Your bedding will get stained and ruined eventually so you don't want to spend too much on high quality bedding, but likewise do not buy the cheapest as it will bobble and tear easily and is often very thin. Fake tan, hair dye and sun cream ruin bed linen and towels more quickly than anything else. Make sure you label all your linen with the property name, especially if you have them laundered by a company – I order personalised school uniform tags which I sew on for any of my own linen or you can use a laundry marker pen. Make sure you launder your duvets at least once a year and change pillows every couple of years. Multi-season duvets are a good idea if storage is limited as it allows you to create different togs for different seasons by clipping different weight duvets together or removing one – e.g. 4 tog for hot summer nights, 10 tog for spring and autumn and put together to create 14 tog for the winter. Alternatively provide 10 tog all year round but provide additional blankets or bedspreads for the autumn and winter. If you have a particularly old or cold house, then you are probably safe just to provide a 13 tog winter duvet all year round with an additional bedspread or blanket for winter. I would still provide a 7 or 10 tog duvet in a bag inside the wardrobe or under a bed in case guests get too hot and wish to change it. I strongly recommend that you have at least one spare single and one spare double/king duvet plus a couple of spare pillows at the home in case of accidents.

Provide a nightstand or bedside unit for each guest with a lamp or reading light – people want room for a drink and their phone at the very least. If space is very limited, then you can get small floating shelves in lieu of a bedside table and plug-in or wired wall lights fitted above the headboard or even beds with narrow storage built in behind the headboard.

Provide a drinks coaster on natural wood bedside tables or those that are liable to stain.

Drawers should be provided if possible – if there is no space for a dressing table then place a generous sized mirror above a dressing table-height drawer unit and a small stool to the side so that it can function as both. Provide a wardrobe if possible – if not then a row of hooks with some wooden hangers at the very least plus hooks on the back of the bedroom door. Try to avoid plastic hangers. A lot of modern wardrobes can be very deep, so you may need to look at getting a joiner or company to make some to fit if space is limited or if you want a modern, streamlined look. Alternatively, older wardrobes, particularly from the 1900s to 1940s tend to be much slimmer, with a short hanging rail facing the wall on each side so that hangers are face-on when the door is opened. (Modern wardrobes are deeper as the hangers usually hang sideways). You can buy these types of short slimline extendable rails on their own and convert any narrower cupboard into a slimline wardrobe by fitting them inside. I usually label my wooden hangers with the property name as they tend to go missing from time to time otherwise, especially skirt hangers as they are very useful and harder to come by.

If you have lots of space then also consider a comfy side chair, luggage rack, dressing table and full-length mirror. Some guests like to have televisions in the bedrooms, but I tend to avoid providing them as there are more things to potentially go wrong and with so many people having tablets and laptops, most people would use these in bed in any case. Parents with small children will generally prefer them not to have unsupervised access to a television. Always provide a waste bin, with liner, and a hairdryer in a drawer, labelled, so that guests do not accidentally pack it at the end of their stay.

Avoid very cheap curtains or blinds if possible as it will downgrade the look of your let immediately. Always provide curtains of a decent thickness, preferably with blackout lining – families with young children will be very glad of these and happier throughout their holiday. They are also less likely to put suction blackout screens on your windows, which tend to leave marks behind. Alternatively, if you buy non-blackout curtains you can purchase blackout liners online which can hook onto the back of your curtains, although you may need to alter their length and/or width. Keep things calm and neutral for modern lets with odd pops of colour if you wish. Richer colours and textures can work well in older period homes. A few feather scatter cushions and a washable throw on the bed, plus some framed prints or artwork on the wall will finish the look. Consider easy to wipe furniture or adding glass protectors on top of furniture – makeup, hot coffee cups and hair stylers all do damage. If you don't have either, then make sure you provide a heat mat for hair stylers and several drinks coasters instead.

Avoid over-styling any of the bedrooms into specific adult or child spaces as it will encourage different types of guests to book with you including families and friendship groups. A twin room needs to be neutral and suited to young and old. Do not put teddies or toys on the beds (why do so many holiday cottages do this?). Make sure each room has a ceiling light and at least one table lamp. I do not provide alarm clocks as the batteries are always running out and most guests use their phones these days - you will also have to remember to change the time when the clocks change. A radio can be a nice touch though – avoid the temptation to put a nice leather Roberts radio or similar on a bedside table. It looks great but will 'go missing' - so many new holiday home hosts make this mistake. I recommend carpet for comfort and quietness in bedrooms. If you want to avoid it then engineered wooden floorboards are probably the next most practical and attractive option, followed by luxury vinyl tiles, but always try to add a few rugs at least in this case, preferably either side of the bed, to stop it feeling too cold and clinical.

Providing a travel cot will potentially win you more bookings as families appreciate not having to bring their own as they can take up a lot of car boot space. However, cots are items which often get forgotten by cleaners and owners in terms of maintenance and I often find them to be dusty and dirty, which is not ideal if guests have a newborn baby. If you do provide one, ensure it is properly cleaned and stored between use. Guests do not generally expect you to provide a baby blanket, pillow or duvet, (baby pillows and duvets should not be used under the age of one in any case), but it is probably worth providing a waterproof sheet and a regular sheet to ensure that the mattress stays clean. Travel cot mattresses tend to be waterproof and quite thin, so the waterproof mattress cover is not essential, although it could save time cleaning the mattress as leaks will happen frequently with babies. Dirty mattresses are a serious hazard for babies so you must ensure they are properly cleaned.

Garden

If your holiday let has a garden, provide an outdoor dining set if there is room. Aluminium furniture requires little maintenance and can be left out all year – Ikea has some good sets and the garden4less website stocks many different types, including more luxurious models. You do not want to be staining wooden furniture every few years or storing it indoors during the winter if you can help it. There are some good wooden furniture dupes available on the market these days – 'Winawood' benches are attractive and look very much like painted wood but are actually made from a heavy type of textured plastic. A parasol is a nice touch for summer months, but choose a weatherproof material as it will frequently be left out in the rain. Avoid soft furnished rattan type furniture or furniture which requires cushions for this reason – even if the cushions are water-repellent, they will not last long, or will start to look tatty, if left out in all weathers and guests will forget to put them away.

A lot of guests really like barbecues, and it can give you the edge over your competition. However, guests rarely clean them after use and cleaners will generally have far much to do on changeover days to have time to scrub grills, so do bear this in mind. It will most likely be you that ends up with this job, unless you have a very hard-working cleaner. I do not provide one for these reasons. If you do wish to provide one but do not intend to clean it yourself, then add a very clear house rule that guests must clean the barbecue after use as you or your cleaners will not be doing it and make sure that you leave the appropriate cleaning tools and products at the home. Even with this house rule, most guests will still leave it in a terrible mess and subsequent guests will complain. I provide a fire pit at some properties which people seem to really appreciate as it allows people to sit around a fire outdoors for socialising and they can toast marshmallows over this if they wish. If you have close neighbours, then I would not recommend providing a barbecue or fire pit as the smoke may greatly inconvenience them. It will also encourage guests to linger outdoors until late and it is not fair to inflict this on neighbours frequently.

Hot tubs are the other big favourite with guests, but ensure you are not disturbing close neighbours and that you or your cleaning company have adequate time to maintain it. You also need to factor in running costs and health and safety for families with young children. A hot tub which is not properly serviced can pose a genuine and serious health hazard for people, in particular through the risk of Legionnaires disease which is spread through dirty warm water.

Avoid potted plants as it is another thing to take care of – you will constantly be watering them in the summer, or your gardener will have to do this. If you have an outdoor tap you may consider adding an irrigation system with a timer to water plants automatically for you. Be mindful of any local, temporary hose-pipe restrictions during dry periods. You can also buy solar-powered irrigation systems and ones which connect to water butts, which is a clever way of utilising rainwater. If there is space and the set up for planting, then definitely provide a few shrubs and flowers. Evergreens are your friend, providing some colour and cover all year round. If you have a very small courtyard garden, then consider slabs or artificial lawn. You will save a lot of money and/or time in this case by not having to mow the lawn or employ a gardener to do so. Do not put wooden decking down as it needs regular maintenance and can be very slippery if not treated frequently enough. If you are keen to have decking then look at the fake wood versions now available – they can be quite convincing.

If you have space, then provide a rotary clothes airer or retractable washing line – Minky lines are very good and easy to fit. Provide a peg basket or bag to encourage guests to put things away after use.

A few plain solar fairy lights or lanterns dotted around help to create a holiday atmosphere and seem popular with most guests. If you can grow some roses or flowers, then do so as you can then provide a vase of free flowers for guests during the summer months which are usually very much appreciated. Guests do like the finer details such as these and respond well to them. Avoid lots of knick-knacks and ornaments as garden decoration is very subjective and one person's taste is usually not another's. Try to avoid any lettered signs, gnomes or fairies etc. A stone bird bath and some bird feeders with some feed provided is a nice touch if your home is in an area frequented by wildlife. Add a bird watching book in the home if you have lots of avian visitors to your garden. Water features can be very soothing, especially in a city or town setting, but try to use natural stone or metal products with simple or classic designs, rather than resin or plastic which can look a little twee.

Gardening will be one of your larger running costs, after cleaning, if you have a medium or large sized garden with real lawn so do factor this into your financial plan at the outset and check gardener availability and costs in advance. Gardeners in rural areas can be very much in demand, from holiday homes or ageing retirees requiring their services, and from a lack of competition – a large garden can cost anything from £50 to £150 for a few hours work per week depending on the size, area and availability of local gardeners. Quite often gardeners will only offer to mow the lawn – if you want weeding and tidying the costs will be quite a bit higher. Finding a gardener who will fully manage the garden and keep on top of weeding and cutting back can be difficult and/or very expensive. You may still find yourself doing a lot of the tidying up, sweeping and weeding. Cleaners rarely have the time to help with any outdoor chores or sweeping and this sort of work is also often overlooked by gardeners. I regularly find myself tidying garden furniture, sweeping and weeding at properties with a larger garden and it makes the whole holiday let appear somewhat neglected if it is not properly maintained. My easiest gardens to manage have been smaller lawn-free ones with a few small borders. Do not underestimate the cost and time involved in a larger, natural garden. If you are inheriting a neglected garden, then you will want to get everything cut back and tidied before letting your home. If you have a simple lawn without steps or steep slopes or separate areas, then it may be worth looking at investing in a robot lawnmower. It will charge itself and can be programmed to mow when you want it to and will save money in the long-term. However, they are expensive and will require some maintenance and there is a risk of theft or damage from guests. Although unpopular with a lot of people, it can be worth considering an artificial lawn for a small garden, it will save you thousands of pounds over the years. Do not buy the cheapest type however as it will look a little too artificial. Wild gardening is increasingly popular, so you could consider going for a naturalistic approach with a larger garden, such as wildflower meadows with a simple path mown through it for access - the main meadow may only need strimming back a couple of times a year, although initially setting up a wildflower meadow can be quite tricky and time consuming. You could have a small tidy section of garden and let the rest go wild in order to encourage wildlife. As long as guests have a seating area and possibly a swing or room for children to play, they most likely won't mind some naturalistic untidiness.

A garden will add a new set of health and safety considerations. Make sure all fences, walls and gates are safe and secure. Also check whether trees are healthy. Ensure there are no poisonous plants growing if you hope to host families with young children. Some plants such as foxgloves and seeds from trees such as laburnums can be very toxic if ingested. If you have natural stone slabs then you will need to treat them with anti-algae spray at least twice a year, if not more, as they can become very slippery otherwise and it is your responsibility to keep guests safe outdoors. If you are planning to allow animals, it is best if a garden is fully enclosed with clearly marked boundaries - be aware that dog urine can discolour lawn. If you have dry stone walls, then warn guests not to let children climb on them as they can collapse from time to time. I would advise against supplying a trampoline or play equipment as sometimes holiday home insurance will not cover injury received on them and it is more work in terms of maintenance. If you do provide them then make it clear to guests in your manual and in advance that any play equipment is used at the guests' own risk and that you will not accept liability for any injury received on it. I would strongly advise against having a pond or body or water in your garden. If it is something you cannot easily remove, then ensure you fence it off completely. If you are lucky enough to have a pool, then ensure it meets all UK safety requirements and is also fully fenced off and enclosed with a safety gate which means that young children cannot access it unsupervised. You will want to invest in a very good filtration system and self-cleaning robot if possible. A pool will also require weekly maintenance and a full cover for the winter. If you have close neighbours, ask your guests to be respectful of them, especially when in the garden, and consider adding a curfew for noise outside. A security PIR light is always a good idea in terms of deterring potential burglars when the house is unoccupied and for guest safety when putting out bins or accessing the home in the dark. You can buy wired or cheap solar/battery run units which respond to movement or that come on for as long as it is dark outside. If your garden has an LPG or oil tank in it then make it clear that guests must not smoke or light disposable barbecues near it.

If your home is in a hiking area, have somewhere for muddy boots or a boot rack outside and a good quality weatherproof mat by the door. For coastal homes, consider somewhere to hang wetsuits outside or store beach equipment as it will save a lot of wear and tear and sand getting inside the home. An outdoor shower or a trug of water to rinse feet or wetsuits can also prevent a lot of damage and mess indoors. If you have any garden buildings or sheds, consider adding a padlock and adding the key to the guests' door key so that they can store bikes or beach equipment inside it. Cycling holidays are increasingly popular, so any kind of cycle store will help increase bookings. You can buy narrow metal units which are designed purely to store bikes, so these could be worth considering if outdoor space is limited. Bikes are high-risk in terms of theft so always offer secure storage for them. Clearly define any parking areas, especially if they are shared or require guests to park in a certain way. Make sure any paths or steps between your car parking and home are clearly lit and safe – warn guests of any steps outside the home before arrival as they may not be expecting them, especially if it is dark. Consider adding handrails by steps. Try to place your key safe (if you use one) somewhere dry and well lit.

Employ a window cleaner and ensure windows are cleaned a minimum of once every six weeks, possibly more in coastal areas. Things like gas and electricity meter boxes, windowsills and outdoor lights and porches often get dusty and full of cobwebs so do not forget to give them a wipe over from time to time as they are often the first thing guests see and help set the tone of your holiday home – if the outside of your holiday let looks a little neglected, it will encourage guests to find fault with the interior. Make sure garden furniture is cleaned every few months or so. A lick of paint on fences and front doors can quickly and relatively cheaply improve the overall look of your home's exterior significantly. Do not neglect these things as first impressions are very important. Finally, make sure you have a clear and attractive house sign and/or number. Ebay and Etsy are very useful for personalised signs in a variety of materials and styles.

General renovation advice

Heating and hot water

If you have gas, oil or LPG central heating then I would strongly urge you to fit a smart thermostat in your home. By linking to the WIFI and your boiler, it allows you to change the temperature remotely, to see the current indoor and outdoor temperatures and to set a limit on the thermostat. You can also set your hot water timing remotely if you have a tank. For guests it will just work like a regular thermostat with which they can alter the temperature, by turning it clockwise and anti-clockwise. I use Nest thermostats and Nest smoke and carbon monoxide alarms which I find very efficient and easy to use. It will save you a small fortune as some guests think nothing of turning the heating up to 25 degrees and then going out for the day or leaving it on high all night. Make sure you add a lock code to your smart thermostat – this way you can set a limit on the maximum temperature setting and select a nighttime temperature if you wish. You can do this on a PC but the phone apps are very user-friendly too. If you do not lock your thermostat, guests will alter the settings and add settings which the subsequent guests may not appreciate – any let I have ever visited with an unlocked Nest thermostat has lots of random programs set by previous guests meaning that the heating is completely erratic. The Nest website will have a list of qualified installers in your area listed on it. It is linked to Google, so bear in mind that if Google fails, unlikely as this may be, your heating and hot water may as well – this has happened to me once. Sometimes if there is a power cut you may need to reset the thermostat and re-link it to the boiler, but you can usually do most of this remotely. I recommend limiting the temperature to 21 degrees with a minimum safety temperature of 9 degrees and having the hot water heated for a few hours in the morning and in the evening. I turn the temperature down to 12-14 degrees from midnight and select this temperature hourly on the app until around 4 or 5 am in case there are any early risers who want the heating on – people will likely turn the heating up in the middle night if they pop to the loo otherwise. For New Year's Eve, Christmas day or any other special holidays, I push back the lower temperatures until the early hours as people are more likely to stay up later on those sorts of occasions. I also push back the timing for temperature reduction at weekends and for short breaks as people tend to stay up later then as well. I do not recommend using the Nest 'eco' setting. It works by sensing if there is movement in the house – this is via guests walking past the thermostat or your smoke alarms, but I find that it does not always pick up on this and will turn itself down when people are in the house. Also, do not use the ambient timing setting – this means that if you set the heating to 18 degrees at 6am, the boiler will click on anything from 30 minutes to several hours before then as it factors in the time it will take for the house to reach that temperature *by* 6am and guests may be woken very early by the boiler and radiators firing into life. You can ask if guests have any heating requirements, (i.e. for it to come on at a certain time in the morning) in advance of their stay. Some guests resent not having full control of the thermostat, but it is completely necessary in my experience. Try not to be too mean with the settings and if a guest tells you they are not warm enough or there's not enough hot water, then do raise the maximum setting or boost the water. I find overseas guests often struggle to get warm, especially in older homes, even on warm summer days, so I will alter my settings in this case and raise the maximum temperature. Make sure your loft is fully insulated and that you have double glazing where possible as you will save a lot of lost heat this way. Letterbox draught excluders and door trim draught excluders can also stop your home losing a lot of heat unnecessarily. Combi boilers can be very efficient for smaller homes and will mean that you do not need a hot water tank, but I would not recommend them for larger properties. Make sure your boiler and hot water tank (if you have one) are sufficient to requirements in terms of number of guests and quantity of water. Most water tanks will run low on hot water if several guests have full baths in quick succession, even if the hot water is permanently on – and I have to tell this to guests when they ask why there isn't sufficient hot water sometimes. I ask guests not to alter the boiler settings as I set them to the recommended most energy efficient settings and tell them not to switch off the broadband router at night as this will stop your thermostat and boiler communicating with each other. Ensure that you have your boiler and any other gas appliances serviced annually and that you obtain a landlord's safety certificate each time, as this is a legal requirement.

    You must install smoke and carbon monoxide alarms in your property. If you have a wood burner, gas fire or open fire, ensure that there is a carbon monoxide alarm in the room. Ideally you should also put one near your boiler as well. Smart smoke and carbon monoxide alarms will alert you if there is a problem at the house, which is useful if you are not around. Sometimes guests might light a smoky fire and the Nest app will alert you to the fact that the alarm has gone off, but it will then let you know when the smoke is clearing. It also tests itself weekly and has an emergency power back up with a light that glows in an emergency and when you walk past it in the dark. Wired smoke and carbon monoxide alarms are generally recommended for any kind of home or let property, but many will still require batteries as well, so always ensure you have spares in the home. Mark any fire exits clearly.

If your home does not have gas or LPG then you will be looking at electric radiators, underfloor heating or a ground heat source pump. Electric radiators can be incredibly expensive to run (as can gas and LPG), so choose as energy-efficient a model as possible. The very cheap ones do tend to go wrong quite quickly in my experience. I would recommend smart electric radiators for the same reasons as recommending smart thermostats in centrally heated homes – it will give you some control over the heating and allow you to save a lot of money over the years. Older programmable manual radiators and storage heaters can be fiddly to use and guests are likely to leave them on continually, on a high setting, so these are worth replacing with something more modern and energy efficient during your renovation. Ground pumps have mixed reviews and usually work best in well insulated more modern properties – it can be a big investment, but if you plan to hold on to your property for some years it may be worth investigating. Wet (hot water) underfloor piped heating is generally a lot more efficient and cheaper than wired flat underfloor heating. Not all flooring types will be compatible though.

If your electrically heated hot water tank has an accessible control panel, then I would recommend that you set it to come on in the mornings and evenings and ask guests not to alter the settings. However, they are still likely to, so you may wish to consider a smart device in this instance or making the control panel physically inaccessible in some way. Most hot water tanks have an immersion heater switch, so again ask guests not to use this unless it is an emergency, as it will work out very expensive, will make your water piping hot and will most likely be left on by accident (applies to gas hot water systems too). Label the switch clearly with the instructions not to use it. If there is an emergency regarding the control panel malfunctioning, or the boiler not working, then you can instruct guests to use the immersion switch to obtain hot water.

Always supply an emergency fan or electric heater of some kind in case your boiler stops working or in case your oil or LPG runs out unexpectedly, if you use them. I would ensure that any additional emergency electric heater devices are hidden in a way that means they can only be accessed by guests in an emergency – i.e. inside a locked cupboard with a number code padlock, otherwise they will be used regularly and dramatically increase your electricity bill. If your home uses oil or LPG then I strongly advise that you have a smart gauge fitted to the tank – quite often the energy supplier will have access to the reading remotely meaning that they will automatically schedule a delivery of fuel when it runs low, or you will be able to see the current reading remotely. Oil tanks often have a plug-in gauge so that you can see the oil level from inside the home it serves. If these options are not possible due to lack of an outdoor WIFI signal etc., then at the very least ensure you sign up for a monthly top up service of LPG or oil, meaning that you will hopefully never run out. Fuel tanks can look unsightly in a garden so consider planting some evergreen shrubs in front of it (not too close – you need to leave room for access) or putting a natural willow screen or piece of trellis in front. If you are on a system which requires you to contact the company for a top up once you are running low, always ensure you have a full tank well before Christmas or New Year, as there is always a run on it at this time of year and deliveries can get delayed, especially if the weather is poor.

Windows, doors and locks

I strongly recommend fitting solid internal doors, preferably with three sets of hinges (including a central hinge), rather than two (one top and bottom). Hollow construction doors are more likely to get damaged and can be tricky to repair. You can update internal doors with paint – if you have old wood veneer type doors then a coat of primer will allow you to paint over them, if you're not happy with the existing finish. New door handles can also improve the look of your doors – I would recommend changing any old tarnished bright brass lever handles for chrome, black, antique brass (older properties) or brushed chrome ones for more modern homes. Use adequate screws and fittings and be wary of fitting round doorknobs which can sometimes have tricky mini grub screw fittings which can come out over time. A surprising number of door handles seem to get pulled off and broken in my experience. I think this partly unfamiliarity with everyday mechanisms which differ from guests' own ones back at home – front door handles seem particularly prone to this, especially if they're traditional lever type handles. I think guests force them upwards, as some UPVC door handles work, to lock them, and end up breaking them. This is a real nuisance on a changeover day or if the guest gets locked inside or outside of the property, so make sure your front door is especially strong and possibly add a little laminated sign above it about the correct use of it – overseas guests will appreciate clear instructions for locking/unlocking doors. Never assume that guests will work out simple operations. Always provide an additional spare key somewhere on the property which can be accessed in an emergency – I often provide a second more hidden key-safe in case of emergencies, such as when guests have taken the keys home with them, or if a key snaps off in the lock, which also happens quite regularly. Be wary of Yale latch type door mechanisms which automatically lock the door from the outside when the door shuts as guests will invariably get locked out due to a gust of wind if they have not put the latch on. I recommend a deadlock instead where possible. You may want to consider a keypad entry system on the front door – Nest and other smart technology providers also provide these. I would be wary, however - if something goes wrong with the technology, you may have a situation which is much more difficult to deal with than finding a spare key. Key collection can be a major headache when setting up a holiday let within a block of flats or apartments. If the reception or main entrance operates by keypad then you can forward this number to guests, although many buildings use an electronic fob, so that can make things trickier. Concierges will be reluctant to allow anyone into the building without a key or if they are not the owner of an apartment and may not be happy to hold keys for your guests. In this case you will need to see if there is anywhere suitable on the exterior of the building or by a car parking space where you can fit a key safe. Do not assume that the building allows this – it may contravene the building's rules and terms. I often see blocks of flats with a whole host of unofficial key safes attached to a side wall, but I imagine they don't have official 'permission' for this and could be removed at any time. Also, you will have to mark your key safe in some way to link it to your flat.

I would not recommend that you fit bedroom locks in homes that are likely to be booked by families, although it may be appreciated by homes aimed solely at adults or groups of friends. If you have a housekeeping cupboard at the let, then I recommend you put a lock on this and keep a spare key for yourself and your cleaner, if you use one. Alternatively consider using a key code padlock. Some guests will happily help themselves to all your supplies otherwise.

Window safety is very important in holiday lets. On one hand, you should always provide a fire escape window on upper storeys of houses, which means that at least one window should open fully in case the staircase is blocked in some way. However, you also need to ensure that there is not a risk of children accessing fully opening windows. It is easy enough to fit restrictors to most windows – some can be locked, so I would do this and provide the key, out of reach of small children, to open the window fully in an emergency with a sign explaining what to do in the event of a fire nearby. Any low-lying windows on upper storeys which guests could theoretically fall against should be constructed from thicker glass – check that your window installer is aware of the legal requirements in these cases. Most flats and apartment windows and balconies should automatically fulfil any legal requirements regarding opening sizes, heights and access, but always check the mechanism and condition of them in any case. I think window safety is one of the most overlooked issues with holiday lets. I have seen numerous holiday homes with inadequate safety in this area with windows one, two or three storeys high at accessible height to small children or even with chairs or other furniture placed in front of them meaning that a child could very easily climb up to them – these windows often open fully to a street below with no restrictor or safety bars in place. It is a disaster waiting to happen – the law needs to tighten up legislation on this matter urgently.

Most UPVC windows should be fitted with vents these days to avoid humidity, condensation and mould building up in doors. If not, then I strongly recommend adding them. If you have wooden windows, most joiners can easily add a vent within the frame for you.

Paint, wallpaper and wall finishes

I would recommend modern emulsion paint for modern houses as it is hard-wearing and easy to wipe clean. Many paint brands offer different formula paints specifically for kitchens and bathrooms which are even harder-wearing and easy to wipe clean. I find that wall areas close to ovens and bins require frequent cleaning and paint touch-ups, so a kitchen specific paint is probably worth looking into. Older buildings often have walls that need to breathe, especially if they are lime-plastered, so look for chalkier water-based natural paints for these kinds of walls. Brands such as Edward Bulmer are specifically aimed for use in old and listed buildings using very natural, breathable ingredients, although they are a lot more expensive than regular paints. Eggshell paints look very nice on woodwork, but satin finishes are slightly shinier and more hard-wearing. Gloss has been very much out of fashion for the last twenty years although it seems to be making a come-back for exterior wood and period kitchens.

I would usually make the paint colour the starting point for any renovation. If you can keep the same wall and woodwork colour running throughout most of the property, then I think this works well and gives it flow and cohesion. 'Safe' colours that are fashionable enough at the moment without being too edgy or liable to date are white, mink, taupe, greige, (somewhere between green and beige), beige and off-whites, mint green, mid-green (not too bright), grey-green and olive greens, mid-blues, grey-blues (navy has been everywhere for five years at least now so avoid), darker teals (in moderation), aubergine (dark reddish purple, in moderation) and yellow (be careful though – darker richer yellows and ochres in period homes and a limited use of light or mid yellow in modern settings ideally). Brown and earthy pinks are having a moment in period homes and can look fabulous if used correctly but choose carefully. I recommend getting colour cards from Little Greene, Farrow & Ball and Mylands as they have some wonderfully inspiring colours. They are quite expensive however, so you may want to mix your own colours at one of the DIY stores. Dulux, Johnstone and Crown paints are starting to cotton on to the period/subtle colour trend so are worth checking out, although stock varies massively online and in store in my experience. Dulux offers some good neutral shades, but some are easier to get hold of than others, so make sure that it is readily available before committing to a colour. Some of the DIY own brands can be quite good if your budget is limited. I would recommend an own brand, or a cheaper brand, matt white paint for ceilings which will keep costs down and look perfectly smart and a white satin or eggshell paint for woodwork if your budget does not stretch to the more expensive paints. Plain white matt emulsion can be very effective on walls in modern and older homes too – you can contrast it with a slightly darker natural shade on the woodwork in this case which can look very nice and work out a lot cheaper.

I generally avoid wallpaper as it can be difficult to repair once damaged or marked. However, some of the modern brands are very wipeable and hard-wearing, so you may want to consider these. A neutral textured wallpaper can look stylish, especially in a modern setting – check out images of modern hotel rooms for inspiration. I would avoid bright, strongly patterned designs as they will not be to everyone's taste, will date quicker and need replacing sooner. You can sometimes get away with painting over existing wallpaper, although there can be a risk of it bubbling from the moisture of the paint. Woodchip wallpaper, popular 50+ years ago, is a nightmare to remove, but it can be done. It will take at least twice as long with a wallpaper steamer compared to other types of wallpaper.

MDF or wooden panelling is incredibly popular now. It can look very smart, but I suspect it will date horribly, especially in modern settings. Modern panelling is not usually real panelling in any case – it is usually wood trims arranged into rectangles on the wall, with the wall and trim then painted the same colour, sometimes with flat MDF backing behind the trims. The other popular type is shaker-frame panelling which tends to look very stark and angular and is currently also very popular. I would only recommend panelling for older homes in general, and then it should be done as real panelling preferably, with MDF or wooden boards and more traditional, substantial mouldings on top. Some online companies specialise in hand carved authentic oak reproduction panelling, but it is very expensive. Tongue-and-groove and shiplap wood or MDF cladding generally seems safe in most kitchens, although this could also go out of favour over time. It is also popular in bedrooms and bathrooms now and can look very attractive painted in period or neutral colours. I think it will always be acceptable in coastal and some rural homes, especially if it is something that was used historically in the local area.

Flooring

Carpet has been a little out of fashion in modern homes and apartments for some years, but it is starting to come back into vogue. Whereas light to mid oak effect laminate was all the rage 15-20 years ago, it is definitely on the wane. Neutral colours are probably safest if you do opt for carpet, although I would avoid grey, along with white, black, red, brown or yellow. Bolder, geometric designs and colours combined with high fashion or mid-century furniture and furnishings can look very exciting, but again, it might not be to everyone's taste. However, if done well, you might be able to corner the younger guest market who will enjoy uploading pictures of your funky rooms to Instagram. I have seen some very attractive vintage inspired interiors using olive greens, oranges and/or patterned carpet. I have also seen coloured carpet used effectively by designers such as Ben Pentreath in period homes where it seems to hark back to mid-century aristocratic interiors – dusty rose and olive green seem to appeal to designers at the moment. However, if you want to attract a wide cross section of society to your let then look for neutral, natural colours such as beige, greige and taupe. Avoid white, ivory or pale cream, as it is too impractical and rather startling in any case. Carpets can make living spaces feel warm and inviting and can greatly reduce noise, especially when used upstairs in two or three storey homes. Hard floors do show up dust quite dramatically, where it can pool in corners and builds up frustratingly quickly. Textured, woven neutral carpets are very popular in modern and period homes and some of them imitate natural seagrass and jute type floorings, which are very popular in period homes but not really suited to holiday homes as they are difficult to clean and will be ruined by a glass of red wine sooner or later. Propylene carpets tend to be cheaper, more hard-wearing and easier to get stains out of. They also won't get eaten by moths, as wool carpet can. Wool carpets can look classier, but some of the polyester carpets have improved greatly in appearance in recent years and they can be very difficult to tell apart from wool. Carpet Right and Tapi are worth a look, although smaller local companies can be surprisingly good value, especially with large off-cuts available at discounted prices which can be used in smaller rooms. I would avoid putting carpet in bathrooms and hallways. Use a decent underlay, especially in high-traffic areas. Avoid looped-type textures as they can be very difficult to get dirt and stains out of. A flatter, easy-to-clean texture or plain finish is usually preferable. Invest in a carpet cleaning machine if possible as you will most likely want to fully clean them at least once a year. Alternatively hire a professional carpet cleaning company. I find that the modern carpet cleaning machines are very easy to use, and it will work out much cheaper over time if you do it yourself. Carpets can be dry within a few hours, especially if you put the heating on. Always wear a mask if taking up old carpet as it will shed a lot of nasty dust and bacteria in the process.

Luxury vinyl floor tiles (LVT) are currently very popular, especially in modern homes and apartments. It is not cold to walk on and tends to be non-slip and hard-wearing and can be a very good substitute for real ceramic tiles or wooden flooring. Companies lay it tile by tile or plank by plank and often add 'grout' strips to their tile effect vinyl to increase its realism. It isn't too difficult to fit, but I strongly recommend that you get a professional in for the best finish. Amtico and Karndean are very good quality and have a reputation for being hard-wearing but can be pricey - many flooring and carpet shops supply their own version which can be much cheaper. I would avoid the pale grey wood effect tiles as they are incredibly popular and likely to date quickest. Flat vinyl sheet flooring can be a cost-effective flooring and comes in a variety of styles including tiles and floorboards but will not be as realistic as LVT and is not usually as hard-wearing. It looks a little cheaper and old-fashioned but could be a quick fix solution if your budget is tight or if you have a small utility or hallway area to cover. If you are planning to lay LVT on top of existing flooring or tiles then you may need to have your floors laid with a screed first to create a flat, uniform surface.

Engineered wooden flooring is usually easier to lay, cheaper and more practical than real wood flooring. It is less affected by atmospheric changes and humidity. Generally, the thicker the wood, the more expensive. This will allow you to sand it back and re-seal it over the years, whereas a thinner engineered wood will not withstand as many sand backs and as much wear and tear. Darker floors and wood are becoming more popular again after many years out of favour and you will find engineered wood flooring in every tone and type of wood. I would avoid very dark flooring as it tends to show imperfections and dust more easily. Small areas of damage including dents and holes can usually be made good with a little wood filler without having to sand the entire floor back, but you may find if the floor gets a lot of heavy use that it might require a full refurbishment after five to ten years. I would avoid using engineered wood in kitchens and bathrooms as it should not be regularly exposed to water and moisture and will deteriorate more quickly in a kitchen with the odd glass and bowl being dropped on it. High heeled shoes can damage it as well. LVT and engineered wood can often have underfloor heating fitted underneath them, although I have stayed in properties where the sound of engineered wood expanding and contracting from the underfloor heating causes it to snap and crack quite loudly. Alternatively, some people consider laminate wood flooring an ideal solution, being relatively cheap, easy to fit and generally more hard-wearing than wood, and not quite as synthetic as LVT flooring. It was very popular around twenty years ago, then seemed to fall out of favour slightly as engineered wood became more popular. Engineered wood is slightly more liable to damage so this may be why laminate wood flooring is becoming popular again for many landlords and property owners. Again, avoid using it in humid and wet environments.

 I would recommend ceramic tiles where possible for hallways, kitchens and bathrooms in most properties, or LVT, but I would be more inclined to use LVT in modern homes rather than older homes. I think it is best to see tiling in the flesh, so it is worth checking out any local tile showrooms or buying sample tiles from online sellers. Unlike natural stone floors, ceramic will rarely require sealing, and is easier maintenance and will not get as stained or damaged as natural stone floors. It can be a little cold on feet, so consider some underfloor heating in kitchens and bathrooms if possible. Avoid underfloor heating being fitted under fridges, freezers and where you will place a bin (basically the edges of a kitchen). Some ceramic tiles mimic wood planks which can be a compromise when you want a maintenance-free hard floor with the charm of wood. Try to buy anti-slip tiles where possible, especially for bathrooms. Consider using a mid to dark grout as white and ivory coloured flooring grout will get very dirty and require frequent cleaning or covering up with grout paint. If you are keen to use natural stone flooring, I would consider a darker slate if possible. Limestone and marbles can look beautiful but will get damaged and stained. There are products which can help protect them and repair them, but quite often if the polished surface is damaged (easily done with acidic drinks or cleaning products) then it will require re-polishing and sealing usually by a professional company such as Tile Doctor.

Whichever type of flooring you choose, *always* ensure that you buy some spare tiles, be it ceramic, LVT or laminate wood, in case of damage that cannot be repaired.

If you have hard floors in living rooms or bedrooms, then I would recommend adding a rug or two to soften the effect and to make the spaces feel warmer and more welcoming. Do not forget to use rug grip which is suitable for hard floors. I find the Rugseller online very good for all different budgets and types of rugs. Alternatively, if you have an older home, check out local auctions for unique old rugs which can be very reasonably priced. They may require specialist cleaning though, so do not forget to factor this into your costs. If your home allows pets, then definitely consider washable rugs – Ruggable sells a large range of rugs in different styles which can be machine washed. Remember that some rubber backings and rug grips can discolour vinyl flooring over time.

Safety and security

Along with smoke and carbon monoxide alarms, it is usually a good idea to add a fire blanket for kitchens and a small fire extinguisher somewhere in the home. Add clear warning notes about any potential dangers in the home.

Something often overlooked by holiday lets and hotels is the danger posed by toppling furniture. There have been numerous tragic cases of young children pulling furniture or furnishings down on to themselves. I always recommend attaching chests of drawers, shelving units, dressers and wardrobes to walls so that they cannot be pulled over. Lighter weight flat-packed furniture is more likely to be pulled over, and Ikea usually provides 'anti-topple' fixings to avoid this danger, but you will want to consider using this for most tall, slim furniture. Do not ever have free standing mirrors if you plan to rent your home to families. Ensure any heavy mirrors or fittings are adequately supported and affixed to walls.

The most common dangers in and around a home, as already outlined, include slippery algae-covered stone paving, slippery untreated decking, fully-opening accessible windows on upper storeys, fireplaces without screens and slippery internal floor tiles. Another consideration is steep or uneven steps where people are more likely to misplace their footing. Older homes tend to have steeper, more uneven internal steps. In this case, I think you must fit carpet or a securely fitted stair runner at the least to lessen the chances of a serious fall, along with a handrail. If there is insufficient room for a protruding handrail, then consider a rope rail affixed at points on the wall. Hard wooden or stone steps represent quite a serious risk for young and old.

I think that candles are an unnecessary risk and would never provide them, apart from for emergency use during a power cut – have them somewhere only accessible via a code in this case and ensure that any candle holders are robust and fit the candle properly. Alternatively, and for greater safety, provide a couple of emergency battery or wind-up lanterns in case of a power cut. Holiday makers are more likely to use candles than regular homeowners as they want to create a nice atmosphere over meals and when relaxing. If you want to provide ambient lighting then consider indoor fairy lights or LED faux candles which are increasingly convincing, many with moving, flickering flames.

I typically avoid burglar alarms if possible as they complicate matters in terms of cleaners, tradespeople and guests potentially setting them off. Even if they are not in use, their battery can run out over time, or they can malfunction and go off in any case and can be difficult to stop (as I have discovered). A security light, good quality door locks and secure fencing and boundaries can greatly decrease your chance of being burgled in any case. Always remind guests and cleaners to close all windows and doors after stays or changeovers. If you have glass patio doors, always ask guests and cleaners not to leave door keys inside them as burglars will think nothing of smashing one of the door panes in order to unlock the door from the inside. If you have security cameras at the property, then you must ensure that they do not point into neighbours' homes or gardens, and you must forewarn guests via your holiday let listing and/or website as well as having a notice at the property. A smart doorbell, such as the 'Ring' doorbell, can alert you to activity by the front door and notify you of any arrivals or deliveries, but not everyone will appreciate being filmed. You could consider only having it switched on when the property is vacant, for security purposes. If you have any CCTV at your property, it must be clearly marked and you must forewarn guests and include it on your listings information.

If your property is very remote and rural with no mobile phone signal, then you should provide an emergency landline phone and specify that it is for use in emergencies only. Ensure you provide the phone number for the property in advance so that guests' families and friends can contact them if necessary. Do this, even if your property has WIFI, as guests need to be able to contact the emergency services.

Decor and wall art

Avoid the temptation to overdo ornaments and wall art. Some tasteful framed prints or original art, especially artwork depicting local landmarks or scenery, is always a nice touch, but two or three pictures per medium sized room should be more than adequate. The Range is good for reasonably priced frames, as is Ikea, Amazon and Ebay. If you have any good quality photographs, consider using one of the many online printing companies to create larger good quality paper prints which you can then frame. Avoid very cheap plastic frames with Perspex glass – they will cheapen the look of your interior for the sake of a relatively small saving. Landscapes and still life are safest in terms of subject matter, avoid any avantgarde figurative art if possible. Do not be tempted to buy any of the jokey or 'life affirming' slogan type hanging signs - they are a pet hate for many people. Avoid rainbow-coloured Highland cow art, even if your home is in Scotland. If you have a coastal home try not to overdo a nautical theme – i.e. twee seaside ornaments including lifebuoys, mermaids, shell art, coastal slogan signs and so on. A large glass vase filled with local shells or pebbles and some nice local landscapes is better. Likewise, avoid cartoonish sheep and rainbow highland cow art for rurally located homes; although popular with lots of people, not everyone will appreciate it. It can be fun buying up lots of cheap ornaments and decorations, but judging by guest feedback on negative reviews, guests find it very annoying if the home is cluttered with these knick-knacks, especially if basic items or cleanliness are lacking, by contrast. It is another thing for you or your cleaner to dust as well.

Feather scatter cushions and throws or blankets on beds and sofas will make the home more welcoming but remember to launder them from time to time. Ensure that throws and blankets are shaken out after each changeover at the very least and possibly sprayed with antibacterial fabric freshener if possible. Synthetic cushion inners are rather rigid and cannot be plumped up luxuriously like feathers. Try to buy cushion inners that are at least an inch smaller than the actual cushion cover for a full, luxurious cushion. Some soft furnishings need gentle washing or dry cleaning, so bear that in mind in terms of cost and time. Synthetic materials such as shiny faux silk, faux suede and velvet, scratchy polyester and microfibre should be avoided, if possible, as they will cheapen the look of your interiors. Try to stick to cotton velvets, cotton and linen. Avoid real silk as it will get stained and is hard to clean. Avoid dry clean-only heavy bedspreads as they will get dirty and will be cumbersome and expensive to dry clean. If it is not spotless you are opening yourself up to a higher chance of complaints and negative reviews.

Try to provide at least one full-length mirror in your home and additional smaller mirrors in most bedrooms and bathrooms. A large decorative mirror in a small living space can help create an illusion of spaciousness – ensure you use several strong screws to take its weight though.

Lots of holiday homes use fake flowers and floristry arrangements, but I would avoid them as they rarely look convincing and tend to gather dust. Some fresh flowers and leaf stems from a garden can be a lovely touch, but unless your home is aiming at a luxury market, guests do not generally expect fresh flowers. A good compromise can be dried flowers and grasses which are having a bit of a renaissance now with online companies offering a wide variety of products which can be mixed and matched into your own all-year round arrangement. They will probably need replacing after a year or two. A combination of dried flowers, dried eucalyptus and corn or decorative grasses can look good, especially in a country setting. Something starker, such as plain eucalyptus or grasses, is probably better suited to a modern home or apartment. Avoid real plants as they will not be sufficiently watered or cared for.

Key points

- Do not underestimate renovation costs – always allow a contingency fund. Even full house surveys miss things.
- Holiday homes take a battering from guests – you need finishes and furnishings to be as robust and damage-proof as possible, especially if you allow pets or are in a coastal location.
- Consider keeping existing bathrooms and kitchens and updating the tiling, appliances, taps, flooring and decoration. There are companies who specialise in bathroom and kitchen facelifts, and you can buy replacement drawer fronts and cupboard doors from many DIY and online stores.
- Keep things fairly neutral and light. Avoid strong dark colours. Try to use at least three complimentary colours in your scheme with one being a neutral colour that can be carried throughout the home. Colour can be added via accessories which can be changed more easily than sofas and curtains.
- Avoid clutter, ornaments and decorative wall signs.

- Avoid grey or too much grey in your colour scheme.
- Avoid wallpaper.
- Free standing kitchen appliances are always preferable to integrated ones.
- Use ceramic or LVT flooring in kitchens and bathrooms where possible. Avoid natural stone finishes that will get marked and stained.
- Avoid pale quartz and marble kitchen worktops as they will get stained.
- Try to provide easy-to-clean and heat resistant furniture.
- Check that your boiler and any gas appliances are safe – you will need a landlord's safety certificate supplied as part of the boiler service.
- Leave appliance manuals for guests in a folder – any tricky oven or grill instructions should be noted nearby.
- Install as large a fridge and freezer as possible.
- Buy beds in as large a size as possible – many people expect king-size these days. If you have room for a super king-size bed, then consider buying one.
- Do not present any rooms as children's rooms.
- If you have more than one double room, then ensure at least one is set up as a twin room.
- Always put waterproof mattress protectors on beds with a regular protector above them which can be washed more regularly. Mattresses will be quickly ruined otherwise.
- Buy decent quality mattresses, preferably pocket sprung. Avoid memory foam.
- Ensure your kitchen is as well-equipped as possible.
- Provide decent pans and knives. Avoid non-stick pans except for frying pans.

- Provide silicone or nylon kitchen utensils to avoid pans being scratched - they are much more hygienic than wood too.
- Install a bath if there is room. If there is no room for a separate shower, then install a thermostatic shower over the bath. If your home is single level or a ground floor dwelling, then consider a walk-in shower instead of a bath.
- Do not buy cheap taps, they always malfunction within a year or so.
- Avoid tiled bath panels.
- Buy a standard sized and shaped toilet plus at least one spare toilet seat. Buy rubber bung toilet seat hinge fittings for a more secure seat.
- Provide adequate seating for all your guests – do not try to squeeze in more beds or sofa beds if the home can't comfortably accommodate additional guests.
- Be wary of sofa beds – it can be worth considering for a one-bedroom property but ensure there is enough living space and an easy bathroom arrangement if you do.
- Consider buying sofas with washable covers and buying a spare set of covers and/or additional seat covers.
- Check out Ebay and auction houses for furniture bargains.
- Always supply table lamps in every room. If there is a shortage of surfaces, provide a standard lamp instead. Ceiling lights can be too harsh and bright.
- Most people expect a Smart TV these days.
- Do not leave any expensive equipment and small appliances at the property.
- Do not include any portable items of sentimental or high value.

- Have any fireplaces and wood burners checked by a HETAS registered installer to check they are safe and that chimneys are properly lined.
- Always fit wired-in smoke and carbon monoxide detectors and ensure you have them in rooms with fireplaces and wood burners. You can buy smart detectors which notify you of any problems via an app. I use Nest smoke and carbon monoxide alarms.
- Provide local books and information, general fiction books and some games and toys for families.
- Buy robust dining chairs, preferably with easy to clean seats or cushions.
- A study area or desk is worth adding if at all possible.
- Install blackout-lined bedroom curtains or blinds.
- Provide a dining set for gardens if you have room. Avoid potted plants unless you have an automatic irrigation system in place.
- Barbecues are very popular with guests. Consider a noise curfew if you have close neighbours.
- Provide an outdoor rotary or retractable washing line and clothes pegs if at all possible.
- Avoid wooden decking. Ensure it is properly maintained if you have it.
- Fence off any open water, ponds or swimming pools.
- Gardening will be one of the bigger running costs if you have a natural lawn. Check the costs and availability of local gardeners before committing to a home with a medium or large sized garden. Many gardeners will not weed or tidy.
- Bike stores are very popular with many guests.
- Smart thermostats are very useful for holiday lets – you can limit the temperature and set it to turn down at night and control the hot water. Remind guests not to

switch off the router at night otherwise the water tank may not be heated.
- Consider installing smart energy efficient electric radiators and/or underfloor heating if you don't have gas at the property.
- Solid internal doors are always preferable to hollow build doors and much less likely to be damaged. Add hooks to the back of all bedroom and bathroom doors.
- Consider adding instructions on front door locks and handles as they do get broken quite frequently through misuse. Keep a spare front door handle and lock in case a replacement is required at short notice. Avoid latch self-locking type front door mechanisms as guests will regularly lock themselves out by accident.
- Set up a second hidden emergency key.
- Consider fire escape windows on upper storeys but ensure that children cannot easily access any fully opening windows.
- Ensure windows have vents where possible.
- Use robust wipe-clean paints in hallways, stairwells, bathrooms and kitchens. Consider chalkier breathable paints for older properties.
- Avoid strong vintage looks or quirky styles unless you are adept at interior design.
- Consider polypropylene carpets instead of wool as they will be harder wearing and moth resistant.
- Avoid figurative or quirky art.
- Only consider a hot tub if someone can maintain it weekly.
- Choose low maintenance garden furniture and avoid furniture which requires large cushions.
- Heating will be one of your other biggest costs, along with other utilities and cleaning costs. Try to maximise your property's heat efficiency.

Chapter Ten
Top tips for running your let

House manual

I recommend providing an extensive local information guide for your holiday home as well as a house manual. You will save yourself a lot of time and bother if guests can access all relevant information in one place. For your house manual you can either print out the information and put it inside one of those A4 presentation files with plastic sleeves for each page or get a laminator and laminate the information. The advantage of laminated information is that you can easily wipe it over if it gets dirty and it won't get crumpled either. I find that sometimes paper information is removed from the sleeved A4 file and gets stained and crumpled. However, it is quicker and easier to replace any outdated information with the plastic file option. Some hosts simply leave one sheet of A4 paper with all key information listed on it, although it will be minimal at one page and will most likely need replacing each changeover. It is worth starting your manual with an introductory short 'welcome' message along the lines of thanking the guest for booking with you, hoping they have a wonderful stay and not hesitate to get in touch if they have any problems or questions.

What to include in your house manual:

- Your contact information, or the agency's, if you use one, preferably with an out-of-hours emergency number. Also provide an email address and ask that

guests email you in the first instance and to only call in an emergency. I very quickly regretted telling guests not to 'hesitate' to contact me by phone if they had any questions or problems as some people would constantly call about every little thing.
- Basic important house rules, e.g. no smoking, pets, shoes off in the hallway etc. Any requests regarding noise curfews and neighbours. This will be replicated in your terms and conditions, but anything important should also be repeated here.
- WIFI network and password. Also print this out and put somewhere prominent so your guests do not all have to keep accessing the file.
- Instructions for check-out – i.e. where to put the keys and requests to lock all doors and windows, wash up kitchenware and put out the rubbish and recycling, for example. Give check-out times here as well. Remind guests that they must vacate by the time requested as they may be charged otherwise for your cleaner's time and if their late departure impacts on the arrival of any subsequent guests. Remind guests to check that all drawers and wardrobes have been emptied, and that any food is removed from the fridge, freezer and cupboards. So many guests think they are doing you or your cleaner a favour by leaving food and drink behind, but it is usually just another thing to deal with and is not appreciated. I find a simple bullet-point list of things to do on departure day works well at reminding guests of these expectations.
- Instructions on how to use the heating and hot water. You cannot make these clear enough in my experience. I have had people claim they cannot use the heating when I can see via my smart thermometer app that they haven't even tried turning it to adjust it. You need to

give them simple step-by-step instructions, telling them where the thermostat is and that you turn it clockwise and anti-clockwise, for example. Some guests may find it slightly patronising, but you have to allow for guests that are not familiar with some things.
- Bins and recycling instructions – I also use stickers on the bins themselves so that overseas guests in particular know what goes where. Let them know what days bins and recycling are collected and if they need to move them out for collection. Generally, guests will forget, so it's always best to have bins and recycling permanently placed in a roadside location where they will automatically be emptied, unless you are around to always do it.
- Information on parking and on bike storage if you provide it.
- Any appliance information including cleaning and maintenance information – i.e. how the TV, washing machine, dishwasher and oven works. Always warn guests about access to adult content on the TV if you have access to Netflix or similar, in case they have children. Include any important instructions for any unusual fittings and appliances, especially things like a macerator toilet system which will get blocked if used incorrectly. If it's something that will cost a lot of time and money to fix if it goes wrong, then ensure you also have a sign up by the appliance itself, preferably with an illustrated warning or user diagram for non-English speaking guests. If your oven is a little fiddly to use (I find modern electric hobs not overly easy to use), then give clear instructions here and put up a sign up next to the oven. I also tell guests where my appliance folder is, where I keep any appliance manuals. If you have an Aga, keep a separate user manual to hand in the

kitchen for this as most guests have no idea how to use them – and even those who do are likely to play with the controls and trip the fire valve by accident.
- Fire safety – let the guests know what smoke and carbon monoxide alarms you have and what to do in the event of a fire. Tell them about any fire escapes and the location of your fire blanket and extinguisher if you have them.
- The location of the fuse box and any operating instructions for it. What to do in the event of a power cut – the location of emergency lanterns or candles.
- Give the location of the water stop cock.
- Give clear instructions on using the wood burner or fireplace use if you have one.
- Give clear instructions and safety information on using any outdoor equipment, especially hot tubs. Re-iterate that you cannot be held responsible for any injury received on equipment and that guests use it at their own risk.
- List any potential health and safety dangers to be aware of, especially for children and politely remind your guests to monitor their children in certain situations.
- Medical and health emergency information including the nearest doctor, hospital and medical advice phone numbers, followed by fire and police emergency contact information.
- The nearest dental practice with contact details.
- I also include a section on breakages, damage and low supplies as part of my house information, even though it is reiterated in my terms and conditions, as guests rarely read these. I add something along the lines of; 'We understand that accidents happen. Please inform us of any breakages so that we can fix/replenish before the next guests' arrival. If any items are broken or any

supplies running low, please let me know. Spare bulbs can be found in the utility room cupboard and spare batteries in the kitchen drawer. If items are missing or appear damaged through excessive force or deliberate misuse, we reserve the right to request payment to cover incurred costs.' It is very helpful if guests can replace a dead battery or light bulb as and when it happens, so make sure your guests know where these things are – cleaners will rarely notice if something like this needs attention. It means that guests are less likely to complain or contact you as well if something needs attention. It is worth leaving some basic tools such as screwdrivers, a radiator key and Allen keys in case something simple needs repairing – some guests will immediately demand that you fix a wobbly chair, whereas others will tighten the screws on it themselves and never mention it. I never bill guests for broken glasses or odd pieces of crockery and view it as wear and tear, although some guests will offer to pay or even leave some cash on the table at the end of their stay. The clause about costs incurred through misuse or excessive force with appliances and fixtures is important as guests are more likely to treat them with more care this way and/or to check how things work before using them.

- It is worth making it very clear what your expectations are in terms of how clean and tidy your home is left and anything which should be done before departure, with a polite reiteration of the fact that you reserve the right to bill guests for additional cleaning if the house has been left in an unusually poor condition or if it becomes clear that house rules have been broken leading to additional cleaning and maintenance being required.

- Provide a copy of your terms and conditions at the end of your information file.

Local information file

Some hosts tack on a few key sites of local interest onto their house manual, but I like to provide a second separate laminated file for local information. I also provide information on the nearest supermarkets, shops, garages, cash machines, pharmacies, taxi firms, recommended pubs, cafes, restaurants and takeaways in this file. I list key attractions, in order of proximity, with a guide to the distance and/or driving time. Pick up any local leaflets or booklets free from your local tourist office and leave some in a basket or leaflet holder. Lots of leaflets can get rather jumbled up and messy, so if your local tourist office offers a single booklet guide to the area, try to collect a pile of these and leave one out for each new guest or when it needs replacing. Try to include a range of interests in your local tourism information such as sports, shopping, walking, cinema, arts, history and so on. Guests love personal recommendations so don't be shy to let them know about your favourite pub or shop. One of the most common questions I am asked is 'please can you recommend a good local pub?' If you live in a popular walking or hiking area then you may wish to provide some walking guidebooks, although they do tend to disappear over time as guests often take them home by accident. By adding a clear label with the property name and address this makes it less likely to happen, or guests are more likely to return it by post. Local walking guidebooks can be worth buying discounted or second hand on Ebay. Alternatively, create some handy A5 laminated walking guides for popular local walks. If you live in a coastal area, compile a simple list of local beaches with distances from the house and a basic description of facilities and features, along with parking advice. I would put this in a frame or on a wall for guests to photograph - you do not want them to take it in the car and forget to return it at the end of their holiday. I have seen some coastal properties make an artwork out of the local coastline map, and incorporate information about local beaches within it, which is a nice touch. Hosts with homes situated in areas famous for walking or mountains could consider using a similar wall mounted map or even a 3D mountain map with different walks highlighted on it.

When a guest books directly with me I always email them a PDF file of local information straight away - guests should have the option to book restaurants and activities well in advance, if possible. If your listing site does not have the option for a local virtual guidebook or a file attachment option, then include some of the basics in your booking confirmation email, particularly grocery shopping and local pubs and restaurants as it will save you a lot of time answering the same few queries over the years. Always use PDF attachments as everyone should be able to easily open this type of file. You can export any type of Word file as a PDF.

I also recommend creating a PDF file for directions and access to your property – you may find you can upload it to some listing sites, but you should also attach it to emails sent just before your guests are due to arrive when dealing with direct bookings. It can be helpful to attach photos of any access roads, parking and/or the location of the key safe.

Customer service, damage deposits, complaints, responding to reviews

You must grow a thick skin when running a holiday let. You will encounter difficult and rude guests at some point, and it is helpful if you are prepared for this. However unreasonable someone is being, try to stay calm and reply in a professional, reasonable tone. If you get riled and respond angrily you will usually just end up escalating a situation. By having clear terms and conditions in place you will hopefully protect yourself against any complaints or unreasonable compensation demands. Difficult situations are sometimes easier to deal with on listing sites as payments and cancellation terms are enforced by the listing site rather than by you. It can feel more personal and antagonistic when you're dealing with a private booking. I always try to be as reasonable as possible and deal with each problem on an individual basis. Terms and conditions are very helpful in protecting you financially, but I will sometimes be flexible if it seems that a guest has an unusual or legitimate reason for not being able to fulfil some element of their booking or needs to cancel due to serious illness or similar. I have waived payments in the past when guests were trapped in a holiday home for an extra night due to a raging storm outside – they didn't really have any choice so I would not charge for this. Other hosts will still charge regardless of the situation, but it creates a very bad feeling and guests are unlikely to return or recommend your let to family and friends as a result. Word of mouth and recommendation is a powerful tool for most holiday lets – having a reputation for being fair and reasonable is not a bad thing.

If guests behave badly, are demanding or deliberately break house rules then you need to respond accordingly – a damage deposit is a very good idea for this reason. Very few guests will willingly pay up extra due to damage and will simply leave a bad review in return if you ask them to, so usually it is not worth pursuing unless the damage is substantial and if you can prove that the recent guests were responsible. You will need proof of the damage or house rules being broken – always take photos immediately on entering the property if there is evidence of damage, theft or broken house rules. You can complain and file reports on most listing sites as well, although I would only recommend going down this route if the situation is particularly bad as guests will invariably deny everything and will leave a poor review in return. Luckily, I do not find many guests behave particularly badly. I usually have a couple of guest groups leave the home in a worse than average, dirty condition each year, and the odd item will go missing, but substantial damage is rare. Reviews and feedback are usually more important in terms of success with your let than trying to claw back some financial compensation, so I usually make a calculated decision to say nothing in these cases. I find that private bookings generally behave better than guests from listing sites, especially if I take a damage deposit in advance. If you happen to live on-site or close by and meet your guests face-to-face then the potential for problems and poor behaviour seems further diminished, because the transaction becomes more personal, and it is harder for guests to treat the let with the disdain and lack of respect which is more common from anonymous guests. Airbnb is generally fine as guests are vetted and you can turn down potential bookings if you are not happy with the guest's previous feedback, or lack of it. My most problematic guests are usually via Booking.com where there is less vetting and reviewing of guests, but even here most are fine. Bear in mind that requesting a damage deposit will deter some guests from booking, so you may want to avoid it, especially in the early days of establishing your business when it is more difficult to fill your calendar. I generally do not request one for smaller lets, especially those that only sleep two, as generally I have a lot less trouble from these types of holiday lets – also, you are in direct competition with hotels for couples' stays and hotels will not be requesting damage deposits. Because I almost never retain the damage deposit, even if things have been left dirtier or worse than usual, I could remove it as a requirement and probably increase my bookings, but the risk then is that you will find more guests leaving the property in a poor condition as they are not worried about deposits being retained. The power of the damage deposit really lies in giving guests an incentive to leave the let in a reasonable condition. The larger a holiday let and the more people it sleeps, then the more reason to request a damage deposit in my view – there is a greater risk of events and parties happening, even if you have a policy against them, and the wear and tear from a larger number of guests will be worse. It is noticeable that large, high-end properties often request a large damage deposit, especially if it has expensive furnishings.

Most of the free listing sites have an option to state a damage payment amount limit which could potentially be charged to guests for damage caused to the let, after their stay, but the listing site will require substantial proof which may well be contested by the guest and the listing site may not be able to insist that guests pay it. It may deter guests from booking, but it may make guests think twice about leaving the property in poor condition or taking any items. Guests will also almost certainly leave you a bad review as soon as the listing site contacts them to discuss damage to the property – a bad review will cost you far more than any compensation you might receive in all likelihood.

A damage deposit is something that you can experiment with, as it will be different for each host and type of let – try adding, adjusting and removing damage deposit requests on different listing platforms to see if it impacts your booking numbers. If you are fully insured, it should not be something that concerns you too much in any case – if you were to have the nightmare experience of a party group that completely trashes your home, you should be covered in any case – a deposit of £100 or £200 will not cover that kind of serious damage. Some booking sites offer their own insurance as well, but I would always strongly recommend that you are fully insured regardless.

Very few listing sites will remove a negative review, in my experience, however unreasonable or unfair you think it is. You usually have a right to reply however, so you can hopefully minimise or negate any untrue or unfair comments here. Again, keep your tone friendly and professional – angry accusatory responses will put off other potential guests more than anything else. Do counter any unreasonable claims with facts or mitigating factors in your response, whilst keeping your tone calm and polite. If your guest's comments sound angry and personal and your response is calm and measured, most other potential guests reading the exchange will deem the complainant to be the unreasonable one. If the complaint is genuine and relates to something that was overlooked, missing or dirty, then you may need to own it and apologise whilst reassuring guests that the issue has been dealt with. Hopefully your guest will message you before leaving negative feedback – if they have a genuine complaint which you can see is something which warrants compensation, then you may want to offer a partial refund, but always with the caveat that they do not leave negative feedback in return. Some hosts offer a promised discount off future stays as compensation, but this is not always popular with guests, as they are unlikely to want to return somewhere if they have really had a below-par experience there. If it is a relatively small complaint, then it might be worth considering this as you lose nothing up front and can potentially encourage a repeat booker. You need to assess each guest and situation as it arises. Most listing sites will award your let an overall 'score' which is an average of all your reviews, and some will automatically push the most positive reviews to the top of your listing page, although guests usually have the option to look at reviews chronologically as well. Some listing sites, such as Booking.com, will not initially score your property until you have a certain number of reviews from which to get adequate data and/or will not share the first handful of reviews with guests until you are more established. This avoids your business being destroyed by one early bad review.

Always apologise profusely, even if a guest's complaint is relatively minor, as this is often enough to take the wind out of the sails of an angry or slightly disappointed guest. I would only consider offering compensation if I agreed that the issue was something severe enough to have spoiled a holiday or if an apology does not mollify the guest. For 'an act of God' – e.g. terrible weather, a boiler breaking down unexpectedly and so on, then I do not think you have to offer compensation as it is something beyond your control. If you do your best to make your guests comfortable in difficult circumstances, to remedy any problems or to refund the affected nights if the home becomes uninhabitable due to a severe problem, then I do not think you need to offer more than that. Some guests will demand full compensation for the entire stay if something like this affects part of their holiday, but I would push back against this, especially if you refund them for the affected nights of the stay. If a guest messages you at the start of the stay regarding the level of cleanliness then you should do your best to remedy this as quickly as possible. If you use a cleaner or cleaning agency, then I would ask that they return and make good. If a guest complains about a lack of supplies and sundries, again, I would request that the cleaner returns to sort these out. If this is not possible for any reason, then try to arrange a next day delivery of the missing items or offer to refund the guest any costs they incur by having to buy basic supplies themselves (e.g. toilet roll, bin bags, kitchen roll, dishwasher tablets etc). One of the biggest complaints for guests staying in luxury accommodation is when basic supplies are missing - if people are paying a lot of money for a luxury experience, they do expect a sufficiently well-stocked home. Even the most modest property should have all the necessities to hand.

Keep a list of 'bad' guests – it will hopefully prevent you accidentally allowing them to stay at your property again. The independent listing sites try their best to deter you from cancelling or rejecting bookings, but if you have good reason to, such as previous poor behaviour or damage to your let, then usually they will waive any potential penalties for cancelling a booking, especially if you cancel straight away. Some listing sites allow you to block certain guests from re-booking.

It is usually worth replying to positive reviews as it shows you to be an engaged, friendly host and will encourage other potential guests to book. If you have a guest that has behaved a little badly or left things in a poor condition, you may want to warn other hosts in your review of them on the sites which invite hosts to review guests. Keep your tone reasonable and professional and avoid any kind of personal comments. Some hosts are very good at not saying too much but allowing other hosts to be able to read between the lines of a slightly lacklustre review of a clearly difficult or messy guest. Guests will generally not be able to read your review of them until they have left one for you, or until a certain amount of time has lapsed if they choose not to leave a review, so there should not be the opportunity for 'revenge' reviews on listing sites. However, bear in mind that guests can score you on additional categories, such as WIFI, room view and bed rating on Booking.com some time after they have left their main review – I have noticed where guests have been a little difficult on messaging or are unhappy with your response to their review that a low score on one of these additional ratings often appears soon afterwards. It is petty, but unfortunately rather typical. Also bear in mind that anyone can currently leave reviews on Google and Trip Advisor, so these sites are liable to be used for revenge reviews by guests, but it is a rare occurrence.

With most private booking platforms which you would use on your own website, such as Freetobook, you usually have the option to choose which reviews you wish to publish. It can be worth sharing positive feedback quotes on your website and on social media. One of the best things about private bookings is that you can control your reviews and feedback and guests cannot hold you to ransom with the threat of a bad review. The ever-present threat of negative reviews is one of the most stressful elements of running a holiday let as your business and income can be directly impacted by them. Guests' expectations and demands have never been higher, and you will never please everyone completely. Even guests that have not been unhappy with their stay sometimes leave misleading or incorrect comments in their reviews which can deter other guests from booking but listing sites do not usually allow guests to change their reviews once they have been submitted. It is always worth asking guests for feedback after their stay, as some people will not tell you the things that they did not like or thought could be improved, without being prompted. You could even consider emailing a review form for private bookings, post-stay or leaving a paper survey form at the property. Sometimes guests can go a little overboard, specifying every little detail that was not 'perfect', so try not to take all feedback too seriously. I was once told that guests did not like the position of the afternoon sun in October in the gardens at one holiday home - I was not quite sure what I could do with that feedback!

The other most common complaint or issue with guests will be regarding cancellations. You will have to state your cancellation policies on free listing sites and holiday agency sites, and I recommend you also have clear cancellation terms on your own website – you should ensure that any cancellation terms on booking platforms linked to your website are identical. I always recommend that guests take out holiday insurance in case they need to cancel, on my terms and conditions and on any invoices, but few people do. A more flexible cancellation policy will certainly equate to more bookings, but you will have more cancellations and more admin to carry out as a result, so it is something that has to be weighed up and experimented with over time until you have a system that works for you – do not underestimate your time in dealing with cancellation admin. Ensure you always have a record of the cancellation terms that your guest agreed to at the time of booking, particularly for private bookings, in case you make any changes to your terms and conditions between them booking and the start of their holiday – booking platforms which you may incorporate to your website such as Freetobook usually state these on the automatically generated booking confirmation in any case. If you do not use a booking platform on your own website, then ensure that all terms and conditions are listed and agreed to in some kind of format or on the invoice. Always state that 'guests agree to all the terms and conditions on our website by proceeding to book' on your invoice or booking confirmation. Guests will often try to get you to waive any cancellation fees for a variety of legitimate reasons, on private and listing site bookings, but it is up to you how you respond. It can be worth moving a guest's booking rather than them losing a deposit, as long as you have sufficient notice to re-book the original dates. I have added a clause in my terms and conditions recently which states a specific small administration charge if guests wish to change dates, within a certain timeframe (meaning guests cannot just move their holiday at very short notice, penalty-free). However popular your holiday let and its location, it still becomes increasingly difficult to re-book dates at short notice, so late cancellations are likely to hurt your business and you should have measures in place to protect yourself from this. People can be very unreliable in my experience and will think nothing of letting you down at the last minute if they can get away with it, penalty-free. Some listing sites such as Booking.com offer you the opportunity to give different rates depending on the type of cancellation policy in place – i.e. it costs less to book a property where the cancellation policy is more limited or there is no refund in the event of the guest cancelling, or you can pay more but have the right to cancel, free of charge, closer to the start of the holiday. Listing sites will sometimes contact you on behalf of a guest who wishes to cancel last minute and ask if you would consider waiving any fees, but you are not obliged to, and it is up to you whether you want to refund or not.

Quite often when I have made kind gestures and waived fees or offered reductions that I was not even obligated to, I have not even received so much as a 'thank you' from guests, so I am a lot firmer these days – good deeds are rarely appreciated unfortunately. I once offered a free night to a guest who arrived a day late due to not arranging transport in advance and was rewarded with negative comments regarding the lack of a certain unnecessary kitchen appliance, and they left over three hours late, leaving my cleaner waiting outside. Another time I let a family book at half the usual rate as they were visiting a family member in hospital nearby and I felt very sorry for them – that was until departure day when I went into the home to find it filthy with pans, food and dishes piled up in the kitchen. From further communications with them it became apparent that they were very well-off and certainly not in need of any special discounts in any case. I always try to be a reasonable and kind host, but I have learned over the years that it is rarely worth being overly generous unfortunately – you will end up feeling embittered if you try to be 'kind' all the time. You are running a business at the end of the day and not a charity.

Another thing worth mentioning here, whilst on the subject of being a kind and generous host, is that family and friends will ask about staying at your holiday home, especially if it is in a popular holiday destination. They will often phone you, rather than email, which can make it difficult to discuss money and prices without having time to think. Whilst you may be more than happy to let close family members stay at your holiday home for free, I do not think it unreasonable to charge distant family and friends to stay. At the very least charge them for the cleaning, laundry and running costs, which can be quite substantial. I knew one host who let some distant cousins stay for free at her let during peak holiday season. It turned out that they had invited additional friends, whom she did not know, and they then asked to extend their stay by several more days. The kind gesture did not appear overly appreciated as she found out after they checked out, with the house left in a dirty, messy state - they had also disturbed neighbours with a lot of noise outside during the evenings. The host admitted that she would not expect distant relatives to gift her several hundred pounds or more, so she should not have felt obliged to do the equivalent. The running costs of a holiday let are not insignificant and you need to optimise your profits during the summer months to cover these and to make a profit, so be especially wary of giving away too much during peak months. If an acquaintance or family member phones you to enquire about booking your let, make an excuse that you cannot talk straight away and ask them to email you the dates they are interested in; this buys you time to decide if you wish to offer a discount and if their suggested dates suit your calendar and stay requirements. If it is possible to check prices and availability on your own website, the only reason for people to call you is usually because they are angling for a discount or freebie. For distant family and acquaintances, I would not offer more than a 10-20% discount. For close family you may feel differently, but I still do not think it unreasonable to charge for cleaning, laundry and heating costs which can be substantial. Do not assume friends and family members will treat your holiday home any better than anonymous guests either – if they offer to do the cleaning or bring their own linen, do not agree to this, as I can guarantee that the property will not be left in an adequately good enough condition for the next guests. There is a genuine risk of you falling out with your nearest and dearest as well if they break house rules or leave your property in a poor state – it is usually best not to mix business with family and friends. Also bear in mind that stays involving friends or family at zero or discounted rates will not count towards your annual occupancy targets from the perspective of HMRC. Check for the latest guidance on this from HMRC directly.

Your other main issue in terms of complaints or problems will be in the case of something going wrong at the property during the guests' stay. Again, ensure you are covered in your terms and conditions by including a clause that states that you will do your best to remedy or fix any problems but cannot promise that it will be done immediately or during guests' stays. Always have an emergency plumber's number to hand in case of leaks or boiler issues and you should arrange for a tradesperson to visit as soon as possible if there is an issue which is a health and safety concern or means that the property is uninhabitable or about to become so. If an appliance breaks down you will need to get it repaired or replaced as soon as possible, especially if it is something like an oven or fridge. If the problem is important and severely impacting the guests' stay and cannot be remedied quickly then you will simply have to cut the holiday short and refund the guest for any nights not stayed. For things like washing machines, TVs and dishwashers then you need to try to fix them or replace them, but I would not say that these sorts of things are 'essential' and therefore if it is not possible to do this within the guest's holiday then a profuse apology should be sufficient. Companies selling electrical appliances such as AO.com will often be able to send out an appliance within a day or two if necessary and can often install it and remove the old one for an additional charge. If one toilet or sink is broken but you have others at the property, then again, I do not think it is unreasonable if you cannot get it fixed straight away as the guests have other options. A partial refund or promised discount off future stays could be offered if you think it likely to pacify your guest or reduce the likelihood of a bad review. If you are suitably sorry and prompt in your communications during any difficulties at the let, then most guests are understanding and reasonable. However, some guests will treat holiday homes like hotels and assume anything can be fixed immediately – you need to remain calm and polite with your communications and let them know what steps you are taking to remedy any problems and apologise if it cannot be done during their stay.

Maintenance and repairs

A good handyman is very useful for most small problems, and I would encourage you to arrange for things to be fixed quickly where possible, especially as it means that the next guests will not arrive to find the same problem. Alternatively, if you are close by, then I would recommend that you go over to fix any small items and quickly as possible, or to at least look at them to see if they can be fixed. It is not uncommon for guests to report broken or malfunctioning items and for it to turn out that they were simply using them incorrectly or had in fact broken them through misuse. For this reason, I now sometimes preface a promise to send over a tradesperson, when there is a reported problem, with the clause that the guest could be billed for any travel or site visit costs if it turns out that the visit was unnecessary. For example I had a guest demand that a plumber be sent over 'immediately' to fix the lever which switches the taps from a bath to shower function – when I apologised and replied that of course I would send over a plumber as soon as possible, but also mentioned the fact that guests could be billed for the plumber's call out fee if it turned out that there was not an issue requiring attention, she suddenly found that she could turn the lever after all, it was just a little stiff. I have had a lot of false and inaccurate reports of broken items and appliances over the years and have learnt to not always assume that the guest is correct. Check whether they are using the item in question properly and if they have referred to the house manual or appliance manual before assuming something is broken.

Keep a basic set of tools, safely away from children, at the let which should include a range of screwdrivers, including a few different sizes of Philips and flat-headed screwdrivers, a set of Allen keys, a hammer, some screws, bolts and nails, a small wrench, some superglue and/or No More Nails glue and an adjustable spanner at the very least. Always have some spare batteries, bulbs and fuses to hand as well, plus some spare curtain hooks (they often get snapped off and broken when guests open curtains a little too roughly). The guests with more initiative can usually fix any small problems with these tools and it will save you a lot of time and bother. Make sure you have your own set of these tools to hand as well in case any of the house ones go missing – it is usually worth having one of those clever Swiss army-knife types of multi tool on your person for most visits to a holiday let as you can fix most little things as and when you notice them this way. It is a good idea to have a more comprehensive tool box for more complex repairs which should ideally also include a drill, rawl plugs in varying sizes, box spanners of varying sizes (very useful for tightening hard to reach bolts and tightening loose taps), a tube of white silicone, a grout brush, some grout reviver paint and small paint brush, some wall filler, graphite for stiff locks and keys, sandpaper and a scraper tool. Most squeaky door hinges can be remedied with a little wipe over with some olive or vegetable oil. Also keep tins of spare paints and a paintbrush to hand. Have a box of wood and metal screws in differing sizes, some spare grub screws if you have any fixtures in the house which use them (usually doorknobs and bathroom fittings use them), and some spare nuts, bolts and washers in varying sizes – you can get very reasonably priced sets on Ebay and Amazon. It is worth having a spare toilet seat, some spare toilet seat fittings, and a spare shower seal to hand as well as these things commonly break or need replacing quite regularly. Keep a sink and toilet plunger to hand, also accessible to guests, as blocked toilets and sinks are another regular occurrence and this will hopefully save you paying up for a plumber in most cases. You will need a proper toilet plunger – a regular cup-shaped sink plunger will not be adequate for most toilet blockages – Amazon is very good for these, check the reviews for the best plungers. Keep a bottle of sink un-blocker to hand as well. And again, always think of the safety of children when storing tools and materials.

Cleaning and general maintenance

Always leave a basic set of cleaning products in the holiday let – most guests will not use them, but some will, especially if they are staying for longer. Leave a bathroom spray, some antibacterial spray, glass spray, floor cleaner solution, some spare cloths and sponges, bleach, dishwasher salt and rinse aid, a duster, some spare pedal bin liners and bin bags. Ensure guests have access to a vacuum cleaner, mop and dustpan and brush. Some guests like to carry out their own clean at the start of their stay even if everything looks immaculate and some will clean at the end of their stay, although this is very rare. Ensure that any cleaning products that could be hazardous to children are kept out of reach.

Even if you use a cleaner or cleaning agency, I recommend that you try to visit the property every couple of weeks at the very least to carry out any deeper cleaning, maintenance and supply top-ups. The things most commonly missed by cleaners are; smudges on windows, dust and dirt on walls or woodwork, dirty shower filters, loose toilet seats, loose bathroom and shower fittings, dead batteries and bulbs, crumbs under sofa cushions, dirty stove glass, dirty toilet and basin pedestals, under-bed dust and debris, dirty place mats, crumbs in kitchen drawers particularly in the cutlery tray, food splashes on hob tiles and kitchen cupboards, dust in bedroom drawers, food splatters on the edges of dishwashers, clogged dishwasher filters, dirty oven trays or grill trays, liquid hand soap which requires topping up, messy patios and paths which require sweeping and tidying. Check all supplies including salt, pepper, oil, foil, dishwasher tablets, bin bags, washing up liquid, hand soap, toilet roll, kitchen roll, sundries including shampoo/conditioner, tea, coffee, sugar biscuits and so on. Cleaners are usually extremely pushed for time and will rarely notice everything. These little things soon add up and become cumulative and the property can appear very neglected if you do not step in to carry out these tasks every few weeks. The holiday lets with the best reviews will generally have a very hands-on, observant host or an excellent cleaning team which carries out additional checks and regular deep cleans. If you do not have time to keep an eye on these things then you could ask your cleaner or cleaning company (or even a neighbour if they are looking for a little part time job) to carry out additional checks or deep cleaning when the let is unoccupied and consider providing a checklist for the above, but it will involve additional costs. Never skimp on basic sundries - you will spoil people's holidays and earn yourself some poor reviews if you do. Turning up to a home without bin bags, washing up liquid, dishwasher tablets, adequate toilet roll, soap or bin bags is very unpleasant for guests as they require these items straight away and will have to go shopping immediately if they are not provided. Some guests will make a point of putting unbagged rubbish in empty bins and leaving the washing up for the cleaners if these things are not supplied, especially for short stays.

Ensure that pillow and mattress protectors are laundered at least monthly and that duvets are laundered annually. You should consider replacing pillows every other year. Aim to clean carpets with a machine once a year. Annually you should be getting boilers serviced with a landlord certificate provided and any chimneys swept. If you have a garden, then ideally carry out a proper tidy and cut-back in the late autumn and early spring. Stone flags and decking should be cleaned or sprayed to prevent slippery algae forming on them a couple of times a year - you can buy effective anti-algae sprays online. Try to clean scatter cushion cases and any bedspreads or throws every few months. Older dark furniture should be waxed once or twice a year and any natural stone floors re-sealed every three to four years. Agas should be serviced every 6 to 12 months.

Other things to provide

Always have a working torch or two to hand for guests, or a wind-up lantern in case of power cuts or issues with the fuse box. You may decide to leave some candles as well for this reason but make it clear that they are only for emergency use, and ensure that they have safe, well-fitting holders or lanterns. Plug-in night lights are much appreciated by families with young children. Some night lights have a removable torch which continuously charges when the night light is switched on - this can be very useful in an emergency or power cut. Make sure you include information on the location and workings of the fuse box as well in your house manual. Consider leaving an emergency electric heater of some kind in case of central heating malfunctioning for any reason, although I would recommend having it hidden/locked up in some way so that it is not used in general as your electricity bills will increase noticeably if it is.

Leave at least one spare duvet and a couple of pillows in case of damage to the ones in use, plus a bag of spare mattress and pillow protectors for all beds - you may want to have these accessible only to the cleaners as guests sometimes like to raid spare linen supplies if they have additional unplanned guests or visitors who decide to stay overnight. Children are frequently sick so you may want to consider leaving some emergency single bedding just in case – but you will need to remember to check if it needs replacing from time to time.

It is a good idea to leave a basic first aid kit somewhere including some plasters and bandages. Some hosts also leave an emergency kit for commonly forgotten items such as toothbrushes, mini tubes of toothpaste, razors, female hygiene products and pain killers. These can be much appreciated by guests, although some will raid the box simply as they feel they have a right to do so, and it is another thing to remember to top-up from time to time.

Always provide a Christmas tree for most of December – artificial is more convenient in this setting. Avoid glass decorations as they are easily broken by children. Some additional fairy lights can be nice in living rooms and bedrooms, and some holly and ivy in an arrangement or vase if you have it to hand. It can be a nice touch to provide a pumpkin to carve for Halloween, with an LED tealight to go inside, and some chocolate eggs or Simnel cake at Easter. Guests appreciate these little seasonal extras. Consider leaving a bottle of bubbly and a cake or chocolates for guests celebrating an important birthday.

Consider a welly stand, boot store and boot scraper for rural areas popular with walkers. For coastal areas, consider including some basic beach equipment - guests may take some home accidentally, but you will also find items are donated or left behind as well. Nothing too fancy - just some buckets and spades, a windbreak, body boards and fishing nets, for example. Consider supplying a picnic rug or two and some beach towels for coastal areas as many seaside hosts complain that bed throws, towels and living room blankets frequently get damaged or lost by being taken to the beach. Also consider some plastic storage trugs for wetsuits or swimwear indoors to save them being draped over furniture and beds along with outdoor hooks to hang them on. Walking books and laminated print outs of walking routes, coastal maps with information on local beaches and any vouchers for local businesses are also a nice touch. Always supply a city or town map for urban homes - preferably one that can be kept by each new guest.

If you want to be very family-friendly, then consider supplying a travel cot which can be easily packed away when not in use. I advise supplying a mattress sheet with this at the very least. Most parents will supply their own baby's blanket or sleeping bag. Most travel cot mattresses are waterproof and should be cleaned properly after each stay. Given the health risks associated with used and dirty mattresses for babies, particularly newborns, I am personally very wary about supplying cots, as they are often overlooked by cleaners, and I simply tell guests to bring their own instead. Highchairs, stair gates and plastic bowls, spoons and sippy cups will be appreciated by parents of babies and toddlers. Plug covers, night lights and plastic corner protectors are another nice touch if you want to welcome babies to your home. You could even consider supplying a baby bath but ensure that it is properly cleaned between use. A regular bath and anti-slip mat are usually sufficient for most babies. Do not leave teddies on the beds, unless they are brand new ones which are intended as a gift for children and ensure that they are suitable for babies if you do not know the ages of the children staying.

Pet friendly hosts often supply a few dog biscuits or treats and somewhere comfortable for them to sleep, plus a clean bowl of water. Consider supplying an easily washable sleep blanket or two which can be changed after each stay.

The number of electric vehicles is increasing all the time, but it can be difficult for guests to find convenient charging points. An EV charging point can be a real bonus for guests with electric vehicles but do bear in mind the associated costs of providing this, which can be very high. You could add an additional fee to cover vehicle charging or have a system in place whereby you only make it available to guests by prior arrangement and an additional cost. I do not offer EV charging currently but will point guests in the direction of the nearest EV charging station instead. I have had guests ask about running a charging cable from the home to their car, but I do not allow this due to the potential trip hazard and fire risk this entails. You might wish to include a clause about this in your terms and conditions, to be on the safe side.

The most common complaints from guests

Over the years that I have run holiday lets I have amassed a list of guests' top bugbears - the things that annoy them most frequently about hosts or the holiday home they are staying in. Avoiding these common mistakes will immediately elevate you above the competition:

- Insufficient toilet roll - this is THE most common complaint from guests. Guests use a surprising amount. Do not leave a large accessible store of it, as it is also the most commonly stolen item. At the very minimum, leave two rolls per WC, possibly four, if you are feeling generous. Buy in bulk to reduce costs. The goodwill that enough toilet roll generates from guests usually means that it is also beneficial to you to provide more rather than less.
- Blunt knives - lack of decent knives always comes up in the top ten annoyances for guests. Provide some decent sharp knives. Provide a knife sharpener for guests, if you wish, but bear in mind that most sharpeners are

intended to be used on smooth knives - if guests use them on serrated knives (which they will), they will damage them. Consider sharpening them yourself every few months.
- Too many signs - an Airbnb host was recently ridiculed online for having laminated signs on display all over their house - from cupboards with signs telling guests not to open them, to shelves with crockery telling guests not to touch or use it, and even a large A4 sign telling guests to be careful when using the table as it used to belong to their grandmother. The odd sign next to a tricky to use appliance or an item which constantly confuses guests or leads to emails and phone calls is a good idea, but people also want to relax on holiday and not be surrounded by signs and rules.
- An overbearing host living on site or close by - people do not want to feel watched and scrutinised on holiday. Even a host who thinks they are being friendly by popping in several times to suggest day trips or who spends the first hour of the guests' arrival showing them how everything works, can feel very overbearing. Most guests want to relax and value their privacy. Be very wary of having any CCTV or a smart video doorbell as most guests will not be happy to be filmed, even if you declare the use of these devices in advance. Do not let yourself into the holiday home when guests are staying there unless it is an emergency. Do not knock on the door and then immediately enter.
- Dusty homes and dirty kitchenware. It can be difficult for a cleaner to get everything done, especially on a same day changeover. You may need to pay your cleaner to do a monthly deep clean or you may need to go over and ensure that all furniture has been dusted

and hoovered underneath. Also check all the crockery and kitchen equipment from time to time.
- Lack of sundries, especially in the kitchen. Guests get very annoyed when certain things are not included. Most will expect dishwasher tablets, washing up liquid, bin bags, a new sponge and cloth, foil, baking paper, clingfilm, salt, pepper, oil, a few tea towels, some tea, coffee, sugar and milk, kitchen roll and soap in the bathrooms at the very least. Any additional items will generally score you extra points. Failing to provide basics like bin bags, soap, dishwasher tablets and adequate toilet roll will almost certainly ensure you are marked down in reviews and end up with dirty bins where guests have empty loose rubbish into them, along with unwashed kitchenware, if guests do not have the means to clean it.
- Lack of kitchen equipment. Always provide too much rather than too little equipment. Most people choose self-catering specifically because they want to self-cater! There is nothing more annoying than a shortage of pans, utensils, dishes, plates and glasses. Guests' other pet peeve is mismatching old crockery - buy basic simple white crockery in bulk. Buy non-stick frying pans when they are on offer as these usually get destroyed within a year or so and need frequent replacing.
- Uncomfortable beds. Old, lumpy mattresses, very soft or very hard mattresses will all be noted by guests. Do not scrimp on mattresses! I recommend pocket sprung mattresses.
- Thin curtains and a lack of window coverings - try to provide good quality thick curtains if you use them. Blackout lining is preferable for most people, especially families with young children who will wake up

horribly early otherwise. Hosts often overlook the fact that people do not want to be woken by the sun in the early morning - so many have inadequate window shutters and blinds as well or inaccessible roof lights or Velux windows which cannot be covered. So many guests leave early due to this problem. Your white shutters and blinds might look very stylish and minimalist during the day, but they may ruin your guests' sleep.
- Doggy smells. It is a little inevitable in a pet friendly home that there may always be a whiff of dog about the place. However, not everyone will appreciate it, especially those without pets. If you allow animals, ensure you have strict rules about where they can sit - do not allow them on beds or sofas. Have removable sofa covers that you change frequently and a powerful vacuum cleaner which is good for picking up pet hair.
- General neglect. Guests will notice an overgrown or messy garden, dusty corners, broken and missing items and so on. To receive good feedback, you either need an excellent housekeeper or to be on top of these things yourself. Regular checks are essential. You will find yourself topping up supplies and tidying missed areas on most visits if you plan to be involved in running the let. If not, pay your housekeeper to do a monthly deep clean and an inventory and supplies check.
- Lack of hot water and heating. If you have a smart app to control heating and hot water, ensure that you have it set to realistic and comfortable levels. The absolute minimum limit for a thermostat should be 21 degrees, but I usually set it to 22 degrees, especially in older homes, which can feel cold for overseas visitors. Consider having your hot water on for most of the day (8am to 11pm) or set it to come on twice a day for

several hours each time, at the very least, in the morning and late afternoon. Guests like to take baths, and if you have a larger home, you need to allow for lots of people taking regular baths and showers at different times of the day. A lack of hot water and inadequate heating will sour guests' impression of your home very quickly. A combi boiler is a good idea for a smaller property as it provides hot water on demand.

- Musty smells or overpowering air fresheners. Try to air your property between guests or ask that cleaners open a window during the clean - ensure they close them again afterwards though. Avoid reed or plug-in fragrance diffusers as some guests are allergic to them or dislike artificial scents. The natural reed type diffusers invariably get knocked over by guests and cleaners and the oil can peel off paint or varnish on surfaces. There are some effective aerosol air fresheners around these days - Febreeze and Oust produce 'fresh air' scents which are good at clearing bad smells without leaving an overpowering fragrance in their place - always keep some in your locked supplies cupboard in case of a particularly pongy house guest. Good cleaning practices and annual carpet cleaning should hopefully mean that your home does not smell bad. Check bins are clean when empty as a split kitchen bin bag or bathroom liner can create a horrible smell which is hard to locate. Do not place a kitchen bin on top of underfloor heating as this will also smell very bad.
- Previous guests' medications being left in drawers. This can be a real danger for children, check all drawers for any items that might have been left behind.

The most frequently stolen and lost items

Unfortunately, most holiday let owners will experience theft from time to time. Most guests are thoroughly decent, but there will be the occasional group who feel that they have a right to take items home with them. Some items will be picked up by accident on check-out. I have never openly accused a guest of theft, as sometimes items can be mislaid, or accidentally taken home. It is worth labelling as many items as possible, either with professionally printed stickers or a simple black sharpie - avoid having ugly visible labels over everything though. I would never leave portable items of sentimental value or great monetary value at a property. I view small losses as part of my running costs. Large items will hopefully be covered by your insurance, but due to rules on excess payments and premiums, it is not usually worth claiming for small items. Using my own experience and a recent online poll from other holiday homeowners, here are the items which most frequently go missing;

- Umbrellas. Easily taken by accident when taken in cars and on day trips. I no longer provide them.
- Tupperware. I think guests often use it for picnics and accidentally take it home, or they pack up unused food in it at the end of their stay. I no longer provide it as it all disappears within a few months. Ensure you have foil and cling film so that guests can cover and wrap food in dishes instead. Guests will empty and take plastic storage pots and boxes containing supplies for picnics and food, so try to use things like open baskets or containers without lids for sundries and supplies to deter this - I used to use a plastic box with a lid for dishwasher tablets at my properties, but these frequently went missing, which is surprising, as the box would retain a strong chemical smell I imagine.

- Emergency chargers and adaptors - some hosts like to leave a range of phone chargers and adaptors for their guests, but they usually disappear within a few months. You will find that you inherit a few as well although these should probably be disposed of as they might be faulty.
- Plug-in streaming devices. Many hosts report that these go missing quite frequently. They are small, portable and have some value. I have had an Amazon Firestick removed from a TV, and many other hosts have reported similar items, such as Sky boxes (which are quite large) going missing. I recommend avoiding these where possible and having a simple integrated smart TV instead, with no additional plug-ins. Some hosts have had TVs stolen as well, so do not buy a top of the range Bluetooth speakers and audio equipment. These seem to disappear quite regularly. Do not buy state of the art equipment, and ensure you label the equipment you do provide, preferably permanently, on the base.
- Toilet roll. Hosts who have an accessible store cupboard for cleaners frequently find their entire stash of 24 toilet rolls or more disappears within a few days. Keep any stores locked but provide a minimum of two spare loo rolls per toilet.
- Wooden hangers. These are probably taken by accident, although I did once have all my wooden skirt hangers removed by one guest. I now label these.
- Towels and bathrobes. I hire laundry so do not notice the odd towel going missing, but hosts who provide their own linen report towels to be a commonly stolen item. You may find yourself with a large bill for missing linen when your contract with your laundry hire company comes to an end.

- Paperback books. This is a contentious issue on online forums. I only buy cheap charity shop books and do not mind if guests take them whereas some hosts are incensed when they do. Many guests assume that they can take them or view books on shelves as a book swap service and will often leave their own behind. Be wary of leaving any rare or expensive books. Consider adding a little note about feeling free to take a book, but to perhaps leave another in its place so that there are always some to hand.
- Maps. Ordnance survey maps and similar can be quite expensive to buy. Guests like to have them in walking areas, but they always disappear within a few months or get damaged beyond use by the rain or from being stuffed into rucksacks.
- Laundry pods. These are quite expensive, and some guests will take them all. Consider leaving just a couple or a cheaper large bottle of detergent with a laundry ball instead.
- Hairdryers. I think these are often mistakenly packed, especially if they are in a drawer. Consider putting them in an official hotel-style labelled hairdryer bag.
- Cutlery. I think it often gets thrown away by accident, especially teaspoons, so ensure you have lots of matching spares.
- Cooking pans. A lot of hosts report all their pans either being destroyed through misuse or going missing completely. Buy decent mid-range pans that are durable but not too covetable.
- Keys. Guests often leave with keys accidentally or lose them on days out. Always have emergency spares hidden somewhere at the property and consider billing them for new ones to be cut, as these costs add up. I am

always having to get new keys cut. Consider adding the cost of new keys to your terms and conditions.
- High quality bedding. A number of hosts reported good quality sheets and pillowcases going missing, and several blamed their housekeeper as it was swapped for cheaper bedding. This could be a mix up if a cleaning company is dealing with bed linen for several properties. If you do supply your own bed linen, consider labelling it.
- Small ornaments, quirky items and unique or expensive pottery. Many hosts report losing small decorative items and quirky or expensive pottery in particular. Some guests seem to take a shine to a particular object and take it home as a souvenir. If you provide decorative items in your let, ensure that none of them have great value. It is generally best to avoid cluttering your home with too many ornaments in any case. Do not provide expensive crockery and mugs as they will get lost and broken.
- Batteries. Many hosts reported batteries being removed from remote controls and even smoke alarms, which is very dangerous. They assumed that guests needed them for other items. For this reason, always have a supply of AA and AAA batteries in a drawer. I don't find that they all disappear and I'd rather guests took one or two of these rather than removing them from an essential appliance in the home. I find that more go missing during Christmas breaks, probably for children's electronic toys.

Quiet periods and longer stays

You will generally find that your let is much quieter between November and March. This is a good time to catch up with maintenance, partial redecoration and improvements. If the house is going to be empty for a week or more then ensure that you empty the kettle and keep the heating on low – at least 9 degrees, to prevent burst pipes and mould forming. If you use a smart heating and hot water app then it is easy to turn off the hot water temporarily and to change the heating schedule remotely – do not forget to turn it back on in time for the next guests though – old houses can take a day to reach optimal temperature during the winter if they have been empty for a while. It can be worth offering shorter stays, such as two nights, if the changeover costs are not too high, and more generous discounts for longer stays during off-peak season. Do not forget to factor in higher heating costs though. Lighting does not burn through as much electricity as some people think, especially if LED bulbs are used, so consider leaving a lamp or two on for security as well or use plug timers or smart bulbs. Although most cleaners are happy to leave a pint of milk for the next guests, consider providing some UHT milk sachets or a bottle of filtered milk (lasts much longer) if there is a gap before the next guests arrive as cleaners will not always be happy to pop back just to leave fresh milk and it might not be economical for you to do so either if you have to drive over especially.

Some hosts find that offering longer stays can be an effective way to fill quiet periods. You can add weekly and monthly discounts on most listing sites, and Airbnb's new professional tools allow you set tailored discounts for a range of long stays. Just remember that stays over 31 days will not count towards your annual occupancy rates and may impact your status as a holiday let, over time. However, this might not be a problem, if your revenue from longer stays outstrips what you would have otherwise made with shorter breaks, even if some of the financial advantages of being classed as a holiday let are lost. Some hosts believe that avoiding short breaks completely, all year round, can be more financially rewarding. This obviously depends on the type of let, its location and target audience, but some hosts have reported higher returns and occupancy when setting a minimum stay requirement of one week. They report that a lot of short breaks end up 'blocking' the calendar, preventing guests who wish to stay longer from booking. Just bear in mind that longer-term guests will expect larger discounts, the longer they stay, and may want a weekly clean and fresh linen, so do factor in these costs. It could be worth experimenting by allowing longer stays for a month or two on your calendar to see what happens.

Keeping accounts and records

Keep clear accounts for spending and revenue. Spreadsheets are usually the best way to go in terms of tracking costs and revenue and will save you a lot of time when it comes to filling in your end of year tax form, especially if you have clear coded systems for the different types of payments going in and out of your account. Keep files on your PC for any warranties, received and sent invoices and keep a box file of important paperwork including any paper receipts, invoices and warranties. Your business could be audited at any time, so it is a good idea to have an organised, transparent system in place.

Keep a paper calendar file for your property with stays marked on it and preferably a spreadsheet of cleans for your cleaning company, if used. Update both immediately after each new booking as it is very easy to lose track of guests and stays and there is nothing worse than having an unexpected or double-booked guest turn up to your property. I usually check my online and paper calendars each week to ensure everything is up to date and check with my cleaner that they have the cleans marked down for that week as well as they sometimes miss things or forget to add cleans to their own rotas.

If your holiday let journey is starting with any kind of renovation, then keep a separate spreadsheet to keep track of those costs and a file of invoices and warranties relating to any of the renovation work – these costs may be offsetable against your income and carried over into the next tax year and beyond if necessary. Always seek professional advice on this and/or consult with HMRC as tax rules are subject to frequent changes.

Do not forget to include incurred costs, as well as all running costs, in your expenses section of your spreadsheet or records, including petrol money/mileage for any travelling you do to the business. Remember that you cannot claim expenses that have a dual purpose for business and personal use. Ensure you have a bank account solely set up for your business with its own debit card. If you forget to use your business debit card or account to make a business payment, then always reimburse yourself as soon as possible and make a note of this in your accounts.

Keep a record of all stays, including the number of separate stays and occupied nights, as this will help you fill out tax returns and keep an eye on whether you are fulfilling the required occupancy rates to trade as a furnished holiday let.

Key points

- Provide a house manual and local information guide at your property as well as emailing local information to guests at the time of booking (for direct bookings).

- Keep all communications with your guest as friendly and welcoming as possible.
- Deal with difficult guests in a polite, professional manner.
- One of the most common issues is guests requesting to cancel without financial penalty. I always advise at the time of booking that guests take out holiday insurance, so you are not obliged to waive any cancellation fees.
- Damage deposits are a good idea for private bookings, especially for larger properties.
- Include a set of your terms and conditions at the holiday let.
- Reply to any negative or factually incorrect reviews calmly and professionally and negate any false claims.
- Apologise profusely for any problems or complaints, however small.
- Only consider compensation for severe issues or if a guest's stay has to be cut short due to the property becoming uninhabitable due to a large problem.
- Kind and generous gestures are not always appreciated by guests or repaid in kind with good behaviour unfortunately.
- Decide if you will be prepared to offer free or discounted stays to family and friends in advance. Free and discounted stays by friends and family will not count towards your occupancy figures.
- Find a good handyman. Provide some basic tools at the holiday let and have your own toolkit to hand.
- Always double check if guests are using items or appliances correctly before sending over someone to repair or fix them.
- Always leave a sink and toilet plunger at the property.

- Visit your let at least once a fortnight if possible, or once a month at the very least, to carry out maintenance and deep cleaning.
- Annual maintenance can include cleaning carpets, servicing the boiler (legal requirement) and having a gas certificate issued, washing duvets and pillows, sweeping chimneys, cutting back gardens, spraying stone flags or wooden decking with anti-algae treatments.
- Guests love attention to detail and seasonal extras such as Christmas trees and decorations, Halloween treats and/or pumpkin, Easter treats etc.
- Use quiet periods to carry out maintenance and improvements. Leave the heating on low to prevent burst pipes and mould forming. Consider using UHT milk sticks or leaving filtered milk if there is a longer gap between guests' stays.
- Keep clear accounts for revenue and costs.
- Keep detailed renovation accounts.
- Keep a record of all stays, including number of stays per month and number of occupied nights. Your own stays, or those of family or friends at zero or discounted rates, should not be counted.

To conclude

Setting up and running a holiday let in the UK can be an exciting and rewarding venture. By following the advice provided in this guide, you are well-equipped to navigate the process and maximise the success of your holiday let. Investing in the right property is key to attracting guests and generating a steady income. Consider the location, amenities, and target market to determine the most suitable property for your holiday let. Additionally, focus on creating a warm and inviting atmosphere through tasteful decor and essential amenities that cater to the needs of your guests.

Marketing plays a vital role in the success of your holiday let. Utilise various online platforms, social media, and professional photography to showcase your property and attract potential guests. Maintain an informative and visually appealing website to provide comprehensive details about your holiday let, including pricing, availability, and any unique selling points.

To ensure a positive guest experience, prioritise effective communication and excellent customer service. Respond promptly to inquiries, provide clear instructions, and be readily available to address any concerns or issues that may arise during their stay. Attention to detail and a personal touch go a long way in creating a memorable experience for your guests, leading to positive reviews and repeat bookings. Always aim to increase direct, private bookings in order to maximise profits and reduce the stress of listing sites review systems.

Managing the operations and finances of your holiday home requires organisation and careful planning. Establish fair and competitive pricing, maintain an up to date booking calendar, and streamline administrative tasks through the use of electronic and paper calendars and spreadsheets. Regularly review your finances, including income, expenses, and potential tax obligations, to ensure profitability and compliance with applicable regulations.

Lastly, remember that continuous improvement is essential to staying competitive in the holiday let market. Seek feedback from your guests and use it to improve your business. Stay up to date with industry trends and adapt accordingly to meet changing guest expectations. With dedication, attention to detail, and a passion for hospitality, your holiday let can become a sought-after destination for travellers in the UK. Embrace the journey, learn from your experiences, and enjoy the satisfaction of providing a memorable and enjoyable holiday experience for your guests.

Wishing you the best of luck for your holiday let journey,

Samantha

Printed in Great Britain
by Amazon